FORMATION BADGES OF WORLD WAR 2

By the same writer:

Badges on Battledress: Post-War Formation Signs
Coronation and Commemoration Medals, 1887–1953
The Origins of Military Aldershot
The Story of Aldershot: A History of the Town and Camp
The Story of Bisley: A Short History of the N.R.A. and Bisley Camp
The Story of Catterick Camp
A Surrey Village and its Church: St. Pauls-in-Tongham
On Wings of Healing: The Story of the Airborne Medical Forces, 1940–60
Minden, 1759

The frontispiece shows:
The 1945 Christmas card of 30 Corps District, depicting on the shields of the knights the badges of the formations then forming part of the Corps District — the 5th, 43rd and 51st Divisions, the 1st Canadian Division, the 8th Armoured Brigade, and the 1st Polish Armoured Division.

FORMATION BADGES OF WORLD WAR 2
Britain, Commonwealth and Empire

Lieutenant Colonel Howard N. Cole,
OBE, TD, FRHistS

Arms and Armour Press

To Pauline
whose badge was
a Red Cross.

Published in 1985 by
Arms and Armour Press Limited,
2-6 Hampstead High Street,
London NW3 1QQ.

Distributed in the USA by
Sterling Publishing Co. Inc.,
2 Park Avenue, New York,
N.Y. 10016.

British Library Cataloguing in Publication Data:
Cole, Howard
Formation badges of World War Two.
1. Great Britain. *Army* – Medals, badges,
decorations, etc.
I. Title II. Series
355.1'4 UC535.G7
ISBN 0-85368-078-7

Formation Badges of World War 2 is based upon
a book first published in 1946 (by Gale & Polden
of Aldershot) under the title *Heraldry in War:
Formation Badges, 1939–1945*. Three editions
appeared – in 1946, 1947 and 1950 – in each of
which small additions and amendments were
made. Publication for the present work was
taken over by Arms and Armour Press. The
present volume has been completely revised
and reset, taking note of corrections and
amendments that continued research has
brought to light over the years. It thus
represents a completely new work, but based
upon the previous volumes. This new impression
of 1985 omits the colour plates of the earlier
printing; these now appear on the jacket.
The author died in 1983, and so the preface
remains that of the original edition.

Printed and bound by R. J. Acford,
Chichester, England.

Preface

My interest in formation badges dates back for more than 30 years to 1941. I was, at that time, a G.S.O.2 in a Staff Duties branch of the War Office. One of my duties was to deal with the equipment of the Maritime Anti-Aircraft Artillery. These gunners were then putting up a magnificent show in the Battle of the Atlantic and around the 'seven seas', and it was decided that the time had come for these sea-going soldier gunners to have some distinguishing badge of their own. I was talking this over with my opposite number at the Maritime A.A. Headquarters, then in Cockspur Street, and made a few suggestions, offering to make some rough sketches. He agreed, and that evening I set to work, producing four ideas: (a) Drake's Golden Hind in full sail. (b) A Mariner's Compass. (c) Britannia. Each of these with the Gunners' motto "Ubique" on a scroll incorporated in the design. (d) A Naval fouled anchor in red, with a white rope, on a black ground, with the initial letters "A.A." in white, one "A" on either side of the anchor.

The last design was subsequently accepted, mainly due, I understood, to the simplicity in reproduction as opposed to the other rather ambitious designs. I well remember first seeing the finished article on the sleeves of two Maritime gunners at Waterloo Station and hoping that they were not too critical of their new badge! Shortly afterwards I went out on the big Home Forces Exercise "Bumper", as an observer, and soon found that a knowledge of formation badges was essential in keeping touch with troop movements during mobile operations. Details were available at the Information Room, and my rough notes on that occasion formed the basis of those which have over many years of research grown into this book. The collection of badges soon followed. I had moved to Northern Command as a S.O.R.E. when I started to collect specimens of the badges of formations in the area, and this collection steadily grew to over two hundred and fifty. It was from those specimens that I drew the line illustrations for the original editions of *Heraldry in War*. Others were drawn from rough sketches made at odd times; the 116th Independent Infantry Brigade was sketched in 1945 by the bridge at Wesel on the Rhine; British Troops in Norway at a Transit Camp; the 36th Division at Woking Station, and so on. In some cases it is admitted that they deviated slightly in detail from the "sealed patterns", or technically, from the "heraldic" aspect, were not quite correct. This can be accounted for by the fact that some were drawn from stencilled designs on vehicles or from locally manufactured badges.

The conventional heraldic tinctures introduced early in the seventeenth century for use in engravings and drawings in line were, I regret, not adhered to in the black and white illustrations which are confined to outline, black and with but few exceptions, a single tint, and so careful reference has been made throughout, in the text, to the actual colours of the designs.

The first edition of my book *Heraldry in War,* the foundation stone for the present work, was published in 1946. It was a slender volume. My researches continued and the scope of the work increased as it was successfully published in two further editions. Over 20 years have now passed since the publication of the third edition of *Heraldry in War* and the book has been long out of print. I have over the years been able to refer to records, war diaries, regimental histories and official archives to check on detail and establish indentification; have entered into correspondence with collectors, serving and ex-officers and NCOs; with commanders of formations; and with Regimental Headquarters, Librarians and Curators of Museums. The results of these contacts have confirmed details and provided information which has now been included, and this leads me to feel that with the present volume now entitled *Formation Badges of World War 2* is a comprehensive record of the formation badges of the formation of the 1939-45 war – at least as far as British, Dominion and Indian formations are concerned. There is, as in the previous editions, a section dealing with the formation signs of our 1939-45 war allies, but, it must be appreciated that in this section, the badges described and illustrated are, particularly so in the case of those of the American Army, but a selection of those worn.

The interest in formation signs has grown over the years and become a new, and wide field of interest to the collectors of militaria. Many private collections were started and built up by those who found in the formation badge scope for research, an inspiration for study and, a fascinating hobby. In 1950, the Military Heraldry Society was founded on the initiative and enthusiasm of Major John Waring of the Durham Light Infantry, and, the Society honoured me by its invitation to accept the Presidency. The Society was formed with the objects of promoting and fostering a general interest in the study of British and foreign military formation signs and to assist collectors in their research and in the building up of their own collections. The Society has today several hundred members, and it has given me considerable pleasure to be associated with its activities for I have always been convinced of the importance of the formation sign, not only for the purpose for which the signs were originally introduced but for the esprit de corps created within the formation in which the symbolism of the badge or its distinctive form has played a part in identifying the formation with its achievements and, at the same time creating a bond among its wearers.

I take this opportunity of placing on record my thanks and appreciation of the help afforded to me by the many who have assisted in providing, over the past twenty seven years, information which has gone into this book. I thank them sincerely for their interest and assistance in helping to make this an interesting book of reference which it is hoped will be accepted as a contribution to our military historical records.

Howard N. Cole

Contents

Introduction

Although the practice of wearing distinctive signs or badges goes back to earliest times,—"It was the Carians[1] who first taught the wearing of crests on their helmets and devices on their shields" (Herodotus – Book 1)—Heraldry, as it is accepted in its association with the introduction of badges and signs of distinguishing marks, dates from the eleventh century. It had its beginnings in military service as required under the feudal system; it developed and thrived during the Crusades and towards the end of the twelfth century, to become established as a means of identification not only on the field of battle but on all military occasions. By the thirteenth century, with the development of body armour, nobles went into battle unrecognizable under this protection. This led to the introduction of the light, distinctive coat being worn over the armour, called a 'coat of arms', on which were displayed the personal symbol of the wearer, such symbols being introduced to ensure recognition – as the colours of the coat could have been the same as others. The distinctive 'arms' were also displayed on the shield, banner and horse-cloths of the wearers.

So descended throughout the ages the practice of wearing distinctive signs of recognition in battle – badges, flags, regimental colours, pennants, and the Formation Sign; although not always conforming to Heraldic practice in design or subject[2], they served their purpose of identification.

Formation badges had their origin in the British Army in the 1914-18 war. In 1914 all vehicles and directional signs disclosed unit identities by inscriptions 'in clear'. When these were removed to prevent identification by the enemy (enabling them to ascertain the composition of the British forces), it soon became apparent that there was a necessity for some form of distinguishing mark or sign to facilitate recognition of Corps and Divisional vehicles and personnel[3].

The adoption of formation signs fulfilled the dual purpose of providing an easily recognisable mark for each formation, while at the same time introducing at the outset a security measure in preventing the disclosure to the enemy of the identity of the formation opposing them. The choice of signs was left to each formation and this soon led to a wider meaning, for it built up the esprit de corps of the Corps and Divisions. The 1914 Army as a whole had, to a very great extent, always thought on a regimental basis; the formation of which a battalion formed part served only as the operational command, and was not regarded as a unit with its own traditions. Men spoke of serving with The Buffs or the Dorsets – not of the 5th or the 12th Divisions. Formation esprit de corps had to some degree been built up during the South African War by the introduction of the Guards and Highland Brigades of Lord Roberts' Force, but between the wars tours of duty only brought the Regular Army into Divisions for training and administration during their tour in any particular garrison. A battalion stationed in the Aldershot Command, for example, automatically formed part of the 1st or 2nd Divisions, but on moving to Colchester it became part of the 4th Division.

The Territorial Force was more closely knit into Divisional pattern and the T.F. formations had a pre-1914 Territorial designation. These designations were retained after the allotment of Divisional numbers and continued when the Territorial Army was reformed in 1921 – e.g. the 42nd (East Lancashire) Division.

The adoption of the formation sign did much to boost morale and men came to feel proud of their badge.

Signs used in the period 1914-18 were limited mainly to armies, corps and divisions: many became famous and have since taken a rightful place in the records of our national military history. Among the best-remembered are the red fox of General Sir Hubert Gough's Fifth Army, the eye of the Guards Division, the double-three domino of the 33rd Division, the 36th (Ulster) Division's red hand, the 'HD' of the 51st (Highland) Division, Wat Tyler's dagger of the 56th (London) Division, the 62nd (West Riding) Division's pelican, the anchor of the 63rd (Royal Naval) Division, and the symbolic broken spur of the 74th Division which was composed of regiments of dismounted Yeomanry. Divisional signs were discontinued by the Regular Army after the 1914-18 war, and by 1920 they had ceased to be worn, although a number of Territorial Army Divisions retained their distinguishing badge. In these, all ranks continued to wear their woven formation signs on their service dress. Among these were the 47th (2nd London) Division (until disbanded in 1935)[4], the 49th (West Riding), 51st (Highland), 52nd (Lowland) and 55th (West Lancs) Divisions.

Divisional Signs were reintroduced early in 1940[5], but instructions were given in December of the following year for them to be described as 'Formation Badges'[6].

It was ruled that the signs were to be worn by all ranks of Command Headquarters, Corps, Divisions, Independent Brigade Groups and Independent Infantry Brigades. Designs were chosen and approved by the commander concerned and the War Office notified. It was not long before the coloured cloth patches and woven badges on battledress sleeves became familiar to the Army and, by sight, to the general public. The security aspect of the badges was also considered, and it became even more necessary to guard the secret of the signs; no disclosure of our order of battle could be permitted. Lists of signs were security documents, and the Army took this in its stride. Formations embarking for overseas removed their badges from uniforms and painted over those on the unit transport, before leaving their mobilization centres for ports of embarkation. The only exception to this rule was when 21st Army Group embarked for the invasion of the Continent, straight from their concentration areas in England.

As time passed signs became more widely used. In the period following the evacuation from Dunkirk, when the Army stood on guard around our own coastlines, signs, hitherto confined to Corps and Divisions, were adopted by Home Commands, Districts and by Independent Brigades, in accordance with War Office Instructions. In several countries the Home Guard Formation signs were later introduced for Sub-Areas, Garrisons, Training Establishments and Administrative Units.

The signs chosen fell broadly into six categories. These can be classified as the "heraldic", the "symbolic or emblematic", the "Territorial or Geographical", the "National", the "Animal", and the "Geometric". There was a link between the "national" and "territorial" and "Animal" – e.g. the rhinoceros of the 11th (East African) Division, the panther of 34 (Indian) Corps, and the oyster catcher of Faeroe Islands Force, being but three examples. There was another link between the "animal" and the "symbolic" classes, especially in the case of Armoured Divisional signs (for example, the charging rhino of the 1st Armoured Division, the charging bull of the 11th, or the bull's head of the 79th). The "heraldic" linked with the "national" – e.g. the lion of the 15th (Scottish) Division, the St. David's cross of the 38th (Welsh) and the St. Andrew's cross of the 52nd (Lowland) Division – but this was especially the case in the "Territorial" signs of Districts of the Home Commands, which in many cases were adapted from the arms of the counties they covered. Amongst these were St. Oswald's shield of Northumbria (Northumbrian District), the Scottish lion rampant (all Districts of Scottish Command), and the dragon of Wales (South Wales District). The geometric class of sign was mainly chosen for its simplicity, but some had a link with the formation. In the case of 10 Corps the circle above an oblong was a '10' on its side, the 15 (Indian) Corps had a design made up of three Roman 'Vs', 3rd Division had a triangle surrounded by three others, and 4th Division had a circle with its fourth quarter displaced.

A few formations continued to wear the same sign as was used in the 1914-18 war. The Guards Armoured Division bore the eye of the Great War's Guards Division the 51st (Highland) Division retained its famous 'HD', and the 55th, their red rose of Lancaster. The 42nd (East Lancs) and the 52nd (Lowland) Division had but slight variations of the 1914-18 war signs. Signs were widely used, exceeding the original intention of a distinguishing badge for personnel and vehicles. Routes allotted to formations during operations were often signposted by the Military Police by means of a directional arrow and a stencilled formation sign on a board. Billets, stores and captured equipment were similarly marked – a point in favour of the geometrical sign, the simplicity of which made it possible to be used by the least proficient of artists. The routes of the 50th and 53rd Divisions through France and Belgium could easily be followed by the two 'T's or the 'W' hastily painted or chalked on the walls of farms and villages.

In Army welfare the badges played their part. On the lines of communication of 21st Army Group one frequently saw signs in use in Corps Administration and Rest areas above the entrances to the formation welfare institution. There was the 'Spearhead Club' of 1 Corps, 'The Crusader Club' – the charging knight of 8 Corps – and 'The Bocage', the three trees of 12 Corps. In Germany, after the cessation of hostilities, 30 Corps made good use of their boar barge. One frequently saw hanging above a village Gasthaus a typically British inn sign: 'The Pig at Rest' depicted the boar comfortably seated in an armchair, while the 'Boar at Anchor' by the Steinhudermer Lake in Hannover was another. At Nienburg the 30 Corps badge was perpetuated above the entrance to the Rathaus, in the work of a stonemason who transfor-

med the stone Nazi eagle into a boar and also by a statue of the latter. In December 1945 Lieut.-General Sir Brian Horrocks performed his last public duty as Commander of 30 Corps in unveiling this memorial outside the Corps Headquarters. The boar rested on a stone plinth on which were carved the formation badges of the Divisions which composed the Corps and also the battles in which the formations had participated. The statue was later moved from Nienburg to Luneburg, where it stood outside the British barracks, and when the British Army of the Rhine withdrew from Luneburg the boar was brought back to England. It now stands by the path leading from the main gates to the Staff College, Camberley, where it was placed in December 1958.

Formation badges were stencilled in colour on the fore and rear mudguards or on the tailboard of lorries and trucks; on jeeps the badge appeared on the body below the windscreen on the driving side. The signs linked with the conventional arm-of-service vehicle marking, denoting – for example – a staff car of H.Q. 8 Corps or a 3-tonner of 49th Division, R.A.S.C. The arm of service markings (given in detail in Appendix 3) were painted squares: red and blue halves for the Gunners, black for formation headquarters, red and green diagonals for the R.A.S.C., light blue for the Sappers, etc.

Signs were worn on the sleeves of uniforms except on greatcoats, one inch below the regimental or corps shoulder title on battledress, and immediately above the arm of service strip. These narrow strips, introduced in the autumn of 1940, gave a quick identification of the wearer's arm of the service when wearing the steel helmet with no badges. These distinguishing simple two-inch strips were of coloured cloth: red for infantry, blue and red for Gunners and Sappers, yellow and red for the Royal Armoured Corps, blue and yellow for the R.A.S.C., and so on. (The full list is given in Appendix 2). Infantry battalions wore one, two or three red strips one below the other to indicate the brigade to which they belonged.

It had been ruled when the badges were introduced in 1940 that they were not to be made of metal in view of the shortage of material, and so the formation badges were either woven or were stencilled in paint on cloth. As austerity progressed the latter type became more familiar. Others were of 'local' manufacture; some badges worn by the Eighth

Army were made by Italian civilians, and in some cases were made by the troops thesmselves.

In North Africa and other tropical kit areas, the formation signs were often worn affixed to the sleeves of K.D. jackets by means of press studs (to facilitate laundering) or were worn stitched on to khaki drill 'slip-on' epaulettes for wear on the shoulders of K.D. shirts. In East and West Africa and in S.E.A.C. the badges were worn either stitched to the side of the pugaree or on the turn-up of the felt bush hat.

Formations soon became sign-minded. Some units adopted the Divisional badge on stationery in preference to that of their own regiment or corps. Corps and Divisional signs were the motif of many of 1945's army Christmas cards, a practice since continued. Continental shop-keepers, with an eye to business, soon produced brooches of the badges of the British Liberation Army, and embroidered handkerchiefs also appeared. By the end of September 1944, it was possible to buy in Brussels an enamel brooch of 21st Army Group or Second Army, and others soon followed. Brussels had by that time become very badge conscious. British formation badges were greatly sought after as souvenirs.

The collecting of brass regimental cap-badges as adornments to waist-belts, so treasured by the old soldier of previous times, gave way to some extent in World War 2 to the collection of the cloth patches of formations. The modern counterpart of the cavalry trooper's badged belt was undoubtedly the leather jerkin of the A.T.S. girl, the lining of which was covered with badges carefully stitched on in patchwork style. This method of collecting badges was also favoured by some E.N.S.A. artists, who thus recorded to whom they had given their shows.

Formation badges were a feature of the War Memorial in the English church at Batavia, Netherlands East Indies, unveiled in June 1946 by Lieut.-General Sir Montagu Stopford, G.O.C. Allied Land Forces, South East Asia. This memorial to the men and women of the British Commonwealth killed in Java in 1942-46 was designed by Cpl. R. Roberts, R.A.S.C., subscribed for by Service personnel; and bore the badges of the 15th (Indian) Corps, the 5th, 23rd and 26th Indian Divisions, the 30th Indian Tank Brigade and the 5th Parachute Brigade. Although not strictly a War Memorial in the accepted sense, the D-Day stone on South Parade, Southsea, unveiled in 1948 by Field-Marshall Lord Montgomery, bears above the commemorative inscription the formation badge of Second Army. The formation badges of the 1st and 2nd Divisions[7] are incorporated in the wrought iron gates which lead to the Royal Garrison Church of all Saints at Aldershot – a memorial to the fallen of the two Divisions. The commemorative plaque on the gate post was unveiled on 29th July 1958 by Field-Marshal Earl Alexander of Tunis.

The inclusion of formation badges in memorials was not new to the 1939-45 war: the Divisional signs of the Scottish formations of the 1914-18 war are perpetuated in the Scottish National War Memorial in Edinburgh Castle, which was opened in 1927. There, on the exterior wall of the shrine erected to the undying memory of those Scots who fell in the Great War, are carved the badges of the 9th (Scottish) and 15th (Scottish) Divisions – two of the earliest formations of Kitchener's Army – the New Army Divisions, and the 51st (Highland) and 52nd (Lowland) Territorial Divisions, while the famous 'broken spur' badge of the 74th Division is incorporated in the memorial to the Scottish Yeomanry.

At the junction of Hospital Hill, Knollys Road and Queen's Avenue in Aldershot, the 1914-18 War Memorial to the 2nd Division stands on a high grass bank overlooking the road. The Divisional sign is carved on the rear panel of the base of the stone cross and, in addition, the memorial stands on a base which depicts the sign; this was a black oval with a large central eight-pointed red star flanked by a white eight-pointed star on either side. The two white stars stood for the 2nd Division, and the red star for the 1 Corps – 'The Second Division of the First Corps'.

The base of the Aldershot memorial is rarely seen except by those who go to the top of the mound to see the oval design reproduced in flint, the smaller stars in white stone, and the centred red star (upon which the Memorial cross stands) in red brick.

As the years passed so the formation badges of 1939-45 found their honoured place on the memorials to those who fell in the second Great War, for the soldier of 1939-45 was proud to identify himself with the formation with which he served – and, with its symbol, the Formation Badge. Such is proved by popularity of the ties bearing Army, Corps and Divisional signs which were introduced in the early 1950s in step with the coming of the symbol or motif ties, which have to some extent replaced the traditional regimental ties.

Formation badges have found a place as background decoration at military events. The display of formation badges emblazoned on banners carried in the grand finale of 'Drums', the Army Pageant held at the Royal Albert Hall in May 1946, set a pattern and gave indication of the association of the familiar badges with army pageant of the future.

The formation badge stayed in days of peace, to become to Corps and Divisions (and some Brigades) a symbol of the history and traditions of the formation. The badges were incorporated into pennants flown outside headquarters buildings, and on the car bonnets of senior officers' vehicles.

The formation badge had played an important role in war as a distinctive sign, and, it was indeed a factor in the promotion of morale. That this had been appreciated was no doubt one of the reasons for the continued feature of army uniform in both peace and war – for in September 1948 it was announced by the War Office[8] that formation badges could continue to be worn by all formations of the Regular and Territorial armies. This led in consequence to the readoption of many of the well known wartime badges and the introduction of many new and appropriate designs, a number of which incorporated into the new portions of wartime badges. Designs for new badges were submitted to the War Office for approval in order to avoid duplication and, when once approved, could not be altered without War Office authority.

In addition to formation badges, the introduction of new designs were extended to Regiments, particularly former Yeomanry and Infantry of the Territorial Army which, on the reformation of the T.A. in April 1947 had become units of other arms of the service, in particular of the Royal Artillery. Formation signs were also incorporated into Regimental Royal Artillery Standards introduced in 1946 to the design produced by the College of Heralds.

This book aims at being a comprehensive record of the Formation signs worn during World War II plus those introduced in the latter part of 1945, after 'V Day' and early in 1946 for the re-established Overseas Commands and occupational forces. Reference must, however be made to the badges worn during the war in Korea (1950-53) and in the operations in Malaya (1948-60).

In 1949, the 40th Division was reformed in Hong Kong. The badge of the Division in the 1914-18 war, introduced in 1917, was a Bantam Cock; a similar badge – a yellow cock with red comb, beak and legs on a square royal blue background – was adopted in 1949. It was from this Division that two battalions (1st Middlesex Regt. and 1st Bn. Argyll and Sutherland Highlanders) were withdrawn to form part of the 27th British Commonwealth Brigade with the 3rd Australian Infantry Battalion in the operations in Korea (August – October 1950). In 1951, this Brigade became part of the First Commonwealth Division, formed in Korea, which adopted as its badge an azure blue shield with in the centre, an Imperial crown in gold above the word 'Commonwealth' in gold on a white bar. This was later changed to the word in dark blue, discarding the background panel.

The 29th Infantry Brigade arrived in Korea wearing the same white ring on a square black background badge worn by the wartime 29th Independent Brigade Group, but this was soon discontinued with the introduction of the Commonwealth Division badge.

In the 1948-60 emergency in Malaya the 17th Gurkha Division adopted the badge worn during World War II by the 43rd Lorried Infantry Brigade – crossed kukris in white set on a dark blue background (the wartime Brigade badge was on a dark green background). On their arrival in Malaya, the 2nd Guards Brigade adapted the wartime badge of the 33rd Guards Division crossing bayonet with a Kukri to denote the incorporation of a Gurkha Battalion in the Brigade, and a similar badge was adopted by the 18th Infantry Brigade, an identical design but set on a square red background.

New badges were also introduced during the operations in Kenya (1952-56), at Suez in 1956, in Borneo (1962) in the Middle East and elsewhere.

The practice of wearing formation signs is now firmly established, both in war and peace; there is no doubt that the formation badges, particularly those of both World Wars, have their undisputed place in our military history and will always be remembered by those who wore them during its making....

(IN HOC SIGNO VINCES
In this sign shalt thou conquer[9])

The Badges

HIGHER FORMATIONS

Supreme Headquarters Allied Expeditionary Force (S.H.A.E.F.).
The now well-known emblem of S.H.A.E.F. was worn on the left sleeve only, by all ranks—American, British and Allied—on the staff of General Eisenhower's Headquarters in England, in France (at Versailles and Reims), and finally in Germany (at Frankfurt).

The official description of the badge was given as: the shieldshaped cloth patch, with a black background, representing the darkness of Nazi oppression, bears the crusader's sword of liberation, with the red flames of avenging justice leaping from its hilt. Above the sword is a rainbow, emblematic of hope, containing all the colours of which Allied flags were composed. The heraldic field of blue above the rainbow is emblematic of peace and tranquillity for the enslaved peoples of Europe—the objective of the United Nations. The badge was authorized by General Eisenhower on the 25th March 1944.

G.H.Q. Home Forces!
A heraldic winged lion, woven in gold within a gold border set upon a circular background of red and blue, was the badge of G.H.Q. Home Forces which commanded all formations and units in the United Kingdom, other than those of Anti-Aircraft Command and War Office training establishments—that is to say I.T.Cs. and P.T.Cs. Training Regiments and Depots and Schools of Instruction.

G.H.Q. Middle East?
A brown or gold camel on a black square background was the badge of G.H.Q. Middle East, although yellow paint instead of gold was inevitably used for vehicle marking. The badge was not worn on uniform. Located in Cairo, G.H.Q. M.E.F. (Middle East Forces) provided the main operational and administrative headquarters for all our forces in Egypt (B.T.E.), Palestine, Syria, Iraq, Persia, Cyprus, Aden, the Sudan, Eritrea, Cyrenaica, Tripolitania, and the Dodecanese. The Camel badge was introduced by G.H.Q. M.E.F. was redesignated Middle East Land Forces (M.E.L.F.) in 1946 as being appropriate to all the countries of the Middle East.

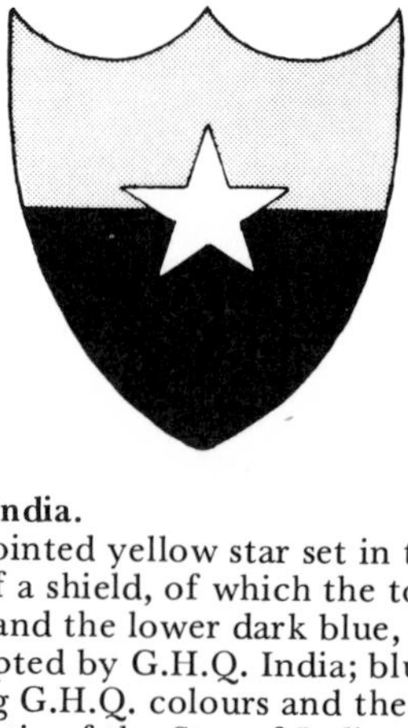

G.H.Q. India.
A five-pointed yellow star set in the centre of a shield, of which the top half was red and the lower dark blue, was the sign adopted by G.H.Q. India; blue and red being G.H.Q. colours and the star emblematic of the Star of India.

Allied Force Headquarters (A.F.H.Q.).
The distinguishing badge of A.F.H.Q. established in Algiers during the North African campaign in 1942 was a saxe blue circle surrounded by a red border and the letters AF in white in the centre of the circle. This Headquarters was in command of all American and British formations in Morocco, Algiers, and Tunisia, and was composed of a mixed U.S. and British staff. After the defeat of the Axis forces in North Africa and Sicily, A.F.H.Q. moved to Italy and was established at Caserta.

Supreme Allied Command, South-East Asia (S.A.C.S.E.A.).
The Headquarters staff of Admiral Lord Louis Mountbatten, the Supreme Commander, South-East Asia, wore as their badge a blue phoenix rising from red flames on a white circular background within a blue border, emblematic of Allied might rising from the ashes of the Japanese-occupied territories of Burma, Malaya, China, the East Indies and South Pacific.

H.Q. Central Mediterranean Force.
This Headquarters was formed upon the disbandment of Allied Forces H.Q. in Italy. It then became the Operational and Administrative Headquarters for all British forces in Italy and the Mediterranean area. Its badge was the (black) torch of freedom with three red flames against a white background the lower portion of which had three thick wavy blue bands to denote the Mediterranean (similar to the badge of 15th Army Group). The design was set in a shield with a black border. It was said that the badge was chosen to commemorate Operation 'Torch'—the code name for the allied operations which carried the war against the Axis into the Western Mediterranean in November 1942.

Allied Land Forces, South-East Asia (A.L.F.S.E.A.).
A.L.F.S.E.A.'s badge was a white shield, on it a red crusader's cross. Behind the shield the wings of victory in yellow or gold and a crusader's sword in white; the whole set on a background of light blue, with a dark blue base. The badge was emblematic of the wings of victory carrying the crusader's sword and shield across the seas to the liberation of enemy-occupied territories and the defeat of Japan, and it symbolized the combined efforts of the three services in this theatre of operations.

11th Army Group.

This formation which became, on
1st January 1945, H.Q. Allied Land
Forces, South East Asia, had as its
badge a yellow sampan sailing on a dark
blue sea, with a red sky. The blue and
red—Army colours—being evenly divided
as the background. The badge illustrated
was that used as a vehicle marking.

11th Army Group was formed in
Delhi in October 1943, under the
command of General Sir George Giffard,
G.C.B., D.S.O. An advance H.Q. was set
up in Delhi whilst Main H.Q. was established at Barrackpore. Main H.Q. and
most of Advance H.Q. was later moved
to Kandy, and it was here that it was
redesignated A.L.F.S.E.A.

Headquarters 15th Army Group.

15th Army Group was formed for the
invasion of Italy and controlled the two
operations in that invasion carried out
by the Seventh American and Eighth
British Armies; 7 plus 8 equals 15, and
this was the reason for the choice of the
number for this Army Group. The formation badge, a white shield set on a red
square, on it three wavy blue lines, was
sponsored by Field-Marshal Lord
Alexander when 15th Army Group H.Q.
evolved into H.Q. Allied Armies in Italy.
In January 1945, H.Q. A.A.I. was
abolished and 15th Army Group
constituted. This was a mixed American
and British formation, composed of the
Fifth (U.S.) and Eighth (British) Armies
under the command of General Mark W.
Clark. Its mixed troops were of many
nationalities, American, British, Brazilian,
South African, New Zealand, Polish,
Palestinian and Italian. The formation
H.Q. took over the A.A.I. badge. It was

this formation that pierced the Gothic
Line, and during the winter of 1944/5
formed up across Italy from the flats
of the Senio River across the Apennines
to the Gulf of Genoa. Its task for the
spring campaign was the destruction of
some thirty enemy divisions in the
north of Italy. 15th Army Group's attack
was launched in the Bologna area in
April 1945, and its drive into the Po
Valley commenced. By 2nd May the
whole country had been overrun, from
the French border to Trieste and northwards to the Brenner. On 4th May the
German forces laid down their arms, and
General Clark accepted the formal
surrender of the German Commander-in-
Chief of all German troops in Northern
Italy and the southern Austrian provinces.

Headquarters 21st Army Group.

The familiar sign of Field-Marshal
Viscount Montgomery's Headquarters
first appeared in September 1943. The
badge worn on both arms of the battledress blouse or service jacket by all
members of the H.Q. Staff of 21st
Army Group was two crusaders' swords
in gold, 'in saltire' (i.e., crossed
diagonally), on a blue cross on a red
shield. The badge was also worn by
G.H.Q. 2nd Echelon, 21st Army Group.

It was 21st Army Group which carried
out the invasion of Europe in June 1944,
fighting its way from the Normandy
beaches to the banks of the Elbe, its
Commander accepting the surrender of
the German Army at Luneburg Heath
on 6th June 1945. When H.Q. 21st
Army Group became, in August 1945,
H.Q. British Army of the Rhine, the
sign continued to be worn by the
staff of the British H.Q. in Germany.

HOME COMMANDS

Scottish Command.
The heraldic lion rampant of Scotland woven in gold on a scarlet background with a central horizontal black band, the colours of a Command H.Q. brassard, was the badge of H.Q. Scottish Command at Edinburgh. Units of the Command other than the H.Q. Staff had the same badge, but with a plain red background.

Nothern Command (U.K.).
A green apple on a small dark blue diamond was the badge of Northern Command, which had its Headquarters in York. The sign was chosen during the time that the former Adjutant-General (General Sir Ronald F. Adam, Bt., G.C.B., D.S.O., O.B.E.), was G.O.C., and, like the badge of 3 Corps, Northern Command's sign was adopted for its association with the name of its Commander—thus Adam's apple.

Eastern Command (U.K.).
During World War II Eastern Command's coastline stretched from the Wash to the Thames, and a similar motif to the South-Eastern Command sign was adopted—on a black square, a white bulldog, denoting tenacity, stood on guard. Eastern Command's war-time H.Q. was at Luton, and its territory covered East Anglia and the Central Midland Counties. Eastern Command reverted to its pre-war boundaries in 1946 to include East Anglia and Kent, Surrey and Sussex, with its H.Q. at Hounslow.

South-Eastern Command (U.K.).
This Command came into existence during the war, and was formed for operational and administrative purposes from the Aldershot Command and that part of the prewar Eastern Command which lay south of the Thames. The Headquarters was near Reigate, and the distinguishing badge of the Command was a tiger's head, the tiger roaring defiance, symbolic of the fact that the Command's coastline of Kent and Sussex faced the German-held French Channel coast. South-Eastern Command ceased to exist at the end of 1944, its territory being divided between Eastern and Southern Commands.

B

Western Command (U.K.).
The yellow cross of St. David of Wales,
with the red rose of Lancaster superimposed on the centre of the cross, within
a red circle on a black background (the
red and black being the Army H.Q.
colours), was the distinguishing sign of
Western Command, which had its Headquarters at Chester. Its boundaries
embraced the whole of Wales and the
bordering North-Western and North-
Midland Counties.

The Western Command Battle School
adopted as its badge the Western
Command Sign but with Rifles (in
brown) with (white) fixed bayonets in
Saltire on The Cross of St. David, and
a torch of learning (yellow torch with
red flame) vertical behind the central
rose.

Southern Command (U.K.).
A conventional representation of the
constellation of the Southern Cross set
on a shield formed the basis of the
Southern Command sign. The colouring
of the shield, forming a background to
the five stars, varied according to the
arm of the service of the unit of the
wearer. In the case of Command Headquarters, the colouring of the shield
was the red and black horizontal bars
of a Command H.Q. pennant and
brassard. This badge was introduced
for use by the Command H.Q. in
July 1940. There were eighteen
variations of this Command's badge,
according to the regimental or Corps
colours of the different arms of the
service. For example, the Royal

Artillery's shield was halved, the
right being dark blue, and the left
half red; the Sappers had a red shield
divided by a dark blue diagonal strip;
the R.E.M.E. shield had three vertical
bars of blue, yellow and red; that of the
R.A.S.C. was half yellow, half dark blue.
In all cases the pattern of the stars of the
Southern Cross was superimposed.

The eighteen variations of the badge
of Southern Command are shown opposite:

The command vehicle marking differed
from the badges worn on uniform, inasmuch as the marking was a rectangle,
divided in horizontal bars of red, black
and red, and with the addition of a fourth
star on the central black band immediately
below the middle star of the central row
of three.

Unit (Arm of Service).	Shield.	Stars.
Command Headquarters	RED, with central horizontal BLACK bar.	WHITE.
Royal Artillery	Divided vertically. Left half RED, right half BLUE.	WHITE.
Royal Engineers	RED, divided by BLUE diagonal bar top left to bottom right.	WHITE.
Royal Signals	Divided vertically. Left half DARK BLUE, right half WHITE.	WHITE on DARK BLUE. DARK BLUE on WHITE.
Royal Armoured Corps	Divided vertically. Left half RED, right half YELLOW.	RED on YELLOW. YELLOW on RED.
Infantry	RED.	WHITE.
Royal Army Medical Corps	MAROON.	WHITE.
Royal Army Service Corps	Divided vertically. Left half DARK BLUE, right half YELLOW.	YELLOW on DARK BLUE. DARK BLUE on YELLOW.
Royal Army Ordnance Corps	RED with central vertical BLACK bar.	WHITE.
Royal Electrical and Mechanical Engineers	Divided in three vertical bars. Left, RED; Centre, YELLOW; Right, DARK BLUE.	DARK BLUE on centre bar. WHITE on side bars.
Corps of Royal Military Police	Divided vertically. Left RED, right BLACK.	WHITE.
Royal Army Dental Corps	Divided vertically. Left GREEN, right WHITE.	WHITE on GREEN, GREEN on WHITE.
Royal Army Pay Corps	YELLOW.	BLUE.
Royal Army Educational Corps	CAMBRIDGE BLUE.	WHITE.
Royal Pioneer Corps	Divided vertically. Left GREEN, right RED.	WHITE.
Intelligence Corps	GREEN.	WHITE.
Army Physical Training Corps	BLACK.	RED.
Women's Royal Army Corps	DARK BROWN with narrow GREEN edging.	BEECH BROWN.

OVERSEAS COMMANDS

Eastern Command (India).
The truncated heraldic head of a horse in white on a square black background was the badge of India's Eastern Command. Eastern Command was the successor to Eastern Army, and was the H.Q. responsible for the operations in the Arakan and elsewhere in Burma until the formation of the Fourteenth Army in November 1943.

The design of the badge stressed the horse's mane, thereby connecting the badge with the name of the formation commander, General Sir Mosley Mayne, K.C.B., C.B.E., D.S.O.

India Command.
Supreme Headquarters, India.
The badge of India Command was a shield divided into three vertical bars, of dark blue, red and light blue, the colours of the Royal Navy, the Army and the R.A.F.; on each bar being the badge of the service—the crest of the Royal Indian Navy; the lion and crown and crossed swords of the Army and the crown and albatross of the R.A.F. is superimposed on a circle bearing the motto 'Per Ardua ad Astra' and surmounted by a crown. The badges were in yellow, and the crowns in red and yellow.

This was a unique Command as it emobodied under one head all three services. The badge was worn by those staffs under the Commander-in-Chief which dealt with the H.Qs. of all three services in New Delhi.

Northern Command (India).
The symbolic compass North Point, as used in cartography, in white set on a red shield divided by a black band, was the badge of this Indian Command. Red and black being the established Army Command colours.

Central Command (India).
A red circle, set within a black equal-sided diamond, was the sign adopted by the Central Command in India. The circle was symbolic of the Centre and Red and Black Command Colours.

Ceylon Army Command.
Superimposed on a background of Command colours, red, black and red, an elephant's head in yellow was the badge of Ceylon Army Command.

Persia and Iraq Command.
Generally known by the accepted
abbreviations 'P.A.I.F.' or 'Paiforce' or
'PAIC' (Persia and Iraq Command), this
force comprised the Tenth Army and its
bases and L. of C., extending, as its
designation proclaimed, over Persia and
Iraq. It conducted the operations which
quelled the Iraqi rebellion of 1941, and
those which expelled the Axis agents
from Persia. Its badge, a red elephant's
head with white tusks, on a royal blue
oblong, was, it was said, chosen in view
of the fact that the first G.O.C. was
General (later Field-Marshal) Sir Henry
Maitland Wilson, G.C.B., D.S.O., M.C.,
universally known by his popular nick-
name, 'Jumbo'. On the disbandment of
'Paiforce' the badge continued to be
worn by H.Q. British troops in Iraq.

West Africa Command.
This Command covered the West African
Colonies—Nigeria, Gold Coast, Gambia, and
Sierra Leone. The Command's badge was
a West African palm tree in black set on
a white rectangular background. The badge
was adopted from that of the Royal
West African Frontier Force—a palm
tree standing on a mount below which
was a scroll with the inscription
'R.W.A.F.F.'.

East Africa Command.
This Command covered Kenya,
Tanganyika, British Somaliland,
Abyssinia and Italian Somaliland.
Its badge was two crossed pangas set
on a green background.

  Its badge was originally two crossed
pangas (machetes) set on a green background. This was subsequently changed
to a scarlet circle, surmounted by a
black ring. Within the circle a pair of
pangas crossed, left over right, each
with a silver blade and black handle.
When used on vehicles the badge was
8 inches in diameter. The black border
was ½ inch in width and the pangas
6½ inches long.

Malta Command.
A white Maltese cross from the arms of
Malta (and the badge of the King's Own
Royal Malta Regiment) set on a shield of
command colours, red, black and red, was
the badge of Malta Command, the senior
military formation of the 'George Cross
Island'.

Malaya Command.
This Command, re-established after the
liberation of Malaya, adopted as its
badge a kris, the native Malayan dagger
with a wavy shaped blade, in yellow
set on a green background.

ARMIES

First Army.

The distinguishing badge of the First Army, commanded by Lieut. General Sir Kenneth Anderson, K.C.B., M.C., worn throughout the campaign in Algeria and Tunisia, was the red cross of St. George on white shield and a crusader's sword superimposed on the upright of the cross. The First Army landed in North Africa in November 1942, and commanded the British formations which cleared Algeria of the Nazi occupying forces, and holding them during the winter of 1942-43 until the final battles in Tunisia which led to the capitulation of von Arnim and the entire German force in North Africa. First Army was composed of the 5 and 9 Corps.

The following description of the First Army badge was given in the Programme of the First Army Thanksgiving Service held in Tunisia for the victory granted to the Allies in North Africa:—

'The Shield: Representing our country— our home set in the midst of the sea, a sure and safe refuge—a land, shaped like a shield, which has stood us in good stead all through the long pages of our history. The base of our strength to-day. "Breathes there a man with soul so dead, who never to himself hath said, 'This is my own, my native land'?"

The Crusader's Cross: The symbol by which all men shall know the ideals and principles for which we stand, no sacrifice being too great in the cause of freedom. For nothing can be higher than the hope expressed by that symbol— persecution, oppression and terror banished, and replaced by Christian peace and toleration. No one can doubt the intention of those who serve and follow The Cross.

The Drawn Sword: Long ago a

Christian soldier gave us an example of the cause for which the sword should be drawn. This example we of First Army endeavour to follow. St. George drew his sword and destroyed a dragon which had enslaved a nation. We endeavour to destroy a dragon which has arisen in Europe which would enslave the whole world. We cannot sheathe our sword until our task be thoroughly finished.'

Second Army.

The Second Army, formed in England in the summer of 1943, adopted a similar sign to that of the First Army, a blue cross being substituted for the red. Second Army was raised for the invasion of Europe, and went ashore in Normandy on D Day, 6th June 1944, forming part of the 21st Army Group. Under the command of Lieut.-General Sir Miles Dempsey, G.B.E., K.C.B., D.S.O., M.C., Second Army saw much hard fighting in the establishment of the beachhead, at Caen, and in the break-out which culminated in the German defeat at Falaise. Then followed the drive across France, the crossing of the Seine and the Somme, the liberation of Brussels, and the sweep up to the banks of the Maas, which was held during the winter of 1944-45. The spring of 1945 saw Second Army engaged in the clearance of the enemy between the Maas and the Rhine, and on 24th March 1945, it was 12 and 30 Corps of Second Army which forced the northern crossing of the Rhine. Then followed the drive across North-West Germany— Munster, Osnabruck, Bremen and Hamburg—and to the banks of the Elbe, which ended in the surrender of the last remaining German armed forces.

Eighth Army.
The existence of the Eighth Army became
known when in November 1941, General
Sir Alan G. Cunningham, G.C.M.G.,
K.C.B., D.S.O., M.C., was appointed to
its command at the opening of General
Sir Claude Auchinleck's offensive in the
Western Desert. The Eighth was formed
from the original Army of the Nile, and
included the 13 and 30 British Corps
with South African, Australian, New
Zealand and Indian formations. It was
engaged in much hard fighting in the
Desert against the combined forces of
the Italians and Rommel's Afrika Korps
throughout 1942, which culminated in
the withdrawal to the defensive line at
the gateway to Egypt. It was at this
time that Lieut.-General (later Field-
Marshal Viscount) Montgomery was
appointed to its command and directed
its efforts into the great victory of
El Alamein in October 1942. Under
his inspiring leadership the Eighth swept
on across Cyrenaica and Tripolitania to
the Mareth Line and thence northward
into Tunisia to the final defeat of the
Axis forces in North Africa. 'The
achievements of the Eighth Army,' said
Mr. Churchill in an address at Tripoli in
February 1943, 'will gleam and glow in
the annals of history.' The Eighth next
saw action in the invasion of Sicily, and
then into Italy where, under command
of the 15th Army Group, they fought
their way northwards across the Sangro,
the Volturno, through the Gothic and
Adolf Hitler Defence lines and finally
in the swift, decisive Po Valley campaign
which culminated in the surrender of
the German forces in Northern Italy.

The Eighth Army H.Q. and Army
Troops wore as their badge the now
famous golden crusader's cross on a
white shield set on a dark blue background.

The Eighth Army badge owes its
origin to the fact that the first operation
in which it went into action had the
code-name 'Operation Crusader'. It
was at this time that the choice of a

formation badge was under consideration
and the name of the operation gave rise
to the choice of a crusader's shield as
a suitable emblem. This, however would
have been a red cross on white shield
and it was considered that this might
lead to confusion with the Red Cross
Signs, flags and vehicle markings of the
R.A.M.C. Field Hospitals, First Aid
Posts and Ambulances. It was decided
therefore to retain the crusader's shield
but to change to colour of the cross
from red to yellow (gold).

The badge was later adopted by H.Q.
British Troops in Austria (B.T.A.)?

Ninth Army.
The Ninth Army was formed in the Middle
East at the end of 1941. It was raised in
the Levant, as the Headquarters for all
forces which might have been used in that
area against a German thrust which it was
anticipated might follow further enemy
successes at the time in Southern Russia.

The badge of the Ninth Army, which
was commanded by General (after Field-
Marshal) Sir Henry Maitland Wilson,
G.C.B., D.S.O., M.C., was a charging
elephant, on its back a castle, from which
flew the red and black flag of an Army
commander. The design was in red on a
black circular background, the elephant,
as in the case of the Paiforce badge,
associating with the formation the nick-
name of its commander—'Jumbo'.

The badge on the disbandment of H.Q.
Ninth Army, was subsequently adopted
by North Levant District?

Tenth Army.
The Tenth Army was raised in Iraq and formed the major part of 'Paiforce' (Persia and Iraq force). It was composed of British and Indian troops and was actively engaged in quelling the Iraqi rebellion in 1941 and in the operations against the Axis elements in Persia. The main task of the Tenth Army was the maintenance of the lines of communication to Russia from the Persian Gulf to the Caspian and the protection of the South Persian and Iraq oilfields. Its badge was a golden Assyrian lion with human head set on a black background. A variation of this colouring was a white lion on a pale blue background.

Twelfth Army.
Twelfth Army H.Q. was first formed in the Middle East, and was an H.Q. set up for the planning of operations in the Mediterranean, it was in fact, the H.Q. of Force 545, the force employed in operation 'Husky'—the invasion of Sicily. Its badge was then a black performing seal on a yellow background, balancing upon its nose a globe showing the Eastern Hemisphere.

The Twelfth Army title was re-adopted in the redesignation of H.Q. 33 Corps in Burma on 28th May 1945 and, under the command of Lieut.-General Sir Montagu Stopford, G.C.B., K.B.E., D.S.O., M.C.,

took part in the final operations against the Japanese which led to the liberation of Burma. It was responsible for the final clearance of the Japanese from Burma after the capture of Rangoon. The formation was disbanded on 1st January 1946 and the Corps and Divisions under its command were incorporated in the Burma Command. Its badge was a Burmese dragon, the chinthe (pagoda custodian) in white and gold superimposed on a background of two red and one, central, black horizontal bar above the Roman figures 'XII' in white.

Fourteenth Army.
A red shield with a narrow white inner border, the centre divided by a black horizontal band on which the Roman figures 'XIV' were inscribed in white, set across a white sword, hilt uppermost, was the badge of the hard-fighting Fourteenth Army, commanded by General (later Field-Marshal) Sir William Slim, G.B.E., K.C.B., D.S.O., M.C. This Army, which was disbanded on 31st December 1945, was formed in November 1943 and was the largest single army of the war. In its time it held the longest battle line, from the Bay of Bengal to the borders of India and China, and fought through some of the most difficult country in the world from Manipur to Rangoon. At one time its strength was nearly a million. It was grouped into three corps, the 4 and the 15 and 33 Indian Corps. A fourth corps, the 34, was formed for the invasion of Malaya, but Fourteenth Army never, in fact, commanded more than three corps, for when 34 Corps was raised, 4 and 33 Indian Corps were under command of the Twelfth Army. The Fourteenth Army's great victories in the Arakan, at Imphal, Kohima, Kennedy Peak, Mandalay, and Meiktila, led to the defeat of the Japanese and the liberation of Burma and Malaya. Fourteenth Army was withdrawn to India in June 1945

to prepare for the invasion of Malaya.
The H.Q. followed 34 Indian Corps to
Malaya in September 1945. The following
divisions served with the Fourteenth
Army: the 2nd and 36th British Divisions,
the 3rd (The Chindits), 5th, 7th, 17th,
19th, 20th, 23rd, 25th and 26th Indian
Divisions, the 11th East African and the
81st and 82nd West African Divisions.

The design of the Fourteenth Army
badge was submitted anonymously in a
competition open to all ranks for the
choice of badge—when it was chosen, it
was disclosed that the artist was none
other than the Army Commander,
General Sir William Slim, and he won
the £5 prize offered for the winning design.

1st Allied Airborne Army.
The badge of this Allied Army was a
light blue shield. At the top the words
'Allied Airborne' in gold on black, in
the centre a white Arabic figure '1'
with gold wings and, at the base, two
gladiator's swords in saltire on red
background.

1st Allied Airborne Army was
composed of British, American and
Polish Airborne formations of which
the following took part in the airborne
operations in North Western Europe in
September 1944: the 1st Airborne
Division (1st and 4th Parachute Brigade
and 1st Air Landing Brigade) with the
1st Polish Parachute Brigade landing at
Arnhem, and the 82nd and 101st U.S.
Airborne Divisions landing in Belgium
and South East Holland.

BRITISH CORPS

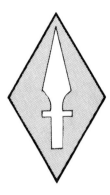

1 Corps.
A white spearhead on a scarlet diamond was the badge of 1 Corps. The design of the badge was adopted because in pre-war days the 1st Corps at Aldershot was the only British Corps permanently in existence, and as such was the spearhead of the British Expeditionary Force, as it had been in 1914, and was indeed again in 1939. The Corps formed part of the B.E.F., going abroad in September 1939, to France. It was among the formations withdrawn from Dunkirk in May 1940. The Corps badge was adopted whilst the formation was part of the B.E.F., and was symbolic of the selection of this Corps as an assault formation. 1 Corps landed in Normandy on D Day, 6th June 1944, and fought across France, Belgium and Southern Holland. The formation formed the first static district of occupied Germany, (1st Corps District) taking over the control and administration of the Rhine Province and Westphalia in the final stages of the campaign.

The Corps was reformed in B.A.O.R. in 1951 and the Corps Sign, as above, was re-adopted.

2 Corps.
2 Corps formed part of the B.E.F., landing in France in October 1939, and in April 1940 it moved forward into Belgium to meet the German invasion. The Corps returned to England via Dunkirk when the B.E.F. was withdrawn from the Continent. The formation badge was said to have been chosen as an association with the name of its commander. Lieut.-General Sir Alan Brooke (later Field-Marshal Viscount Alanbrooke, G.C.B., D.S.O.) and was originally three dark wavy blue bands on a white oblong, symbolizing a brook. The red fish, a leaping salmon, was added to give the badge a more 'watery' effect, and the badge was bordered by a narrow red line.

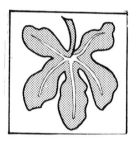

3 Corps.
3 Corps, comprising the 42nd (East Lancs), 44th (Home Counties) and 51st (Highland) Divisions, joined the B.E.F. in France in March 1940 and (without the 51st Division) took part in the operations leading to the withdrawal to and evacuation from Dunkirk. The Corps badge was adopted while the formation was in Northern Ireland. This badge, a green fig-leaf on a white background, was chosen for its association with the name of the Corps Commander, Lieut.-General Sir Ronald Adam (later G.O.C. Northern Command and Adjutant-General to the Forces). In 1943 the Corps embarked for Persia. Moving later to Syria and Egypt, it subsequently served in Italy and Greece, where the Corps H.Q. became H.Q. Land Forces, Greece.

4 Corps.

A black elephant on a red background[4] the badge of this formation was introduce at Alresford, Hants. in February 1940 by the then G.O.C., General Sir Claud Auchinleck who chose the badge of his own Regiment, the 1st Punjabis, —an elephant—as the Corps badge. This Corps H.Q. formed the H.Q. Northern Norway Land Forces in April 1940. The Corps H.Q. was later sent to Iraq. The Corps was moved from Iraq to India in the spring of 1942, and from then onwards was actively engaged in operations against the Japanese, firstly under command of Eastern Army (India) and then with the Fourteenth Army. The Corps saw much hard fighting in the liberation of Burma. It established the Irrawaddy bridgehead and, moving across country, drove the Japanese from Meiktila. The Corps was in the van of the Fourteenth Army in its drive to Mandalay and Rangoon. Finally the Corps came under command of Twelfth Army.

5 Corps.

5 Corps formed part of the N.W.E.F. in Norway in 1940. The formation badge, a Viking ship, was subsequently chosen to commemorate the Corps H.Q's. service in Norway. 5 Corps joined First Army, from Home Forces, in North Africa in 1942, taking part in the operations which led to the final defeat of the Axis forces in Tunisia and the surrender of von Arnim, commander of the Axis forces in Africa, to the Corps Commander, at Cap Bon. 5 Corps next saw service in Sicily and Italy, where it advanced northwards in the Adriatic sector. As part of 15th Army Group, and composed of the 56th, 78th, 2nd (New Zealand)

and 8th (Indian) Divisions, a Commando and two Armoured Brigades, 5 Corps, under command of the Eighth Army, took part in the final operations in the Po Valley which culminated in the surrender of the German armies in Italy.

The badge depicted the Viking ship and sail in white; on the sail a cross in red picked out in black, the design on a black background.

7 Corps[5]

7 Corps was formed in the U.K. in the summer of 1940, and, under the command of the Canadian, Lieut.-General McNaughton, was composed of the 1st Armoured Division, the 1st Canadian Division, and the 2nd New Zealand Division. The Corps was formed for an anti-invasion operational role on the South Coast of England during the Battle of Britain. With the defeat of the Luftwaffe and the German reluctance to venture across the Channel, the emergency passed and the need for this formation ceased to exist, and 7 Corps was disbanded on Christmas Day 1940.

8 Corps.

8 Corps has had two badges. As 8 Corps District (covering the counties of Devon, Cornwall and Somerset) of Southern Command in 1940-42, the badge of a black (Francolin) partridge on a white oval was worn. In February 1943, H.Q. 8 Corps moved to Scotch Corner, near Darlington, in Northern Command. The 9th and 42nd Armoured Divisions were placed under command and a new badge was adopted, the original badge being retained by the newly formed South-Western District which was raised to take over the former 8 Corps area in

South-West England. 8 Corps' second badge was appropriate to the formation's new role, an armoured corps. It was a charging knight in armour in white on a scarlet square. 8 Corps formed part of 21st Army Group, landing in Normandy in June 1944. With the 7th and 11th Armoured Divisions under command it took part in the operations from the beachhead to the Elbe, moving into Schleswig-Holstein on the final defeat of the German armies, where it formed 8 Corps administrative district of the British Army of the Rhine, with its H.Q. at Plon.

9 Corps.
A black 'Kilkenny' cat, back arched in defiance, on an orange square was the first badge of 9 Corps. It was said that the badge was adopted as a play on the '9' and the traditional nine lives of a cat, but it had been chosen by the corps commander, whose home was in Kilkenny. As 9 Corps District of Northern Command, the Corps area covered the counties of Northumberland, Durham, and the North Riding of Yorkshire, until mobilized in 1942 for service in North Africa.

On mobilization it was decided to change the badge, and the black cat was removed from all vehicles and personnel for security reasons before embarkation. The new badge selected in April 1943 in North Africa was a trumpet. The idea behind its adoption came from the biblical motto—'If the trumpet make an uncertain sound who shall prepare for battle?'

'I give you this sign,' wrote Lieut.-General J.T. Crocker, the Corps Commander, in his order notifying its adoption, 'as a trumpet call to duty, the highest of all military virtues, confident that you will all, with me, strive to live up to its great ideal.'

The Corps served in Algeria and Tunisia with the First Army. It was disbanded after the capture of Tunis and the conclusion of the North Africa campaign.

10 Corps.
The official designation of the 10 Corps badge was 'A green square, with a white rectangle in the bottom portion, and a white ball in the upper portion,' but the Corps badge has been worn on a red background, and also on a green semi-circular background. This was one of the Western Desert formations. Composed of the 50th (Northumbrian) and 4th (Indian) Divisions at El Alamein, the Corps pushed forward with the Eighth Army into Cyrenaica and Tripolitania and broke through the Mareth Line defences on into Tunisia to the defeat of Afrika Korps. 10 Corps then formed part of British forces in Italy, and under command of the Eighth Army took part in the final operations in the Po Valley which led to the German capitulation in Northern Italy in May 1945.

11 Corps.
A black and white chequered Martello tower, representing a castle or 'pill-box' guarding England's coast-line, was the badge of 11 Corps. This Corps formed part of Home Forces, and did not serve overseas, being disbanded in the U.K. It was popularly accepted that the badge was chosen as symbolic of the number

of 'pill-boxes' and strong points
constructed by the Corps along the
East Coast whilst fulfilling its anti-
invasion role in 1940 and 1941.

12 Corps.
12 Corps, formed in Home Forces, was
until 1944 located in South-Eastern
Command. Its badge, familiar in Kent
and Surrey, was three trees—foliage
green and black trunks—an oak, an
ash and a thorn, set in a white oval
frame on a black background. The
three trees were chosen to link with
the name of the commander, Major-
General (later Lieut.-General) Sir
A.F.A.N. Thorne, K.C.B., C.M.G.,
D.S.O., and 'the Oak, the Ash, and
the Thorn' in 'Puck of Pook's Hill,'[10]
for it was in the Pook's Hill country
that the Corps was raised. 12 Corps
formed part of 21st Army Group for
the invasion of Europe, and fought
its way as part of Second Army
through France, Belgium and Holland,
across the Rhine, where it was one
of the two assault corps, and in the
sweep through North-West Germany,
Hamburg falling to 12 Corps in the
final operations before VE Day.

During the operations in
Normandy—in the 'Bocage Country'—
the Corps Sign was likened to a
Bocage and the name was adopted
in the Corps Welfare Services, viz:
'The Bocage Club'.

13 Corps.
A leaping red gazelle in a white oval

on a red diamond, with a narrow white
border, was the formation badge adopted
in the Western Desert by H.Q. 13 Corps.
The badge was later changed to a red
gazelle on a white circle on a red
diamond with a narrow white border.
The formation was part of the Eighth
Army in the hard fighting in the Western
Desert in the winter of 1941-42 and,
with the 4th (Indian) and 2nd (New
Zealand) Divisions and a tank brigade
under command, took part in the relief
of Tobruk in November-December 1941.
The Corps took part in the battle of
El Alamein and the advance through
Libya to Tunis. It was 13 Corps which
landed in Sicily and fought at Catania
and cleared the Axis forces from the
island. On 3rd September 1943, the
Corps, then composed of the 5th
British and 1st Canadian Divisions,
landed on the toe of Italy. The Corps
remained in Italy throughout the
remainder of the war and, with the
6th Armoured and 10th (Indian)
Divisions under command, took part
in the final operations in the Po Valley
which brought about the German
surrender on 4th May 1945.[11]

25 Corps.
Formerly the badge of the H.Q. of the
British Troops in Cyprus,[12] the badge was
taken on by 25 Corps. It was a (Cyprus)
lion, passant guardant, as appeared in
the Coat of Arms of Richard Coeur de
Lion, (who took possession of the island
in 1191) in red on a yellow background.

30 Corps.
Another badge adopted in the Middle
East was that of 30 Corps, a black
charging boar set in a white circle on a
square black background. The 30th was
one of the Western Desert formations,

where it distinguished itself in the drive
to Tobruk in November 1941, and
together with 13th Corps bore the
brunt of the fighting against the Afrika
Korps from November 1941 to August
1942. The Corps formed part of the
Eighth Army at El Alamein, where it
was composed of the 50th (Northhum-
brian), 51st (Highland) and the 7th
(Armoured) Divisions. Early in 1944
the formation was withdrawn from the
Mediterranean and returned to U.K. to
join 21st Army Group. Landing in
Normandy, the Corps, under the
command of Lieut.-General Sir Brian
Horrocks, K.C.B., K.B.E., D.S.O., M.C.,
fought across France, Belgium and
Southern Holland to the Rhine. It was
one of the assault formations in the
Rhine crossing and drove deep into
Germany in the final operations.
30 Corps became one of the Corps
Districts of the British Army of the
Rhine, covering the Province of
Hanover, with its H.Q. at Nienburg.

BRITISH ARMOURED DIVISIONS

The Guards Armoured Division.

This formation was composed of regiments and battalions of the Household Brigade. The well-known badge worn by the Guards Division in the 1914-18 war was reintroduced for use by the Guards Armoured Division. The sign, designed by the late Major Sir Eric Avery, Bt., M.C. (who commanded the Guards Divisional M.T. Company in the first B.E.F.), was a white eye (the eye denoting vigilance) on a blue shield, with a red border, the above badge being selected from a number of designs painted on some of the Division's vehicles by the late Rex Whistler!

The Guards Armoured Division was formed in September 1941, and it formed part of 21st Army Group for the invasion of Europe. As part of 8 Corps it landed in Normandy in June 1944, took part in the hard fighting at Caen and Falaise and the dash to the Somme on the break out of the beachhead. It was the first formation to enter Brussels on its liberation in September 1944, and then took part in the operations which cleared the area from the Meuse to the Rhine. Crossing the Rhine under the command of 12 Corps, the Division fought its way across Germany to Bremen and Cuxhaven, accepting the surrender of the latter port shortly before V.E. Day. From the north of Germany the Division was moved back to the Rhineland, where the Guards Division had been in occupation in 1918-19. The Division was converted to an Infantry Division in June 1945. On the 10th of that month the formation paraded for the last time with its armour, and Field-Marshal Montgomery attended the ceremonial parade held to mark the occasion at Rothenburg. Redesignated the Guards Division, the formation then formed part of the British Army of the Rhine.

1st Armoured Division.

A charging rhinoceros (the most heavily 'armoured' animal) in white on a black oval background was the badge of the 1st Armoured Division. The Division joined the B.E.F. in 1940 as part of the forces on the L. of C. in the fighting which took place around the Somme and the Seine. Back in U.K. it formed part of the 7 Corps in South-East England. In 1941 the Division sailed for the Middle East and formed part of the British force in the Western Desert and was engaged in the fighting which halted Rommel's Afrika Korps' drive to Egypt. The Division formed part of the Eighth Army at El Alamein and in the advance across Libya to the Mareth Line, and into Tunisia in the spring of 1943, and was composed of the 2nd Armoured Brigade (The Bays; 9th Lancers; 10th Royal Hussars; and the Yorkshire Dragoons) and the 7th Motor Brigade (2nd and 7th Bns. Rifle Brigade and 2nd Bn. K.R.R.C.). The Division subsequently took part in the operations in Italy, but after the breakthrough of the Gothic Line, the formation was broken up. Its original badge continued to be worn by the 2nd Armoured Brigade[2] and in July 1946, when the 6th Armoured Division was redesignated 1st Armoured, the Division wore the 'mailed fist' badge of the 6th Armoured Division[3].

The original badge of the Division depicted above was a very static animal. The badge was changed in 1942 to the 'charging rhino' shown below.

This was brought about at Khatatba while the Division was refitting prior to the battle of El Alamein, when a Sapper of No. 3 Troop of the Cheshire Field Squadron was repainting the sign board outside Divisional H.Q. he produced a more spirited animal at the charge. The H.Q. Staff liked the change, the rhino's attitude being more in keeping with the formation's offensive role, and so it was universally adopted.

2nd Armoured Division.
A knight's helmet—symbolic of armour worn in battle—in white on a red background was this formation's badge. This was one of the Western Desert formations which took part in the early fighting against the Axis forces in Libya. The Division was formed in U.K. and embarked for the Middle East in November 1940. At the time of its departure it was the only fully equipped armoured formation in Home Forces, but it was a critical time in the Middle East and this bold move paid a good dividend. The Division was disbanded in May 1941.

6th Armoured Division.
A clenched mailed gauntlet in white, on a square black background, was this Division's badge. The formation served in the B.N.A.F. with the First Army during the campaign in Tunisia in 1942-43, and it was this Division which linked up with the advancing Eighth Army in the coastal sector of Tunisia in the final round up and defeat of von Arnim's broken Axis forces. The 6th Armoured served through the Italian campaign, and as part of the Eighth Army took part in the 15th

Army Group's operations in the Po Valley in the spring of 1945. The Division's dash to Gorizia in the last days of the campaign saw the crumbling of the final German resistance in Northern Italy. The Division was subsequently renumbered and became the 1st Armoured Division.

7th Armoured Division.
The 7th Armoured Division, the famous 'Desert Rats,' was the first formation to go into the Western Desert at the outbreak of war with Italy. It was in the sands and barren wastes of Libya that the Division earned its title, thanks to its 'scurrying and biting' activities, and the adoption of the jerboa (the desert rat) as its badge—a red rat in a white circle on a red square. This form was later changed to a brown rat, picked out in white, on a black background. The Division formed part of Field-Marshal Lord Wavell's original desert force, which became the Army of the Nile. It took part in the first offensive against Graziani's forces which rolled the Italians back beyond Benghazi in 1941. Throughout all the desert operations, in General Sir Claude Auchinleck's offensive, and with the Eighth Army under General Montgomery, the Division was to the forefront of the battle—at Sidi Barrani, the Battle of the Omars, Gazala; it took part in the battle of El Alamein, the advance through Libya, and in the final battles in Tunisia which brought the British Armies in North Africa to their goal.

The Division was withdrawn from
the Mediterranean early in 1944 to
participate in the invasion of Europe
with 21st Army Group, and it landed
in Normandy in June. It was in action
at Caen and Falaise and in the
operations in France, Belgium and
Holland which culminated in the
assault on the Rhine and the drive
into Germany. It was the 7th
Armoured Division which formed
the bulk of the British force which
entered Berlin, taking part in the
Victory march before the 'Big Three'
in the heart of the fallen capital, a
fitting end to the long, hard-fought
road from the Western Desert, where
the 'Desert Rats' first went into action.

8th Armoured Division.
Raised in England in 1940, this formation
embarked for the Middle East in 1942. It
did not, however, go into action as a
complete division, although within a few
weeks of disembarking in Egypt one
brigade took part in the Eighth Army's
hard-fought withdrawal to El Alamein.
Not long after the Division was broken
up on the reorganization and redistri-
bution of units and equipment in the
M.E.F.

The formation badge was taken from
the familiar traffic-light signals—the word
'GO' in black on a green circle within a
black square.

The Divisional motto being 'No stop;
Go on.' The badge of the 8th Armoured
Division continued to be borne after the
disbandment of the Division by the
R.A.S.C. Company or the 24th Armoured
Brigade. The Company became the 334
Corps Troops Company, R.A.S.C., and
carried this badge as its vehicle marking
in Sicily and Italy with the 13 Corps.

9th Armoured Division.
This war-formed Armoured Division was
raised in the U.K. in 1941, adopting as
its formation badge the head of a giant
panda. The Division formed part of
Home Forces, and was disbanded at the
end of 1944, when most of its personnel
joined the 21st Army Group

The badge was said to have been
adopted as a pun on the German
'Panzer' Divisions, but the badge was
originally adopted by the 1st. M.M.G.
Brigade and taken from the badge of
the Pandas' polo team in which several
officers of the Brigade had been members.
Major-General Burrows took the badge
with him to the Division on his
appointment to command after
leaving the Brigade.

10th Armoured Division.
A fox's mask in red on a black (or
yellow) circle was this formation's
badge. The Division was raised in the
Middle East, in Palestine in August 1941,
and made up mainly of mechanized
units of the original 1st Cavalry Division,
including the Yeomanry cavalry (of the
4th, 5th and 6th Cavalry Brigades) that
was dispatched to Egypt and Palestine
early in 1940. The Division formed part
of the Eighth Army at El Alamein, and
in the advance across Libya to Tripoli,
the Mareth Line and Tunisia.

11th Armoured Division.
Formed in England during the build-up
of our armoured forces in 1941, the
11th Armoured Division adopted the
badge of a charging black bull with red
horns, eyes and hooves, and a yellow
oblong background. As one of the
armoured formations of 21st Army
Group, with the fitting Divisional motto,
'Taurus Pursuant,' the Division, forming
part of 8 Corps, took part in the heavy
fighting around Caen, the break out of
the Normandy beachhead, the operations
in France, Belgium and Holland which
followed, and finally in the sweep
across Germany to the Elbe which
ended with the German surrender in
May 1945.

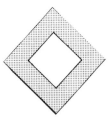

42nd Armoured Division.
This Armoured Division was formed in
1941 by the conversion of the 42nd
(East Lancashire) Division. It formed
part of Home Forces, and continued
to wear the badge of the East Lancs
Division, an equal-sided white
diamond within a larger red diamond.
The formation was disbanded in 1943.

79th Armoured Division.
A bull's head with black and white

markings; red and brown nostrils and
red-tipped horns on a yellow background set on an inverted equilateral
triangle to form the 'V' for Victory,
within a narrow black border was the
badge of the 79th Armoured Division,
which was commanded by Major-
General Sir P.C.S. Hobart, K.B.E., C.B.,
D.S.O., M.C., the Crest of whose arms
was a bull passant.
The Division was formed in England
in October 1942. It was reorganized in
April the following year and converted
to a specially equipped assault formation,
its armoured units being equipped with
'Flails' (for minefield clearance),
'Crocodiles' (flamethrowers), 'Buffaloes'
(amphibious carriers), 'Kangaroos' (for
the armoured lift of infantry), and
many special assault devices. The
Division included the 1st Assault Brigade
Royal Engineers, later redesignated the
Armoured R.E., made up of three
regiments equipped with A.Vs.R.E.
(Armoured Vehicles R.E.), and specially
designed assault bridging and demolition
stores. The formation formed part of
21st Army Group and had a distinguished
record in the fighting from D Day to
VE Day, taking part in the assault
actions of the Normandy landing; at
Caumont, Villers Bocage, Caen, Tilly
and Falaise; at Boulogne and Calais; at
the mouth of the Scheldt; at Breskens
and on the Island of Walcheren; at
Roermond and in the Siegfried Line
at Geilenkirchen; the Rhine crossing;
the Ruhr pocket, and on through
North-West Germany.

BRITISH INFANTRY DIVISIONS

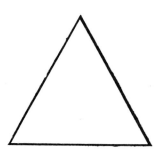

1st Division.

A white triangle was the formation badge of the 1st (Regular) Division. It formed part of the original B.E.F. and embarked for France in September 1939, as part of 1 Corps. It saw much hard fighting in the 1940 operations in Flanders and in the evacuation from Dunkirk. In 1942 the Division joined the First Army in B.N.A.F. (British North Africa Force) and took part in the campaign in Tunisia, thence to Italy, as one of the formations of C.M.F. (Central Mediterranean Force).

The triangular badge on the sleeve was often improvised out of ordnance flannelette, whilst the Divisional Artillery[1] wore the white triangle in the centre of an evenly divided red and blue diamond, and the Divisional Signals[2] the white triangle on a dark blue diamond.

Prior to 1939 the only corps more or less permanently in existence was 1 Corps at Aldershot. The badge of the Corps was a spearhead—the spearhead of the B.E.F. both in 1914 and 1940. The 1st Division therefore took the tip of the spearhead as its badge.

2nd Division.

Two white keys, crossed, on a black square was the badge adopted by the 2nd Division. It was chosen in 1940 by the G.O.C., Lieut.-General Sir H. Charles Lloyd, K.C.B., D.S.O., M.C.

The badge was an appropriate choice, for in the earliest days of the histroy of British arms, it was the practice in time of need for two armies to be raised, one in the South of England by the Archbishop of Canterbury, and the other in the North by the Archbishop of York. The northern army carried on its shield and banners the crossed keys (St. Peter's Keys) taken from the arms of the Archbishop of York.

This was a pre-war Regular division and it formed part of the 1939 B.E.F., serving in France and Belgium until the withdrawal from Dunkirk in May 1940.

The Division left England for India in 1942. After nearly two years training in India it was hurriedly moved to Dimapur on the borders of India and Burma in March 1944. It subsequently became one of the two British divisions with the Fourteenth Army in the victorious campaign which drove the Japanese from Burma.

The Division returned to India in June 1945, and was moved to Malaya at the end of that year. One brigade of the Division (the 5th) formed part of the British Commonwealth Occupation Force in Japan[3]. The badge was subsequently worn by the 2nd Division in B.A.O.R.

3rd Division.

Another Regular Army division which served with the B.E.F. and took part in the heavy fighting in holding the Dunkirk perimeter during the evacuation in May 1940. The Assault Division of Second Army, the 3rd Division landed on the Normandy beaches on the 6th of June 1944. As part of 1 Corps it took part in the establishment of and the subsequent break out of the beachhead and the operations in North-Western Europe culminating in V.E. Day in May 1945. In the autumn of that year the Division was withdrawn from the British Army of the Rhine and embarked for the Middle East.

3rd Division's badge was a red triangle surrounded by three black ones, the whole forming an equilateral triangle.

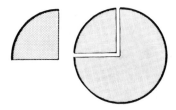

4th Division.

This Regular Division first adopted as its badge the fourth quadrant of a circle in red, but this was later changed to a red circle, with one quadrant displaced, set in a white square. It formed part of the B.E.F., arriving in France as part of 2 Corps in October 1939. In the evacuation in 1940 it held the west flank of the Dunkirk perimeter. The Division later saw service in North Africa with First Army and with the Central Mediterranean Force in Italy and in Greece.

(The badge depicted above was readopted in 1956 on the re-formation of the 4th Division by the conversion of the 11th Armoured Division in B.A.O.R.).

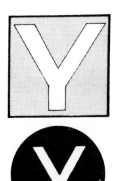

5th Division.

This Division undoubtedly holds the record of the most travelled formation of the war. A Regular Division located pre-war in Northern Command at Catterick camp, it joined the B.E.F. in France 1939. In the spring of 1940 one Brigade (the 15th) was withdrawn to participate in the operations in Norway with the N.W.E.F. The remaining two

brigades took part in the battles in Belgium and North-Western France which led up to the evacuation from Dunkirk. These brigades, under the command of Major-General Franklyn, together with two brigades of the 50th (Northumbrian) Division and the 1st Army Tank Brigade, became 'Frankforce' and were allotted a special role on the flank of the withdrawing B.E.F. In U.K. again, the Division served in Home Forces in England and Northern Ireland until mobilized in 1942 for further service overseas. The formation took part in the occupation of Madagascar, and thence to India.

The next move was to 'Paiforce,' where it formed part of the garrisons of Persia and Iraq. In 1943 the 5th moved to Egypt and joined the M.E.F. In July of that year it embarked for Sicily, and in September went to Italy. It took part in the Anzio landing the following year, and in July 1944, was withdrawn from A.A.I. and moved to Palestine. February 1945, saw the Division back in Italy, but only for a short period, for in March it joined 21st Army Group in Belgium in time to move forward and participate in the final stages of the war in Germany. The Division which was disbanded in 1946, subsequently formed part of the British Army of the Rhine, having been formed from the 7th Armoured Division in April 1958.

The Divisional sign was, during the war, a white 'Y' for Yorkshire to denote its pre-war association with Northern Command. Set on a khaki background, this badge was changed in 1946 and became a white 'Y' on a black circular background.

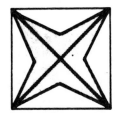

6th Division.

A red four-pointed star set in a white square was this formation's badge. A Regular Division, it was formed in Egypt in November 1939, under the command of Major-General (later Lieut.-General, Sir) J.F. Evetts C.B., C.B.E., M.C. from regular army units serving in the Middle East. The Division saw action soon afterwards in the

Western Desert. The Division established the Bagush 'Box,' East of Mersa Matruh. In June 1941, the Divisional H.Q., was hastily moved to Palestine to take command of the 5th Indian Infantry Brigade (detached from the 4th Indian Division) and other troops then moving into Syria against the Vichy Forces. Other Brigades moved up from the Western Desert came under command of the Division which then came under command of 1 Australian Corps with the 7th Australian Division. At the conclusion of hostilities in Syria 6th Division was composed of the 14th, 16th and 23rd Infantry Brigades with certain Australian gunner and sapper units under command.

The Division's next move was to Tobruk in relief of the 9th Australian Division. The relief of the Tobruk garrison was completed by sea in October 1941, and on the 10th of that month, the 6th Division was redesignated the 70th Division. This was a security measure designed to deceive the enemy and to prevent the changeover in Tobruk becoming known. The Divisional Transport was left in Syria with the 6th Australian Division which for a while used the 6th Division's red star badge.

Inside Tobruk the Division, then commanded by Major-General later Lieut.-General Sir Ronald) Scobie K.B.E., C.B., M.C., had some 25,000 troops under command, including one Australian Battalion (the 2nd/13th) the Polish Carpathian Brigade, the 11th Czech Battalion and the 32nd Anti-Tank Regiment. On breaking out of Tobruk in November 1941, and joining up with Eighth Army troops the Division was withdrawn from the Western Desert to Palestine, from where it was transferred to India Command.

8th Division.
This was a Regular Division, formed from two infantry brigades in Palestine in 1938, and commanded by Major-General A.R. Goodwin-Austen. It remained in

Palestine on the outbreak of war and was engaged in internal security duties until February 1940, when it was broken up. The Divisional H.Q. was disbanded in Egypt on the 26th February 1940. Its badge was a red cross on a blue shield.

9th (Scottish) Division
This second-line Territorial Army Division was raised in 1939 when the Territorial Army was doubled. It was the duplicate Division of the 51st (Highland) Division. It was disbanded at the end of 1940, when the greater part of the formation joined the reformed 51st Division to fill the gaps created by the loss of the 152nd and 153rd Infantry Brigades after their gallant stand at St. Valery-en-Caux.

The sign of the 9th (Scottish) Division was a silver thistle set on a dark blue background within a silver circular border, the same badge as born by the 9th (Scottish) Division during the 1914—18 war.

12th (Eastern) Division.[6]
This was a second-line Territorial Army Division, the duplicate formation of the 44th (Home Counties) Division. It was formed in 1939. It joined the B.E.F. in 1940, under the command of Major-General R.L. Petre C.B., D.S.O., M.C. The Division, less the 36th Brigade, took part in the hard fighting following the German break-through to the Channel ports, going into action on the lower reaches of the River Somme and in

Northern Normandy under the command
of Brigadier R.J.P. Wyatt. Part of the
Division joined up with the 51st
Division and fought with that formation
up to St. Valery. Major-General Petre
had been cut off from his Division
during the German armoured thrust,
and collected together an emergency
force known as 'Petre-Force,' to protect the flank of the B.E.F. from Arras
and along the Canal du Nord. The
12th Division had as its badge a white
diamond. The Division was subsequently
disbanded on the reorganization of the
forces in the United Kingdom.

13th Division.
Raised in Greece during the winter of
1945-46 from the British element of
the 4th Indian Division when that
formation returned to India, the
13th Division adopted as its badge
the Divisional sign borne by the
13th Division in the 1914-18 war—a
black horseshoe, picked out in white,
set on a square red background. The
13th Division had therefore had a
close association with Indian
Formations in two wars. In the
1939-45 war, the British battalions
and Divisional troops came from the
4th Indian Division; whilst in the
Great War the 13th (Western) Division,
composed of new army units, formed
part of the Mesopotamian
Expeditionary Force, where it
served with the Third Army Corps
and was the only British Division in
that force serving with the 14th,
15th, 17th and 18th Indian Divisions.
   It was said that the horseshoe for
luck was chosen as the Divisional sign
to offset any bad luck which, to the
superstitious, may have followed the
allotment of '13' as the Divisional
number.

15th (Scottish) Division.
This second-line Territorial Army
Division was formed in the summer
of 1939 as the duplicate of the 52nd
(Lowland) Division (T.A.). As its
formation badge, the Division adopted
the Scottish heraldic lion rampant,
set in a yellow circle with a white
border, on a black square.
   As part of Home Forces, the Division
manned the coastal area of Northumberland District) until placed under
command of 21st Army Group in the
autumn of 1943. Landing in Normandy
in June 1944, the Division played its
part in the establishment and subsequent break out of the beachhead,
the crossing of the Orne, and the sweep
across France and Belgium to the Maas.
It took part in the operations which
drove the enemy from the west bank
of the Rhine, the crossing in March 1945,
and the drive across Westphalia and
Hanover to the Elbe.

18th Division.
This second-line Territorial Army
Division, duplicate of the 54th (East
Anglian) Division, was composed of
Territorials from Essex, Norfolk,
Suffolk and Cambridgeshire. Under
the command of the late Major-
General Beckwith-Smith, formerly
Welsh Guards (who died in a Japanese
prisoner-of-war camp), the Division
was dispatched from the U.K. to
India in the autumn of 1941. Early
in 1942 it was hurriedly diverted
to Malaya, disembarking at Singapore
a few days before the fall of the city
in February 1942. The Divisional
badge was the conventional sign of
a windmill, to denote its association

with East Anglia, in black, set on an orange background.

23rd (Northumbrian) Division.
A Tudor rose in white, set on a blue (sometimes green) background, was the sign of the 23rd Division which joined the B.E.F. in France in 1940. It was located on the L. of C. when the German penetration into France threatened to cut off the main B.E.F. from its reserves and bases. The Division was allotted part of the line of the Canal du Nord and the Scarpe and formed part of the hastily raised force under Major-General Mason McFarlane (then D.M.I. at G.H.Q. B.E.F.) which was known as 'MacForce'. The formation was evacuated to the U.K. with the bulk of the B.E.F., but was subsequently disbanded.

36th Division.
The Division was originally an Indian Division, although two of its brigades were composed entirely of troops from U.K. The Division was formed early in 1943 as the Army component of the Combined Training Centre in India. At this time the Division wore the badge subsequently adopted by the 33 Indian Corps. In 1943 the 29th and 72nd British Brigades were allotted to the formation, but all the other units were Indian. At this time the Division came under command of the Indian Expeditionary Force and adopted a badge of its own, which was two interlocked circles, one red, one white, set on a black rectangle. The badge thereby incorporated the badges of two of the brigades—the 29th, a white circle, and the 72nd, a red circle.[8] The Division, under the command of Major-General F.W. Festing, D.S.O.,

took part in the operations on the Arakan front in 1944 in support of the 5th Indian Division in the jungle-covered hill country in the area of the Ngakyedauk Pass.

In May 1944, the Division was withdrawn from the Arakan and after a short rest near Shillong in Assam, moved to Ledo, the terminus of the Burma Road, where the formation came under command of General Stillwell's Chinese-American Army, and saw much of the hard fighting in the Myitkyina and Mogaung areas. In January 1945, the Division crossed the Irrawaddy and advanced into the Shan States, and came under command of the 14th Army during the final operations which broke the last Japanese resistance in Burma. After the capture of the Myitkyina and Mogaung airfields in December 1944, the 26th Indian Brigade was flown from India to join the Division. Later this Indian brigade was replaced by the 26th British Brigade, and thereby the formation became the 36th British Division. In June 1945, the Division returned to India and was disbanded.

38th (Welsh) Division.
Formed in the summer of 1939 as a second-line Territorial Army Division, duplicate of the 53rd (Welsh) Division (T.A.), the 38th was composed of Territorial Battalions of the Welch Regiment, The Royal Welch Fusiliers and Welsh Border regiments. The formation adopted as its sign the yellow cross of St. David of Wales, set on a black shield on a khaki background. The Division formed part of Home Forces.

40th Division.
This Division was raised in Sicily in the
autumn of 1943 and was made up of
Overseas Garrison battalions and Lines
of Communication units. The formation
was raised to add to the order of battle
in Sicily at the time that the 50th and
51st Divisions were withdrawn from
the Mediterranean to return to U.K. to
join 21st Army Group. Initially the
40th Division was composed only of
three battalions, the 30th Battalions
of the Royal Norfolk Regiment, the
Somerset Light Infantry and the
Green Howards; each battalion
assumed the role of a brigade, the
Commanding Officers flying
Brigadier's pennants and the
Adjutants signing correspondence
as 'Brigade-Major'.

The formation badges, made up
'on the ground', were an acorn cut
out of brown cloth stitched on to a
white linen square.

It is interesting to note the association
of this badge with the Divisional sign of
the 1914-18 war. This formation sign
was a bantam cock, on it a white diamond, within the diamond was an oak
leaf and an acorn which was added on
G.H.Q. authority to commemorate the
capture of Bourlon Wood.

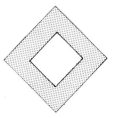

42nd (East Lancashire) Division.[9]
A first-line Territorial Army Division,
this formation was made up of
Territorials from Manchester and
the East Lancashire towns. The
Division formed part of the B.E.F. in
France in 1940 and took part in the
advance into Belgium and the hard
fighting which culminated in the
withdrawal to and evacuation from
Dunkirk. In 1941, whilst under the

command of Home Forces, the
formation was converted to an
Armoured Division and the sub-title
'East Lancashire' was dropped. The
Division did not, however, serve
overseas as a formation, and it was
disbanded in 1943. The Divisional
Engineers remained as a formation
and became the 42nd Assault Regiment, Royal Engineers (later designated
the 42nd Armoured Engineer Regiment),
and formed part of the Armoured
Engineer Brigade of the 79th Armoured
Division.[10]

Following the precedent of the
1914-18 war, when the 42nd (East
Lancs) Division wore as their sign a
red and white diamond, the formation
badge adopted in 1940 by the Division
was a small white diamond superimposed
on a larger red diamond. This was one
of the smallest of the formation signs,
being nine-tenths of an inch in diameter.

43rd (Wessex) Division.
The first-line Territorial Army Division
was composed of the T.A. Battalions of
the Devon, the Wiltshire, the Hampshire
and the Dorset Regiments and the
Somerset and Duke of Cornwall's Light
Infantry. As its badge it adopted the
ancient emblem of the Kings of Wessex,
the heraldic wyvern in gold set on a
dark blue square.

The Division formed part of Home
Forces as part of 12 Corps and as such
in 1943 joined 21st Army Group for the
invasion of Europe. It landed in
Normandy in June 1944, and took part
in the operations which led to the
establishment of the beachhead, which
was followed by the hard fighting at
Falaise, the crossing of the Seine, and
the sweep across France and Belgium.
It formed part of the force which
spearheaded the Rhine crossing in
March 1945, and took part in the final
drive across Germany which led to the
surrender of the German armies in
May of that year.

44th (Home Counties) Division.[11]
This first-line Territorial Army Division
was made up of T.A. units of Kent,
Surrey and Sussex and the County of
London. A scarlet horizontal oval[12]was
the formation sign when used as a
vehicle marking; the red oval sometimes
had a narrow white border. The 44th
formed part of the B.E.F. in 1940,
taking part in the defence of Cassel and
the withdrawal to and evacuation from
the Dunkirk beaches. Dispatched to
the Middle East via the Cape in 1942
it took part in the operations in the
Western Desert and was part of the
Eighth Army at El Alamein, but was
subsequently disbanded on the
reorganization of our forces in the
M.E.F.

45th (West Country) Division.[13]
Drake's drum was appropriately chosen
as the formation badge of this second-
line Territorial Army Division which
was formed as the duplicate division
of the 43rd (Wessex) on the doubling
up of the Territorial Army in 1939.
Like the 43rd it was composed of T.A.
units of the South-Western counties.
It formed part of Home Forces,
serving in Northern Ireland and in
England in an anti-invasion role. The
Division subsequently became a
training formation.

The colours of the badge were:
A yellow drum, red bands top and
bottom, white cords, and with a small
red diamond and dark blue square in
the centre. The drum was set on a
khaki background.

**46th (North Midand and West Riding)
Division.**[13]
A tree, the Sherwood Forest oak, set on
a black square was adopted by the 46th
Division—an apt badge for this
Territorial Army Division composed
of Territorials of the North-Midland
counties. The tree had a brown trunk
and green foliage and was picked out
with a narrow white border. The oak
being emblematic of strength and
reliability.

The 46th Division (T.A.) had ceased
to exist in 1936 when a number of its
original infantry battalions were converted into Anti-Aircraft Brigades R.A.
and A.A. Battalions R.E. in the
reorganization of the Territorial
Army to meet the increasing commitments of A.D.G.B. (Air Defence of
Great Britain). The Division was, however, re-formed three years later when
duplicate formations of the existing
T.A. field force formations were
raised.

The three infantry brigades and the
Divisional Engineers joined the B.E.F.
in the spring of 1940 for duty on the
Lines of Communication, one brigade
in the Nantes area and two near
Rennes. One brigade susequently
joined the main body of the B.E.F.
and was among the last to leave the
Dunkirk beaches; the rest of the
Division was evacuated from the
Normandy and Brittany ports after
the fall of France.

The Division formed part of Home
Forces until the opening of the North
African Campaign in Algeria and
Tunisia, when it joined First Army
and took part in the operations which
led to the final defeat of the Axis
forces at Cap Bon. The Division next
saw action in Italy, where, on 9th
September 1943, it was among the
first troops ashore in the Anglo-
American landings at Salerno under
command of the 5th American Army.
It subsequently took part in the
crossing of the Volturno and the
Garigliano. The Division was withdrawn to the Middle East for four
months to train and rest, but returned

to Italy to take part in the attack
which broke through the Gothic
Line and drove northwards. In
November 1944, one brigade (the
139th) flew to Greece, two battalions
going to Athens, the other to
Salonika. In February 1945, the two
remaining brigades of the Division
joined them from Italy. The Division
returned to Italy in April and formed
part of the Eigth Army in 15th Army
Group for the final operations in the
Po Valley which culminated in the
capitulation of the German forces.
The 46th then crossed the Alps to
form part of the British Army of
Occupation in Austria.

47th (London) Division.
One of the original first-line Territorial
Army Divisions, this formation did not
exist between 1936 and 1939. Prior to
1936 there had been two T.A. Divisions
in London, the 56th (1st London) and
the 47th (2nd London); the latter made
up of County of London Territorials.
The heavy calls on the Territorial Army
for A.A. Brigades R.A. and A.A.
Battalions R.E. to meet the needs of
the 1st Anti-Aircraft Division made it
necessary to reduce the London Divisions
to one; the 56th, being the senior,
remained. The 47th was, however,
reformed in 1939, when the Territorial
Army was doubled. During the war it
formed part of Home Forces, latterly
as a training formation. The appropriate
divisional badge was two red bells with
a red bow (Bow bells of London) on a
dark blue background.

48th (South Midland) Division.
The badge adopted by the 48th Division
was a blue macaw set on a red diamond
within a dark blue oval. This first-line
Territorial Army Division was made up
of Territorials from Gloucestershire,
Berkshire, Buckinghamshire, Worcestershire and Warwickshire. This was the
first line T.A. Division to join the
B.E.F. in January 1940, and took part
in the operations in France and Belgium
until the evacuation from Dunkirk in
May 1940. The 48th Division did not
serve overseas again as a formation. For
the remainder of the war it formed part
of Home Forces, filling, in the later
years, the role of a training formation,
which was adopted in 1942.

The Divisional badge was adopted
in 1940. At the time the Division's H.Q.
was in an old Elizabethan house at
Littlecote, on the River Kennet, two
miles west of Hungerford. In the hall
was a macaw in its cage. When the
G.O.C., Major-General (later Lieut.-
General Sir) Andrew Thorne first
entered the house the bird called out
'Good luck—Good Luck'. This was
taken as an omen, and, when a
formation badge was selected, the
macaw was chosen to commemorate
the incident. It was set on a red
diamond background to link the
badge of the Division with that of
the 1914-18 War when the sign
was a white diamond.

50th (Northumbrian) Division.

Composed of Territorials recruited from
Northumberland and Durham and
Yorkshire, this was a first-line Territorial
Army Division, and saw active service
in France and Belgium in 1940 as the
50th (Motor) Division under the
command of Major-General Le Q. Martel,
seeing much hard fighting in May 1940,
prior to the withdrawal of the B.E.F. to
the U.K. In 1941 the Division embarked
for the Middle East and joined our
forces in the Western Desert, where it
took part in the operations in Libya in
General Auchinleck's offensive, at the
Battle of Knightsbridge and the Omars.
The Division formed part of 30 Corps
at El Alamein and took part in the
victorious advance through Cyrenaica
and Tripolitania. It participated in the
invasion of Sicily and was heavily
engaged in the fighting at Catania. The
50th was among the formations withdrawn from the Mediterranean early
in 1944 and returned to England to
join the 21st Army Group. It took
part in the Normandy landings in
June 1944, and the hard-fought battles
around Caen which led to the
establishment of the beachhead, and
in the battles of the Falaise Gap and
the crossing of the Seine. The Division
was withdrawn from operations in the
autumn of 1944 and returned to
England with the exception of the
Divisional Engineers, who remained
in B.L.A. as G.H.Q. Troops Engineers.
Part of the 50th were, however, destined
to proceed overseas for a fourth time, as
the H.Q. and some Divisional troops
formed the nucleus of the British force
which went to Norway in May 1945.

49th (West Riding) Division.

This first-line Territorial Division was
recruited in the East and West Ridings
of Yorkshire. It first saw active service
in 1940, with the North-Western
Expeditionary Force in Norway. It did
not remain long in the United Kingdom
after the withdrawal from Norway, and
later in the year embarked for Iceland
to form the main part of our force
which held that Atlantic base. The
Division spent over two years in the
garrisons Reykjavik, Akureyri, and
Halfurdurfjord. The formation's
original sign was the white rose of
Yorkshire, which had been the Divisional
sign during the 1914-18 War and was
worn between the wars, but whilst in
Iceland the now familiar badge of the
polar bear on a black background was
adopted. The design depicted a polar
bear with its head pointed downwards
as if looking into the water; this was
afterwards changed, the head of the
bear looking upwards, head thrown
back in defiance. On its return to the
United Kingdom in 1943 the Division
formed part of the force destined for
the invasion of Europe and, as part of
21st Army Group, landed in Normandy
in June 1944. It took part in the
operations in France, Belgium and
Southern Holland, and in the latter
stages of the campaign was under the
command of 1st Canadian Army in
the final liberation of the Netherlands.

The Divisional badge (designed by
Colonel J.M. Grant, D.S.O., O.B.E., who
was a staff captain at the Divisional H.Q.
1938-39) was two capital 'Ts' (for the
Tyne and Tees) in red on a black square,
when looked at sideways the two 'Ts'
formed an 'H', so that the initial letters
of the three main rivers which flowed
through the Divisional area—the Tyne,
Tees and Humber—were represented in
the sign. The well-known 'TT' sign, which
marked the progress of the Division from

Tobruk to Sicily, through Italy and
Normandy, was not lost when the
formation was disbanded. The 74th Field
Regiment, R.A.[16] from the 50th Division
was absorbed by the 49th Division. The
old Divisional spirit was such, however,
that the Regiment was permitted to
add the red 'TTs' to the polar bear badge
of the 49th whilst the 524 Company,
R.A.S.C., the transport company of
151 Infantry Brigade, on becoming a
general transport company also retained
the 'TT' badge and took it into Berlin
on their vehicles with the occupation
force.

51st (Highland) Division.

The first-line Territorial Army Division
was composed of the T.A. Battalions of
all the Highland Regiments. It joined the
B.E.F. in France in January 1940, as
part of the 3 Corps, moving up to the
Belgian frontier and in March taking
over a sector from the French Army.

The Division was detached from the
British zone in April and moved to the
Saar front, where they took over a sector
of the forward defences of the Maginot
Line in the Ligne de contact. The 51st
were in the Saar when the German
attack broke upon the Netherlands and
Belgium, and the Division was moved
up from the French zone at the time
that the German motorized columns
were pouring into the gap where they
had broken through to the Channel
ports. The 51st came up to the attack
on the south of the German line of
advance, going into action at Abbeville
and on the Bresle. The Division saw
much hard fighting, sustaining heavy
casualties as they moved through
Normandy to stem the tide of the
enemy advance: one brigade was
detached from the Division to form
part of 'Arc force' in the defence of
Le Havre and was finally evacuated
from that port; two remaining brigades
(the 152nd and 153rd) being cut off
and trapped, their backs to the sea,
above the cliffs of St. Valery-en-Caux.
It was not possible for them to be
taken off by sea, and with ammunition
almost spent, suffering severe casualities,

and hemmed in by superior enemy
forces, the remains of the Division were
forced to capitulate.

The 51st Division was re-formed in
U.K., with its original remaining brigade
as the nucleus. The Division moved
overseas in 1942 to the Middle East
and went into action at El Alamein
with the Eighth Army, pushing on into
Cyreanaica on the heels of the retreating
Axis forces. On into Tripolitania through
the Mareth Line, the pipes of the
Highland Division were heard in Tunisia
as the 51st moved forward to the final
defeat of the Afrika Korps and their
scattered Italian allies.

The Division took part in the invasion
of Sicily in July 1943, and the landings
in Italy in August. The formation was
withdrawn from the Mediterranean
later in the year and returned to U.K.
to join 21st Army Group for the invasion
of Europe. June 1944, saw the Highland
Division in the Normandy beachhead. It
took part in the break out and the hard
fighting at Falaise, in the dash across
France to the Seine and on to the
liberation of Belgium, the fighting
which drove the enemy back across
the Rhine, and in the final advance
through Germany to the Elbe.

The 51st wore as their badge the
Divisional sign of the Highland Division
of the 1914-18 War: the letters 'HD'
in red joined together within a red
circle on a blue background.[17]

52nd (Lowland) Division
(Mountain Division).

Recruited from the Lowlands of
Scotland, this was a first-line Territorial
Army Division. The 52nd embarked for
France in June 1940, during the critical
days following Dunkirk, and landed at
Brest, Cherbourg and St. Malo. It
formed part of the covering force for
the withdrawal from the lines of
communication immediately prior to

the fall of France. Whilst forming part of Home Forces, the formation was allotted the role of a mountain division and was specially equipped and trained as such. It did not, however, operate in this role and joined 21st Army Group on the Continent in October 1944, taking part in the operations along the Maas, the Rhine crossing, and the drive into Germany. The formation sign was a modified version of that worn by the 1914-18 War. That sign was composed of the cross of St. Andrew on a blue shield, a thistle superimposed on the cross, the shield being set in the angle of a black 'L' (for Lowland) on a khaki background. The 'L' and the thistle were dispensed with in the new badge, the white across of St. Andrew on a blue shield only being worn. The word 'Mountain' in white on a blue ground on a separate scroll worn beneath the shield was added when the formation adopted this special role.

53rd (Welsh) Division.
A first-line Territorial Army Division composed of Territorial Battalions of the Welch Regiment, Royal Welch Fusiliers, K.S.L.I., and the purely Territorial Regiments of Monmouth-shire and Herefordshire. Mobilized in South Wales in 1939, the Division moved to Northern Ireland in 1940, where it remained until 1942. It then moved to South-Eastern Command and later became part of 21st Army Group. Landing in the early days of the invasion of Europe, the Division saw much hard fighting at Caen and Falaise, in the Ardennes, in the Reichswald Forest; took part in the crossing of the Rhine and the sweep across Germany. The Divisional badge was a red 'W', the base of the letter resting on a horizontal bar.[18] On the Divisional transport this 'W' was shown on a green background, but when worn on uniform the sign had a khaki background. It was said that the 'W' stood for Wales, and was also symbolic of the firm base of the attack (the horizontal), the spearhead of the attack (the centre inverted 'V' of the 'W'), and the outflanking

movements (the side members of the letter). It was also said that the badge was symbolic of a Bardic crown, and again that it represented the traditional tall hat of the women of Wales.

54th (East Anglian) Division.
A first-line Territorial Division made up of T.A. units from Norfolk, Suffolk, Cambridgeshire, Herts and Essex. The formation did not serve overseas as a Division, although it was absorbed into the Lines of Communication of 21st Army Group. The Divisional badge was a small red circle, the monogram 'JP' in blue in the centre. These were the initials of the Divisional Commander (Major-General J.H.T. Priestman, C.B.E., D.S.O., M.C.). One brigade of the formation (the 162nd) remained as an independent infantry brigade within 21st Army Group and retained the former Divisional sign as their badge.[19]

55th (West Lancashire) Division.
The red rose of Lancaster, the Divisional sign adopted by West Lancs Division in 1916, was retained by the 55th Division, a first-line Territorial Army formation, composed of Territorials from Liverpool and West Lancashire, between the wars, and continued as the formation badge during World War II. The rose depicted in the badge has five petals inside and five outside; the leaves are arranged five on each side of the stem, thereby repeating the Divisional number '55'. The Divisional vehicle marking did not include the stem and the leaves, and was confined to the Lancashire rose.

In the arm badge the rose was red, with green stem and leaves set on khaki circular background. The 55th did not serve overseas; it formed part of Home Forces, latterly in a training role.

56th (London) Division.[20]
The badge of this London Division was a black cat set on a red background. It was 'Dick Whittington's cat', as well as being a lucky black cat, and the badge was chosen by its original Commander, Major-General Sir Claude Liardet (the first T.A. Officer to command a Division). The 56th formed part of Home Forces until 1942, when it embarked for the Middle East and joined the forces which garrisoned Palestine, Syria and Iraq. The Division joined the Central Mediterranean Force in 1943 and took part in the landings at Salerno and Anzio and the advance through Italy, being well to the fore in the crossing of the Garigliano. As part of the Eighth Army, the 56th took part in the Po Valley campaign, forging through the Argenta Gap, winning the bridgehead over the Reno, and sweeping north-east to the liberation of Venice at the end of the 15th Army Group's victorious campaign in Northern Italy.

59th (Staffordshire) Division.[21]
This second-line Territorial Army formation, duplicate division of the 46th (North Midland) Division, was composed mainly of Staffordshire Territorials, and appropriately selected as its badge one depicting pit-head gear in red, against a black slag-heap on a blue background. The Division served in Northern Ireland and England as part of Home Forces, and joined 21st Army Group for the invasion of Europe. After taking part in the fighting which established the beachhead and the capture of Caen, the Division ceased to exist as a Field Force formation, the personnel going as reinforcements to other formations of Second Army. The Divisional Engineers remained as G.H.Q. Troops Engineers.

61st Division.
This was the duplicate (second-line) Territorial Army Division of the 48th (South Midland) Division. Raised in 1939 to 1945, it formed part of Home Forces. Its badge was a red diamond on a blue background. The Division moved to Northern Ireland in July 1940, being distributed over the counties of Londonderry and Antrim. It later moved to Armagh, Tyrone and Fermanagh. It returned to England in 1943 was mobilized for service in North-Western Europe, but it was subsequently stood down and became a training and drafting Division in Home Forces. The Division was then earmarked for service in the Far East, but due to the collapse of Japan it was not required and was disbanded in 1946.

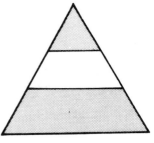

66th (Lancs and Border) Division.
This was a second-line T.A. Division, raised in 1939 as the duplicate Division of the 42nd (East Lancashire) Division

(T.A.), and was known as the 66th (Lancs and Border) Division. The Division was only in existence for a short time, for it was disbanded in June 1940. The divisional badge was never issued, but the design adopted was a light blue equilateral triangle divided by a central horizontal yellow band, the same design as the divisional sign of the 66th Division in the 1914-18 war.

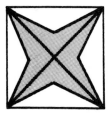

70th Division.[22]

Originally designated the 6th Division, this formation was renumbered 70th whilst forming part of the Middle East Forces in the Western Desert. It formed the garrison at Tobruk in 1941, relieving the Australians whilst the siege was still in progress, and in November of that year made the sortie which linked up with the 1st South African and 7th Indian Brigades during General Auchinleck's offensive. On the relief of Tobruk the Division was withdrawn from the M.E.F. and dispatched to India to meet the threat of the Japanese invasion. Whilst in India Command the formation was reorganized and formed the British element of the 3rd Indian Division (The Chindits). The 70th Division retained the 6th Division's badge when it was renumbered—a red four-pointed star on a white background.

76th Division.

This was a war-formed Division, on a special establishment, forming part of Home Forces, and allotted a training role. Its badge was a Norfolk wherry in full sail, in red, on a black background, the design linking the Division's associations with East Anglia.

77th Division.

This was also a war-formed formation with a similar role to that of the 76th Division. It was composed mainly of battalions of West Country county regiments, and adopted as its badge King Arthur's sword 'Excalibur', held aloft from the water, from the Arthurian legend which had its setting in Wessex. The colours of the badge were: red sword; white arm; and three wavy blue lines to represent the water; the design was on a black background.

78th Division.

This was a war-formed Division which was raised in Scotland in preparation for the North African Expedition, and landed with 'Blade Force' at Algiers on 8th November 1942. The Division had its first main clash with the enemy at Tebourba. As part of the First Army the Division saw much hard fighting, holding the line along the borders of Algeria and Tunisia during the winter of 1942-43, clinging on to Medjez el Bab, and the fierce fighting at Fort MacGregor and Longstop Hill. It took part in the final operations in Tunisia culminating in the surrender of the Axis forces at Cap Bon.

Landing in Sicily on 25th July 1943, the Division fought at Cantanuova, Adrano, Bronte, and Randazzo. Operations in Sicily were concluded on 15th August, and the following month

saw the Division in Italy fighting up
to Larino with the Eighth Army. The
78th were later withdrawn to Egypt,
but only for a short time, for the
winter saw the Division back in action
again in the Apennines. As part of the
Eighth Army in 15th Army Group the
Division took part in the forcing of the
Argenta Gap into Northern Italy, and
in the final round-up of the broken
German Army reached Austria, where
the Division became part of the Army
of Occupation. The badge of the
78th Division was a yellow Crusader's
battle-axe on a black square or circular
background, symbolic of the spirit of
the Crusader.

80th Division.
This was a war-formed Division. Under
command of Home Forces it was located
in Western Command, and had a training
and draftfinding role. The latter function
was said to be the reason for the
Divisional badge, a liner steaming across
the high seas. The ship was red; the
sea and smoke from the funnel in light
blue; the whole design on a yellow
background within a light blue border.

AIRBORNE DIVISIONS

The well-known badge of Bellerophon astride a Pegasus in pale blue on a dark maroon background is worn by all Airborne troops, and there were no separate badges to distinguish between the units of the 1st and 6th Airborne Divisions. The badge was designed by Mr. Edward Seago, the well-known landscape artist. Below the badge on a separate maroon strip is the word 'Airborne', in pale blue. The word 'India', also in pale blue, is incorporated in the badge, below the hooves of Pegasus, when worn by Indian airborne troops. It was in November 1941, that Major-General Sir F.A.M. Browning, K.B.E., C.B., D.S.O., was appointed G.O.C. and the Airborne Forces began to take shape with the formation of the 1st Parachute Brigade. This was the result of the hard work of experiment and development which had commenced in the summer of 1940. February 1941, had seen the first British airborne action. On the 10th of that month the first British parachutists to drop on enemy territory landed in Italy near Monte Volture with the object of destroying the aqueduct water supply of the Province of Apulia. This was followed by the successful airborne action at Bruneval near Le Havre.

From these beginnings the airborne forces grew, and by May 1943, two airborne divisions had been formed in the U.K.

1st Airborne Division.

The 1st Airborne Division first went into action in North Africa in 1942 when, in support of the British First Army landings, the 1st Parachute Brigade were allotted the task of capturing and securing the airfield at Bone; this was successfully accomplished. A second landing was effected at Souk el Arba. Their initial task complete, the formation fought as an infantry division during the winter of 1942-43 when the First Army was holding on to the scattered line from Cap Serrat to Medjez el Bab, Bou Arada and Fondouk. With the collapse and final surrender of the Axis forces in Tunisia, preparations went ahead for the invasion of Southern Europe. The 1st Airborne Division took part in the invasion of Sicily in July 1943: first glider-borne troops landed on the 9th and 10th, and three days later Paratroops were dropped in the vicinity of Syracuse. The Division also took part in the invasion of the Italian mainland, landing at Taranto and pushing forward to the capture of Castellaneta, the Air Landing Brigade occupying Foggia. As the invasion progressed and more men became available, the Airborne Troops were relieved in their forward positions, the Division was withdrawn and returned to U.K.

The formation's next action was in Holland. It was the 1st Airborne which won undying fame at Arnhem during those days, the 17th to 25th September 1944, when, under command of Major-General R.E. Urquhart, C.B., D.S.O., the Division landed in Holland to establish a bridgehead north of the Waal in an attempt to force the end of the war in Europe by a left hook sweep by 21st Army Group into the heart of Germany through the bridgehead established by the airborne troops. The final objective was not achieved, but it was estimated that the operation was eighty-five per cent successful and the efforts of the Division had not been in vain.

The formation was withdrawn to England. In May 1945, it went overseas again, landing in Norway, where the Division formed part of the British liberation forces.

6th Airborne Division.

While the 1st Airborne Division was in North Africa, Sicily and Italy, the 6th Airborne Division, which had been formed in May 1943, was training and being equipped to play an important role in the invasion of North-Western Europe. The first parachutists of the Division landed in Normandy soon after midnight of the 5th/6th June 1944, with the object of seizing the crossings over the River Orne and the Caen canal near Benouville, thereby being in position to help 1 Corps in the protection of the left flank of the British sector. In the hard fighting that followed the Division distinguished itself in the establishment of the bridgehead. When in August the order was given for a general advance, the Division swept north-east to Le Havre and crossed the Seine to Honfleur. The Division was withdrawn to U.K. early in 1945, to prepare for its second airborne action.

This was the assault of the Rhine in March, the Division landed on the eastern banks of the river whilst Second Army made the long assault. The Division then took part in the sweep across Germany, which was halted only by the surrender of the German armies after British troops had reached the Elbe and Schleswig-Holstein. The Division remained in Germany until the autumn of 1945, when it was moved to the Middle East. The 5th Parachute Brigade left the Division earlier. In July 1945, it was dispatched to India to take part in the operations for the recapture of Malaya as part of 34 Corps. This Brigade was one of the first to land in Singapore at the conclusion of operations.

1st Air Landing Brigade.

Symbolic of the composition of the Brigade Battalions of English, Scottish and Irish Regiments—the formation adopted as its badge, a red rose, a thistle and a shamrock, their green stalks and leaves entwined; and set on a maroon square.

ANTI-AIRCRAFT FORMATIONS

Anti-Aircraft Command.
The black bow and arrow, aimed upwards,
set on a scarlet square was the familiar
badge of Anti-Aircraft Command.
Originally the badge was worn only by
the staff of General Sir Frederick Pile's
Headquarters, but in 1943 it was
universally adopted for use by all
formations and units of A.D.G.B.
(Air Defence of Great Britain),
including the Home Guard batteries,
and the use of separate signs (as
previously worn by the three A.A.
Corps and twelve Divisions) was
discontinued.

The A.A. Command badge was
symbolic of defence against air attack,
but its choice was influenced by the
crest of the Gordon family, of which the
sign was a reproduction, which by coincidence appeared above the entrance of
"Glenthorne" at Stanmore, which was
built by a member of the Gordon family
in the nineteenth century and was taken
over as the Command Headquarters, and
the fact that the badge of the first School
of Anti-Aircraft Defence at Biggin Hill[2]
was a kneeling, nude archer, his bow and
arrow pointing skywards.

ANTI-AIRCRAFT
CORPS AND DIVISIONS

Owing to the large expansion of A.D.G.B. during 1940, it was found that super-vision of the A.A. Divisions could not satisfactorily be exercised by H.Q. Anti-Aircraft Command. Three inter-mediate formations, known as A.A. Corps, were accordingly formed on the 11th November 1940.

1st A.A. Corps corresponded with Nos. 10 and 11 R.A.F. Groups and covered the area south of a line approximately Great Yarmouth—Bedford—Bambury—Cardigan. It was composed of the 1st, 5th, 6th, 8th and 9th A.A. Divisions, and was commanded by Lieut.-General S.R. Wason and, after him, by Lieut.-General C.A.E. Cadell.

2nd A.A. Corps corresponded with Nos 9 and 12 R.A.F. Groups and covered the area north of 1st A.A. Corps as fas as a line Scarborough—Ripon—Barnard Castle—Whitehaven. It comprised the 2nd, 4th, 10th and 11th A.A. Divisions and was commanded by Lieut.-General M.F. Grove-White.

3rd A.A. Corps corresponded with Nos. 13 and 14 R.A.F. Groups and covered the area North of 2nd A.A. Corps and included Northern Ireland. It was made up of the 3rd, 7th and 12th A.A. Divisions and was commanded by Lieut.-General H.G. Martin, C.B., D.S.O., O.B.E.

During the night 'blitzes' which were in progress at the time of their formation and which lasted until the 12th of May 1941, all three Corps were kept equally busy. Frequent targets for the enemy in the 1st A.A. Corps area were London, Bristol, Southampton, Portsmouth, Plymouth, Cardiff and Swansea, in 2nd A.A. Corps area Birmingham, Coventry, Liverpool, Manchester, Sheffield, Leeds and Hull, and in 3rd A.A. Corps area Middlesborough, Sunderland, Newcastle, Belfast and Glasgow.

After May 1941, A.A. defences tended to drift southwards. German activity during the rest of the year consisted largely of minelaying along the whole of the East coast, and particularly in the Humber and Thames, and the South and West coasts as far north as Liverpool. In the spring of 1942 the Germans launched the 'Baedeker raids', Exeter, Canterbury, Ipswich and York being among the main targets, and one A.A. Division was transferred from 3rd A.A. Corps to 1st A.A. Corps to meet the changed areas of attack. At the same time there began the series of 'tip and run raids' on the South coast which further increased the commitments of 1st A.A. Corps. By the autumn of 1942 the respon-sibilities of 1st A.A. Corps had grown out of all proportion to those of 3rd A.A. Corps in particular, and, to a lesser degree, those of 2nd A.A. Corps. The time had come for considerable reorganization, and on the 1st October 1942, the A.A. Corps and Divisions were disbanded and replaced by seven A.A. Groups.

The distinguishing badges of the Anti-Aircraft Corps and Divisions were withdrawn in the latter part of 1942, when all A.A. formations adopted the A.A. Command badge.

1 Anti-Aircraft Corps.
This A.A. Corps covered the South of England and adopted as its badge a red eagle in flight, an arrow through its breast, set on a bright blue background.

2 Anti-Aircraft Corps.
A mailed arm, clasping a dagger—symbolic of the Air Arm striking against the enemy in the sky—in blue on a red oblong background was the badge of 2 A.A. Corps, which covered the Midlands and North of England. The Corps was commanded by Lieut. General M.F. Grove-White the crest of whose arms, described in heraldic terms, was 'upon a wreath a dexter (right) arm embowed in

armour holding in the hand a dagger all proper'.

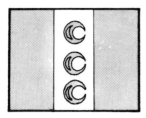

3 Anti-Aircraft Corps.

This Corps area covered Scotland, and its badge was the Corps Headquarters Brassard Colours—red, white, red, with, on the central white division, three red crescents with the points facing right. The adoption of the three crescents resulted from their being a charge in the arms of the General Officer Commanding the Corps; three crescents also linked with the Corps Number and the location of the Headquarters which was accommodated in three Crescents in Edinburgh.

1st Anti-Aircraft Division.

This was the first Anti-Aircraft operational formation and was raised on the 15th December 1935. Composed originally of Territorials drawn from London and the Home Counties, it became in 1938 a purely London T.A. formation. The Divisional badge subsequently chosen was a Dornier, in black, pierced by a sword in red, on a light blue background within a black border. The badge had a distinctive shape—an inverted isocleles triangle, the angle at the apex being squared off. The sword in the badge was taken from the arms of the City of London. An earlier pattern of the badge had a plain khaki background.

Originally covering the area south-east of the line from the Wash to the Solent, the Division, on the outbreak of war, was responsible for the A.A. Defence of London. It was heavily engaged in the night attacks on the metropolis in 1940-41, and was the first formation to use radar for gun control.

2nd Anti-Aircraft Division.

This was the second Anti-Aircraft formation to be raised. It was formed on the 10th December 1936, and was composed of Territorial Army A.A. Units located in the Midlands and North of England. Its badge was a red witch on her broomstick in flight, set on a dark blue background.

The badge was chosen to be symbolic of the formation's motto 'We sweep the skies'.

Badges in these colours were usually embroidered but the badge was also used with the red witch, broom and clouds stencilled in red on a plain khaki background.

Originally covering the area North-West of a line drawn from Harwich and North of London to the Solent it was later responsible for the A.A. Defence of the East Midlands and North-East Anglia.

3rd Anti-Aircraft Division.

A pre-war Territorial Army Anti-Aircraft formation raised in September 1938, and located in Scotland and with the majority of units of Scottish origin, this Division adopted as its badge a white thistle, on a blue square background, the letter 'A' set on either side of the Scottish emblem.

The first German raids on the British mainland in the area of the Firth of Forth were dealt with by this Division.

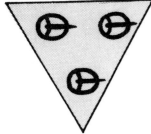

4th Anti-Aircraft Division.
This was also a Territorial Army Anti-Aircraft formation, raised in September 1938, and located in the North-Western Counties. Its badge was a red inverted equilateral triangle; on it in pale blue were three oval buckles. An alternative to this badge was a single buckle in red stencilled on a plain khaki background. The buckles of this formation badge were one of the charges in the coat of arms of the Cadells of Grange[2] (the arms of the Divisional Commander, Lieut.-General C.A.E. Cadell, C.B.E., M.C.). Until November 1940, the Division was primarily responsible for the A.A. defence of Birmingham, but later its main commitment was the defence of Manchester and Liverpool.

5th Anti-Aircraft Division.
This Territorial Army Anti-Aircraft Division was raised in September 1938, and was composed of T.A. A.A. Regiments R.A., and A.A. Battalions R.E. drawn from the Home Counties, the South and West of England, plus a few units from the County of London. The Divisional Headquarters were at Reading, and the badge was a falling Dornier in black, nose downwards, five red flames rising upwards from

the wings and fuselage, the whole on a khaki background. The Division's main commitment was the A.A. Defence of the Portsmouth and Southampton area and dealt with the 'tip and run' raids on the South coast.

6th Anti-Aircraft Division.
A black and white target, with a red arrow piercing the bull, was the 6th A.A. Division's badge. Raised in September 1939, the Division's operational area covered the Thames Estuary, Essex and North Kent.
    The Division was continually in action due to its operational area covering all the main approaches to London. In 1941 it dealt with the minelaying aircraft in the Thames Estuary, in 1942 the 'Baedeker Raids' on Canterbury and the 'tip and run' raids on the South-East coast.

7th Anti-Aircraft Division.
Raised in September 1939, and located in the North-Eastern Counties with its H.Q. in Gosforth, Newcastle, the sword and scales of the seventh sign of the zodiac in red on a blue background distinguished the units of the 7th A.A. Division.
    This formation was responsible for the Tyne-Tees defences and the first mixed battery to score a 'category one' success formed part of the Division.

8th Anti-Aircraft Division.

The 8th A.A. Division's badge was a
distinctive silhouette, in black, of a
German bomber, nose downwards, a red
eight-pointed star superimposed on the
fuselage, indicating a shell burst; the
whole set on a sky blue square background. The Division was formed in
November 1940, and was located in
South Wales and the West of England,
it was responsible for the A.A.
Defences of Plymouth and Bristol,
and Exeter during the 1942 'Baedeker
raids' and 'tip and run' attacks on the
South coast.

9th Anti-Aircraft Division.

An aircraft silhouette in red, on the
back of a black cat, the tail of which,
outlined in red, made the shape of a
figure '9', was the badge of the 9th
A.A. Division, which was raised in
November 1940, and covered the
A.A. Defence of Cardiff and the
South Wales Ports.

10th Anti-Aircraft Division.

This Division's badge was the heraldic
head of a lion in black, outlined in
white, set on a khaki background.

It was adapted from the crest of the
arms of the G.O.C., Major-General
L. Browning, C.B. O.B.E., M.C. who
chose the sign as it was considered
that the lion was a suitable symbol.

The formation was located in
Yorkshire, its main area of defence
being the Humber, for Hull was an
enemy objective not only in the
sustained night raids of 1940-41 but
also in the latter years of the war.

11th Anti-Aircraft Division.

A German eagle, in black and yellow,
with a scarlet arrow thrust upwards
through its breast, the design set on
a khaki background, was the badge of
the 11th A.A. Division. The arrow
being the eleventh sign of the Zodiac—
Sagittarius, the archer. The eagle was
a true German eagle, so much so,
that before the badge became known
there were instances of vehicles from
the Division being held up by the
Home Guard.

The Division came into being just
before the heavy raid on Coventry and
was responsible for the A.A. defence
of Birmingham, Coventry and the West
and Central Midlands in all subsequent
attacks.

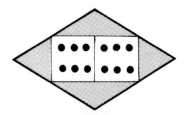

12th Anti-Aircraft Division.
The double six domino, in dark blue
and white, set on a red horizontal
diamond was 12th A.A. Division's
badge. The Division area included the
South-West of Scotland, including the
Clyde Estuary, and the A.A. Defences
of Northern Ireland. The Division
was raised in November 1940, in time
to deal with the attacks on the
Clydeside and Belfast.

COUNTY DIVISIONS (U.K.)

County Divisions were raised early in 1941 for an anti-invasion role, providing an operational and administrative Head-quarters for the grouping of independent brigades and units into operational formations. The County Divisions raised in coastal areas ceased to exist between October and December 1941 when replaced by Field Force formations.

Durham and North Riding County Division.
This Division had as its badge a pair of sheep shears in yellow, on a dark green background, the badge associating the formation with the wool industry of the North Riding of Yorkshire and the North Riding of Yorkshire and the name of the Commander, Major-General P.J. Shears, C.B. The Divisional H.Q. was later redesignated Durham and North Riding Coastal Area.

Dorset County Division.
Three lions passant guardant in black— adapted from the arms of Dorchester and the County Council Arms — set on a circle, right half yellow, left half white, the whole on a square khaki background, was the badge of the Dorset County Division.

Devon and Cornwall County Division.
The arms of the Duchy of Cornwall, fifteen gold bezants on a black shield, with a gold border superimposed on the sword Excalibur, yellow hilt and white blade, set on a dark blue rectangle was this formation's badge; it was subsequently adopted, when the formation was disbanded, by the 73rd Independent Infantry Brigade.[1]

The H.Q. of this County Division the became the H.Q. of the 77th Division in which the sword 'Excalibur' also formed part of the Divisional badge.

Essex County Division.
The three seaxes of the arms of the County of Essex, in white on a red shield or red square background, was this County Division's badge, which was later adopted in design, but not in colour by the 223rd Independent Infantry Brigade.[2]

Hampshire County Division.
A black Hampshire hog, set on a white rectangular or semicircular background, was the badge adopted by the Hampshire Division which was formed from Hampshire Area.

Lincolnshire County Division.
The tulip, the traditional flower of
Lincolnshire, was worn by the Lincolnshire County Division. When the
formation was disbanded the badge
continued to be worn by the 212th
Independent Infantry Brigade? The
badge was a red tulip with green
stem and leaf set on a white
rectangular background, emblematic
of the bulb growing industry of
Lincolnshire, in which county the
Division was raised.

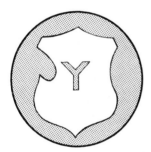

Yorkshire County Division.
The badge of this County Division was
a red 'Y' on a white shield, set in a red
circle. On disbandment in December 1941
the Divisional H.Q. was redesignated
East Riding District?

Northumbrian County Division.
Formed in February 1941 and disbanded
in December of that year, this division
wore as its badge St. Oswald's shield
with six yellow and red vertical bars.
The shield set on a dark blue background?

CANADIAN FORMATIONS

Canadian Military Headquarters (C.M.H.Q.).
The gold maple leaf, the national emblem of Canada, set on a black circle within a golden border was the appropriate badge of C.M.H.Q. which was established in in England in the autumn of 1939 to command and administer, other than operationally, all the Canadian Forces in the U.K. and the European theatres of operations. The H.Q. was located in Cockspur Street, London near Trafalgar Square. The badge was also worn by all base units in the United Kingdom which came directly under command of Canadian Military Headquarters.

First Canadian Army.
The first Canadian Army was raised in England on 6th April 1942, having under command by the end of that year the 1 and 2 Canadian Corps, comprising the 1st, 2nd and 3rd Canadian Divisions and the 4th and 5th Canadian Armoured Divisions. The 1 Canadian Corps with the 1st Canadian Division and the 5th Canadian Armoured Division left the United Kingdom in 1943 to come under command of the Eighth Army in the invasion of Sicily and Italy. First Canadian Army, with the remaining Canadian forces in the U.K., then came under command of 21st Army Group for the invasion of Europe, and the formation went ashore in Normandy in June 1944. After the break-out

from the beachhead the Canadian Army was allotted the coastal route in the sweep up the Channel coast through France and Belgium as far as the Scheldt estuary. During the winter of 1944-45 First Canadian Army was located at Tilburg in Southern Holland; it then moved forward to Grave, near Nijmegen, for the operations which drove the enemy from the Reichswald Forest and to the north bank of the Waal. Following the Rhine crossing the Canadian Army swung north and west into occupied Holland and fought westwards in the final operations which led to the capitulation of the Nazi forces and the liberation of Holland.

The First Canadian Army's sign was a scarlet horizontal diamond with a centre band of dark blue, this representing a combination of the 'patches' of the 1st and 2nd Canadian Corps, which were red and blue diamonds respectively. A different badge was used for vehicle markings and directional signs. This was a yellow maple leaf superimposed on a red background with a central black bar.

1 Canadian Corps.
With the arrival in U.K. of the 2nd Canadian Division, which was completed in December 1940, 1 Canadian Corps was formed to command the 1st and 2nd Canadian Divisions, then in England. The Corps was located in South-Eastern Command. It embarked for the Mediterranean in 1943, landing in Italy in September in command of the 1st Canadian Infantry Division and the 5th Canadian Armoured Division. The Corps took part in the hard-fought advance through Italy, including

Cassino and the piercing of the Adolf
line. The formation was withdrawn in
March 1945, to North-West Europe to
join the 1st Canadian Army in Holland
in time for the closing operations which
led to the final liberation of the
Netherlands. The formation badge was
a scarlet horizontal diamond, in keeping
with the colour worn by the Canadian
Corps in the 1914-18 war.

2 Canadian Corps.
The 2 Canadian Corps was also raised in
England when the Canadian Divisions
numbered five with the arrival of the
4th Canadian Armoured Division in
1942. Forming part of 1st Canadian
Army, the Corps took part in the
landings in Normandy, the establishment
of the beachhead, and in the general
advance was allotted the coastal
forward route through Dieppe and
northwards along the Channel coast
to the Scheldt. Throughout the winter
of 1944-45 it was on the right flank
of 21st Army Group and took part in
the operations which drove the enemy
to the east bank of the Rhine and finally
from Holland in the last stages of the
campaign in North-West Europe. The
Corps badge was a dark blue horizontal
diamond.

CANADIAN DIVISIONS

The Canadian Divisions, as in the 1914-18 war, all wore a similar sign, a rectangular cloth patch, called the 'battle patch', the colour varying for each formation as follows:—

1st Division . . . .   Red.
2nd Division . . . .   Royal Blue.
3rd Division . . . .   French grey.
4th Armoured Division . . .   Dark green.
5th Armoured Division . . .   Maroon.

1st Canadian Division.
(Red patch.)
This was the first Canadian formation to proceed overseas from the Dominion. The first troops arrived in the Clyde on 17th December 1939; there were 7,500 all ranks, the forerunners of the 335,000 Canadian troops who finally landed in the United Kingdom. The 1st Division was then commanded by Major-General (later General) A.G.L. McNaughton. In 1940 part of the Division was warned for duty in Norway, but although it moved to Scotland in preparation for embarkation to Trondheim, the operation was cancelled. In May 1940, the Division received orders to join the B.E.F., but following the German breakthrough to the Channel coast, these too were cancelled. The 1st Canadian Infantry Brigade of the Division, finally embarked for France in June, landing in Brittany a few days before the fall of France. The Brigade had moved up from Brest to the Le Mans area, only to be evacuated a few days later. Back in England it formed part of the 7th Corps, then forming up for its anti-invasion role in South-East England. The Division subsequently formed part of 1st Canadian Corps, and the Canadian Corps District. Selected units of the Division were withdrawn in 1941 to participate in the Spitzbergen expedition, and in 1942 other units took part in the Dieppe raid.

The Division left England in June 1943, landing in Sicily in July. In September it formed part of the invasion force which landed on the toe of Italy, and under command of the Eighth Army it distinguished itself at Orona, in the Liri Valley and the break through the Gothic Line. In March 1945, together with the other Canadian forces in Italy, it was withdrawn to join the First Canadian Army in North-Western Europe and took part in the final operations leading to the defeat of the German Army and the liberation of Holland.

2nd Canadian Division.
(Royal blue patch.)
The Division arrived in England in August and September 1940; some units, including two infantry battalions, did not arrive until December, having served several months after leaving Canada with the British troops in Iceland. The formation was concentrated in Surrey and Sussex in the Canadian Corps District. 2nd Canadian Division formed the main part of the force which took part in the first major assault on Nazi-occupied Europe in the raid on Dieppe, distinguishing itself in the fierce fighting on the beaches and the town defences. The Division Commander, Major-General J.H. Roberts, was the military force commander during the operation. The Division returned to Europe in June 1944, as part of First Canadian Army in 21st Army Group, and took part in the break-out of the Normandy beachhead, the Falaise battle, and the sweep up the French Channel coast, taking Dieppe and the Channel ports up to the mouth of the Scheldt. Thence into Holland, taking part in the operations which drove the Germans from the area south of the Waal, and finally, in the last phases of the campaign, in the liberation of the remaining Nazi—occupied territory of Holland.

Soon after its arrival in England, the Division adopted as its formation badge a royal blue patch upon which was a gold (or Yellow) letter 'C', the Roman figure II in the centre of the 'C'. This badge was subsequently superseded by the plain royal blue 'battle patch' to conform with the other Canadian divisions. The use of the 'C II' badge was, however, continued to distinguish the Division's installations and welfare organizations.

3rd Canadian Division.
(French grey patch.)
The 3rd Division left the Dominion for England in July 1941, and took its place in the Canadian Corps with the 1st and 2nd Divisions. Its first active service was in the invasion of the Continent in June 1944, where it went ashore in Normandy as one of the assault divisions, winning distinction in the fierce fighting around Caen and later in the Falaise battle, the advance through France and along the Belgian Coast, and finally in the liberation of Holland following the defeat of the German occupying forces.

The 3rd Canadian Infantry Division (C.A.O.F.) constituted the Canadian Army Occupation Force in Germany after the war, and, as such, was distinct from the 3rd Canadian Division referred to above, which returned to the Dominion after the cessation of hostilities. In order to distinguish between the two formations personnel of the occupation force wore a French grey bar below the formation patch.

4th Canadian Armoured Division.
(Dark green patch.)
Arriving in the United Kingdom in the autumn of 1942, this Division also formed part of the First Canadian Army in the invasion of Europe, going ashore on the Normandy beaches, participating in the battles of the beachhead breakout, and forming the armoured spearhead of the Canadian drive that cleared the Germans from the Channel coast and from Holland.

5th Canadian Armoured Division.
(Maroon patch.)
Originally designated the 1st Canadian Armoured Division, the 5th Armoured left Canada in June 1941, to join the Canadian forces in the United Kingdom, where it remained until the late autumn of 1943, when it embarked for the Mediterranean. The Division landed at Naples in November 1943, and with the 1st Canadian Division formed part of the 1 Canadian Corps in the

operations leading up to the assault and break through the Gothic Line. In March 1945, the Division was withdrawn from Italy and joined the Canadian Army in Holland for the final phase of the war in North-West Europe.

1st Canadian Armoured Brigade.
A black horizontal diamond²with a red centre band was this formation's badge. The Brigade participated in the invasion of Sicily and subsequent operations in Italy. It joined 1st Canadian Army in North-West Europe in 1945.

2nd Canadian Armoured Brigade.
Also a black horizontal diamond, but with a dark blue central band, was the badge of the 2nd Canadian Armoured Brigade, which formed part of the First Canadian Army in the campaign in France and Belgium and in the liberation of Holland. The horizontal diamond badges of the 1st and 2nd Canadian Armoured Brigades, described above, were the badges worn by the personnel of the brigades. The vehicle markings were of similar colouring, but the shapes were oblong, with a yellow maple leaf in the centre.

1st Canadian A.G.R.A.
This Army Group R.A. formation wore a red and blue patch, the central blue band having a red zigzag line similar to that in the R.A. Regimental tie. The formation formed part of 1st Canadian Army and served in North-Western Europe.

1st Canadian Corps R.C.A.
The Artillery of the 1st Canadian Corps wore a similar patch in red with a central blue zigzag bar.

2nd Canadian A.G.R.A.
This formation wore a similar badge to the 1st Canadian A.G.R.A. It is a dark blue patch with a red zigzag line.

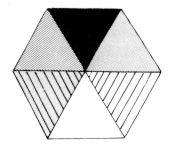

Canadian Army Pacific Force.
This formation was to have comprised one division (the 6th Canadian) and details and was made up of Canadian Army volunteers for the Japanese War. Organization of the force was proceeded with after the defeat of Germany and volunteers from the Canadian Army overseas in Europe returned to the Dominion. The force was to have been organized on American lines and equipped in the U.S.A. Advance parties had reached Fort Knox, Kentucky, when owing to the collapse of Japan, it was decided that the force would not be completed and volunteering closed on the 15th of August 1945. All ranks actually posted in Canada to C.A.P.F. wore a hexagon, three inches in diameter, of six equal segments, reading clockwise, red, blue, French grey, green, maroon and black; the division between the red and black segments being at the top centre. The colours were representative of the Divisions of the Canadian Army overseas except the black, which represents the independent armoured brigades.

Hong Kong Service Badge.
This badge was not in any sense a formation badge, although it was worn on the sleeve in the same manner. It was not issued until 1945, and was worn by all Canadian Army personnel who had served in Hong Kong in 1941, and issued to them as soon as they arrived at the reception camps in British Columbia on repatriation to the Dominion. In the Canadian Press it was called a 'battle patch', and it was proudly worn by all Canadians, who were among the first of the Dominion troops to see major action in the 1939-45 war. The badge was composed of a red circle approximately two inches in diameter with, in the centre, a white embroidered Chinese style monogram 'HK'.

AUSTRALIAN FORMATIONS

Most Australian formations adopted as
their badges the national animals and
birds of the Commonwealth, the
kookaburra, emu, parakeet, swan,
kangaroo and koala bear. With few
exceptions, all the Australian badges
incorporated a boomerang in the design.
The badges were used as divisional signs
and vehicle markings; combinations of
coloured patches being worn on uniforms
as distinguishing marks for personnel.
The coloured shoulder patches of the
Australian military forces were first
adopted in the 1914-18 war. Coloured
flags were used to distinguish unit
lines in large camps, and these were of
different shapes and colours. The use of
these coloured geometrical shapes was
later extended and small replicas of the
designs were taken into use for wear on
uniforms. The small coloured patches
worn on the sleeves vary in shape
according to the branches of the
service, and combinations of colours
denote the brigades of division and
battalions of brigades and so on.
The Militia divisions of the Australian
Army wore, between the wars, the
coloured patches borne by the
Australian Imperial Forces of the
1914-18 war. To distinguish units of
the 1939-45 A.I.F., a narrow grey
border was added to all formation and
unit patches.

H.Q. Australian Imperial Forces M.E.F.
A badge similar to the General Service
capbadge of the Australian Common-
ealth Forces was adopted by the Headquarters of the A.I.F. in the Middle East.
The design was in yellow on a blue background. The badge does not, as is
popularly supposed, represent the Rising
Sun. It originated from the badge of the
first regiment of Australian Light Horse,
who served with the Imperial Forces in
South Africa (1899–1902), which had

been designed to represent a trophy of
arms—swords and bayonets surrounding
the crown.

Australian Imperial Forces
Base Area M.E.F.
The Base area of the Australian Imperial
Forces in the Middle East adopted as its
badge a dingo above a boomerang. The
design in white on a black background.

First Australian Army.
First Australian Army was raised in 1942
in Melbourne under the command of
Lieut.-General Sir J.D. Lavarack. From
1942 until 1944 it was located in
Australia. In August 1944, it embarked
for New Guinea where the formation
took over the operational and administrative responsibilities of New Guinea
Force, and also the command of all
Australian troops in the Solomon
Islands, New Britain and Aitape. Its
badge was the black swan of Western
Australia in white, set above a white
boomerang on a black background.

Second Australian Army.
Raised in October 1942, the Second

Australian Army did not serve outside
the Commonwealth. Its H.Q. was located
at Ivanhoe in Victoria, and later at
Parramatta, New South Wales. Its badge
was a horse set above a boomerang.

1 Australian Corps.
This Corps was formed in the Middle
East in April 1940, under the command
of Lieut.-General Sir Thomas Blamey.
The Corps was withdrawn from M.E.F.
in 1942, and took part in the operations
in New Guinea.

2 Australian Corps.
This formation was raised in 1943. It
was later redesignated New Guinea Force'
and assumed the administrative and
operational responsibility for all
Australian activities in New Guinea. In
1944 it was reconstituted as a Corps
and relieved the XIV American Corps
at Bougainville. The Corps badge was
a parakeet's head above a boomerang.

3 Australian Corps.
This Corps H.Q. became H.Q. Western
Command, Australia, and included the
Western Australia lines of communication
Area. Its badge was a black and white
magpie.

1st Australian Armoured Division.
Raised in Australia in 1941. This
formation was redesignated in 1943 the
1st Armoured Brigade Group, and saw
active service in the operations at Buna,
Port Moresby and Milne Bay. Its badge
was an armourclad arm and hand holding
aloft a battleaxe in white on a black
background.

2nd Australian Armoured Division.
Formed in 1942 from the 2nd Australian
Cavalry Division, which for a short period
was designated the 2nd Australian Motor
Division, this formation badge was a
scorpion. The Division did not serve
outside Australia.

3rd Australian Armoured Division.
Formed in November 1942, from the
1st Australian Motor Division, this
formation badge was a mounted knight
in armour. The Division did not serve
outside the Commonwealth.

2nd Australian Division.
This Division, raised in February 1942,
served in New South Wales and in Western
Australia. The formation badge was a
penguin set above a boomerang.

1st Australian Cavalry Division.
1st Australian Motor Division.
The 1st Australian Cavalry Division,
comprised of the famous Australian
Light Horse Regiments, was reorganized
in March 1942, and redesignated the
1st Australian Motor Division. Its badge
was a greyhound leaping above a
boomerang. The formation later became
the 3rd Australian Armoured Division.
(See above.)

3rd Australian Division.
This formation, raised in 1942, saw much
hard fighting in New Guinea in the
operations which culminated in the
defeat of the Japanese at Salamaua and
in their strongholds in the Buna area and
around the Huron Gulf and the Markham
Valley, and later at Bougainville in the
Solomons. A koala bear and a boomerang
was the Divisional badge.

1st Australian Division.
Formed in December 1941, in New South
Wales, this Division served in Australia.
Its badge was an athlete with raised
javelin set above a boomerang.

4th Australian Division.
Raised in 1943, this formation was
designated York Force, and in October
1943, assumed command of the Torres
Strait area, where it remained until
September 1944. It was disbanded the
following month. The formation badge
was an echidna above a boomerang.

5th Australian Division.
This Division, which was raised in 1942 in Queensland, saw operational service the following year in New Guinea, taking part in the hard fighting at Kouriatum, Bobdubi and Salamaua. From April to September 1944, it took part in the operations in the Alexishafen area and at Hansa Bay and Sepik River. In October 1944, it moved to New Britain. A boar's head above a boomerang was the formation badge.

6th Australian Division.
This Division sailed from Australia in January 1940, to join the British Forces in the Middle East, and formed part of General (later Field-Marshal) Lord Wavell's original force which sept the Italians back from the Egyptian border in our first offensive. Bardia, Tobruk, Derna fell to the 6th Australian Division; they captured Giarubub and forced the surrender of Benghazi. The Division was withdrawn from Libya to form part of the force which was dispatched to Greece in 1941. Following the evacuation the Division moved to Crete and then back to Egypt. It also took part in the operations in Syria against the Vichy forces.

Withdrawn from the Middle East in 1942, the Division was moved to Ceylon to meet the threat of a Japanese invasion. The Division returned to Australia. It next saw service in New Guinea at Buna, Salamaua, the Danmap River, and at Wewak.

The Division's well-known badge was a white kangaroo leaping above a white boomerang, the two on a black background.

7th Australian Division.
This Division first saw service in the Middle East in the Western Desert, one Brigade taking part in the defence of Tobruk. The Division also took part in the operations in Syria, and was then withdrawn to Australia.

The 7th Australian Division played a prominent part in the recoquest of New Guinea in the hard fighting around Finschafen and Lae, the operations in the Markham and Ramu valleys and in the Madang area and at Hansa Bay. The badge of the Division was the Australian bird the kookaburra, perched on a boomerang, set on a black background. This badge was changed when the Division was allotted an airborne role and a kookaburra in flight was adopted. Although an airborne formation, the Division participated in operations in New Guinea mainly in an infantry role. In consequence, humorists depicted the kookaburra wearing heavy boots when the sign was used as a vehicle marking.

8th Australian Division.
This Division formed part of the Empire forces in Malaya at the time of the Japanese invasion. It arrived at Singapore in February 1941, and on 14th January the following year, was in action against the invaders, withdrawing fighting a stubborn rear-guard action across the Johore Strait, back to Singapore and

was part of the force which was forced to capitulate on Singapore Island at the fall of Malaya. An emu above a boomerang was the formation badge.

12th Australian Division.
Raised in 1942, this formation later became the Northern Territory force with its headquarters at Port Darwin. It did not serve outside Australia. Its badge was a water buffalo set above a boomerang.

9th Australian Division.
This formation served in the Middle East and took part in the hard fighting in the Western Desert; at this time the Division wore a 'T' shaped cloth patch as its formation sign? It formed part of the Eighth Army at El Alamein, but was withdrawn from the M.E.F. early in 1943 and in February sailed for Australia. Back in Australia the Division was re-equipped and was moved to New Guinea, where, with the 7th Australian Division, it took part in the operations against the Japanese-held port of Finschafen, at Lae, in the Ramu and Markham valleys, and at Madang. The Division later saw service in Borneo. Its badge then being a duck-billed platypus above a boomerang.

3rd Australian Army Tank Brigade.
The armour clad head of a knight's charger similar to that of the British 20th Armoured Brigade was the badge of this Australian Army Tank Brigade.

11th Australian Division.
This Division was formed in December 1942, at Milne Bay in New Guinea from Milne Force, and took part in the operations in the Finisterre Ranges and in New Britain. The formation badge was a palm tree.

4th Australian Armoured Brigade.
Formed in 1943 in New South Wales, this Brigade served in Queensland until the end of that year when it embarked for New Guinea and took part in the operations at Buna, Finschafen, Torokina and Wewak, and later in New Britain and Borneo. Its badge was an alligator before a palm tree set above a boomerang. The design in white on a black background.

34th Australian Infantry Brigade.
A badge similar to the general service
cap badge of the Australian Commonwealth Forces,[3] set above a boomerang,
was the sign adopted by the 34th
Infantry Brigade.

NEW ZEALAND FORMATIONS

The New Zealand Formation Badges were used for vehicle markings: personnel being distinguished by combinations of colour patches worn on battledress.

New Zealand Expeditionary Force.
Four red stars set on a square black background was the badge of the H.Q. of the New Zealand Expeditionary Force.

1st New Zealand Division.
A battleaxe was the badge of the 1st New Zealand Division, a New Zealand Home Defence Formation.

2nd New Zealand Division.
The New Zealand national emblem of the fern leaf, in white on a black circular background, was the badge adopted by the famous 2nd New Zealand Division. The formation arrived in the United Kingdom in 1940 under the command of Lieut.-General Sir Bernard C. Freyberg,

V.C., K.C.B., K.B.E., C.M.G., D.S.O., and formed part of the 7 British Corps, after Dunkirk, in its South-Eastern England operational area in an anti-invasion role. The New Zealand Division proceeded overseas the following year to the Middle East. It saw action in the Western Desert and in Greece and Crete, and then back to the Desert, taking part in the hard fighting at Sidi Rezegh. It formed part of the Eighth Army at El Alamein and in the drive through Cyrenaica and Tripolitania to the Mareth Line and on into Tunisia to the final defeat of the Axis forces in North Africa. In Italy the Division added fresh honours to its name. It took part in the final operations of 15th Army Group in the Po Valley. It was the formation that entered Padua and captured Mestre and swept on to Trieste, where it linked up with Tito's Yugoslavian forces advancing from the east.

The Division ceased to exist early in 1946, leaving with C.M.F. only a Brigade Group, intended as New Zealand's contribution to the British Commonwealth's occupational force in Japan.

3rd New Zealand Division.
This formation adopted as its badge the national bird of New Zealand, the kiwi.

The Division was held in readiness in New Zealand in 1942 against the Japanese drive in the Pacific. It later saw service in New Caledonia, and one brigade group saw action in the Solomon Islands.

4th New Zealand Division.
A charging bull was the Divisional badge. The formation did not serve outside New Zealand.

5th New Zealand Division.
A kea's head was adopted by the 5th
New Zealand Division as its badge.
     The Division formed part of New
Zealand's Home Defence Force.

6th New Zealand Division.
This formation was raised in 1942 in the
Middle East, at the time of Rommel's
threat to Egypt. It was raised from units
of the N.Z.E.F. not forming part of the
2nd New Zealand Division Order of
Battle, and was made up from reinforcements, Training Establishments, and
Lines of Communication Units. The
formation was later disbanded and the
units reverted to their former roles or
were absorbed into the 2nd New Zealand
Division.
     The 6th New Zealand Division adopted
as its badge the kiwi, as also borne by the
3rd New Zealand Division in the Pacific.

4th New Zealand Armoured Brigade.
This Brigade was formed in New Zealand
from a nucleus of the 2nd New Zealand
Division which returned from the Middle
East after participation in the operations
in Greece and Crete. The Brigade rejoined
the N.Z.E.F. in the Middle East after
El Alamein, and served in the final phase
of the operations in North Africa. As
part of the 2nd New Zealand Division
the Brigade subsequently served in the
Italian campaign. The formation badge
was a dragon.

SOUTH AFRICAN FORMATIONS

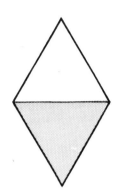

1st South African Division.

This Division was formed in Kenya in 1940 and was composed of the 2nd and 5th South African Brigades. It formed part of Lieut.-General Sir Alan Cunningham's Force which routed the Italians in Somaliland and pursued them in the operations which followed and led to the conquest of Abyssinia. It was this formation which occupied Moyale in the early stages of the advance on the road to Harar and the fall of Addis Ababa, and the final round-up of the scattered Italian Army.

The Division next saw action in the Middle East. It was part of 30 Corps with the Eighth Army in November 1941, and took part in General Sir Claude Auchinleck's offensive. It was at El Alamein in October 1942, and in the advance through Cyrenaica and Tripolitania, in the battles which broke the Axis forces in North Africa.

The badge of the 1st S.A. Division was a diamond. It was divided into halves, the top yellow, the lower green. The Division Subsequently adopted another badge. A square, evenly divided, the top half yellow, the lower green. Superimposed on this background was the black silhouette of a white-tailed gnu, or black wildebeest, once common on the plains of the Transvaal and the Orange River Colony.

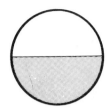

2nd South African Division.

This Division also served in the Middle East and saw much hard fighting with the Eighth Army in Libya. Two Brigades of the Division formed the major part of the garrison in Tobruk when Rommel swept forward in June 1942, and were lost when the port fell to the superior numbers of the Afrika Korps and their Italian allies.

The Divisional badge was a divided circle, the top being yellow, the bottom division green.

3rd South Africa Division.

A cloth patch equally divided; top half yellow, and lower half green, was the badge of the 3rd South African Division. This Formation was raised on 23rd October 1940, under the command of Major-General M. Botha, C.M.G. The function of the Division was the organization and training of those units remaining in the Union for home defence and garrison duties; it also trained reinforcements for the 1st and 2nd South African Division. From 1940 to 1942 the Divisional H.Q. was at Pretoria. It then moved to Ermelo in the Eastern Transvaal, although its units were scattered as far away as South-West Africa. On 4th April 1942, the Division was redesignated 3rd Armoured Division and, on 15th October in the same year it was disbanded, its place being taken by a mobile field force based on Ermerlo.

6th South African Armoured Division.
A green triangle with a yellow centre
was the badge of the 6th South African
Armoured Division. This formation
formed part of the Allied Armies in
Italy from May 1944, until the end of
the campaign, taking part in the battle
of Cassino and the piercing of the
Gothic Line. It was under command of
the 15th Army Group during the final
operations in the Po Valley, driving into
Trevisio in the last stages of the
campaign which led to the German
capitulation.

U.D.F. Repatriation Unit(s).
The head of a springbok in light yellow
and white, picked out in black and set
on a khaki background was the badge
of the Repatriation Units of the Union
Defence Force.

INDIAN FORMATIONS

Southern Army (India).
The Southern Cross, four yellow stars on a square background, evenly divided into three horizontal bands of red, black and red, was the badge of India's Southern Army.

North-Western Army (India).
A castle gateway, symbolic of the North-Western gateway of India, the Khyber Pass, was the badge of the North-Western Army of India. The gateway was in white set on a square background of equal red, black and red bands.

15 Indian Corps.
A geometric design composed of three Roman figure 'V'—for fifteen—in white or black on a red rectangular or circular background, was the badge of the 15 Indian Corps, which was one of the three Indian Corps of the Fourteenth Army during the hardfought campaign for the liberation of Burma.

The Corps was engaged in prolonged and bitter fighting in the Second and

Third Arakan Campaigns. In the Second Arakan Campaign, 1943-44, it inflicted the first decisive defeat that any Japanese force had ever suffered at the hands of the British, breaking for the first time the legend of Japanese invincibility in the South-East Asia theatre.

In the Third Arakan Campaign, 1944-45, which was a series of combined operations, 15 Indian Corps carried out no less than nine combined assault landings varying in size from a brigade group to a divisional operation. These operations culminated in a divisional assault on the Rangoon River which led to the capture of Rangoon itself in May 1945. By the end of the war the Corps had been withdrawn to India to prepare for operations in Malaya, but was eventually moved to the Netherlands East Indies to command the British and Indian force in the area.

21 Indian Corps.
The Corps, which was one of the Middle East formations, bore as its badge the truncated heraldic head of a horse in white on a square black background, similar in design to that of Eastern Command, India.

33 Indian Corps.
The first badge of the 33 Indian Corps

was a black silhouette of the head of the Duke of Wellington on a green background within a red circle. The badge was chosen by Lieut.-General A.F.P. Christison, the Corps Commander, because the operational area allocated to the formation covered much of the territory over which the Duke of Wellington fought when he was in India (1800-1805). The Corps was raised in November 1942, to command the 19th and 25th Indian Divisions, the 251st Indian Tank Brigade, and other formations and units allocated for the defence of Southern India. A sword and trident, crossed, and superimposed on geometrical wings, the design in white on a black or dark blue background, was subsequently adopted on the change in the role of the Corps. The design was also worn on a background of Corps colours of red, white and red.

Intended as an amphibious expeditionary force, the badge was made up of the trident to represent the Royal Navy, the sword for the Army, and the wings for the R.A.F.—a similar motif to the Combined Operations badge.

From 3rd April 1944, to 27th May 1945, 33 Corps travelled a distance of 1,127 miles, from Jorhat to Rangoon, liberating some 55,500 square miles of enemy-occupied territory. The Corps had the task of halting the northernmost Japs' drive at Kohima, following the reopening of the land route to Imphal. By continuous action through the 1944-45 monsoon the Jap 15th Army was driven back across the Chindwin from where the drive to the Irrawaddy was launched, culminating in the capture of Mandalay on 19th March 1945. Operating south on the line of the Irrawaddy the Corps cleared the oilfields area around Yenangyaung to link with troops pushing north from Rangoon on 15th May 1945. The Corps, under the command of Lieut.-General Sir Montagu Stopford, was converted to Twelfth Army at the end of May 1945.

34 Indian Corps.
A leaping panther in black on a circular background divided into Corps colours of two red and a central white band, was the badge adopted by the 34 Indian Corps, which was raised for the invasion of Malaya in 1945. Although this was the badge officially approved for the Corps, the badge actually worn was a leaping black panther on a red circle with a black border.

The Corps was being embarked for Malaya at the time of the Jap surrender. Two of its divisions, however, actually carried out landings in Malaya as had been planned.

THE INDIAN DIVISIONS

2nd Indian Division.

A yellow hornet on a black rectangular background was the badge adopted by this formation, which was raised in Iraq in March 1942. It was said that the formation badge was adopted owing to the prevalence of the hornets in the area at the time of its formation. The Division was formed from No. 2 lines of communication Area (Southern Iraq and South-West Persia). It remained in Iraq as an lines of communication formation.

3rd Indian Division (The Chindits).

A golden Burmese Dragon (a Chinthern–Pagoda Guardian) on a blue circular background was the badge of the 3rd Indian Division—Wingate's Chindits—who made history with their airborne invasions of Burma. The Chindits were first in action in Japanese-occupied Burma as long-range penetration troops in the expedition led by Major-General Orde Wingate, D.S.O. As part of the Fourteenth Army, the Division was subsequently engaged in the Chindwin area harassing and disorganizing the Japanese lines of communication.

4th Indian Division.

The 4th Indian Division was the first formation to leave India. It embarked for Egypt, where it concentrated in the autumn of 1939 and formed part of the original desert force under command of General (later Field-Marshal) Lord Wavell. At Sidi Barrani, the Division shared with the 7th Armoured Division the honours of that complete victory over the Italians. The formation was then withdrawn from the Western Desert to participate in the campaign in East Africa. It joined General Platt's forces in Eritrea, where it took part in the operations leading to the defeat of the Italians at Keren, where the Division fought with the 5th (Indian) Division in securing a complete victory. The 4th (Indian) Division then hurriedly returned to Egypt to meet the threat of the Afrika Korps. One Brigade (the 5th) was withdrawn to Syria, where it took part in the operations against the Vichy French Forces. The rest of the Division remained in the Western Desert where one brigade (the 11th) participated in the action at Halfaya Pass in June 1941. The whole Division took part in the Allied offensive of November 1941, advanced to Benghazi and then withdrew to the Gazala line. In April 1942, the Division was withdrawn from the Desert, one brigade going to Cyprus, another to Palestine, and the third to the Canal Zone. These last two brigades returned to the Desert when Rommel attacked in May 1942, one (the 11th) was lost in Tobruk, but the second withdrew to El Alamein. The Division re-formed at Alamein in September 1942, and took part in the Eighth Army's attack in October. It was composed then of the 5th, 7th and 161st Indian Infantry Brigades, the British element of which was the 1st/4th Bn. Essex Regiment, 1st Bn. Royal Sussex Regiment, and 1st Bn. Argyll and Sutherland Highlanders. After Alamein the Division was not engaged until Tunisia was reached.

There, with only the 5th and 7th Brigades, they took part in the attacks which outflanked the Mareth Line, burst through the enemy's defences at the Wadi Akarit, and were checked in the hard fighting around Enfidaville. Together with the 7th Armoured Division and the 201st Guards Brigade, the Division joined First Army for the last attacks which ended in the complete defeat of the Axis forces in North Africa. The Division next joined the Allied armies in Italy on the Orsogna front in December 1943, took part in the fighting at Cassino in February and March 1944, advanced through Central Italy and was first to break into the Gothic Line at the end of August 1944. Withdrawn from Italy in the autumn of 1945, the Division formed part of our forces in Greece until it returned to India in January 1946.

The Division's badge was a red eagle in flight on a dark blue background, and the Division became known as the 'Red Eagles'. The first badges worn in the Western Desert were the gift of women of the Punjab at the instance of Sir Sikander Hyat Khan, then Prime Minister of the Punjab, who visited the Division in the Middle East.

the line. In September, after Rommel's final attacks had been defeated, the Division was relieved at El Alamein by the 4th Indian Division and moved to 'Paiforce', and in May and June 1942, returned to India with only 9th and 161st Brigades, moving into the Arakan, being one of the two forward divisions in the advance of 15 Indian Corps. The 5th took part in the defence of Imphal and the reoccupation of Tiddim. It formed part of the Fourteenth Army in the final operations in Burma. In April 1945, the Division was withdrawn from north of Rangoon to take part in 'mopping-up' operations until it embarked for Malaya. The Division was first ashore at Singapore, reoccupying the city on the 5th September 1945. Two months later the formation moved to Java where it was engaged in restoring peace among the Indonesians. The badge of the 5th Indian Division was a red circle on a black background. It had been said that the sign was derived from the red circles hurriedly painted on the Division's vehicles in urgent compliance with the order that formation signs were to be so displayed for recognition purposes. Later the Formation Sign was referred to as the 'Ball of Fire'.

5th Indian Division.
The 5th Indian Division, composed of the 9th, 10th and 29th Indian Infantry Brigades, left India in September 1940, and embarked for the Sudan. The Division formed part of General Platt's forces in Eritrea and played a leading part in the capture of Kassala and at Keren. The 5th followed up the broken Italians to the capture of Asmara and Massawa and received the surrender of the Duke of Aosta at Amba Alagi. After this surrender, in July 1941, the Division moved to Egypt, then to Iraq and, by the end of the year, to Cyprus. It relieved the 4th Indian Division with the Eighth Army in the Western Desert, and during April 1942, took part in the costly fighting around Tobruk and in the withdrawal to Alamein, where it helped in stabilizing

6th Indian Division.
This Division was formed in India in March 1941. By October 1941, the Division had moved to Iraq with the 24th, 26th and 27th Indian Infantry Brigades, where it was engaged largely on protection of the supply routes to Russia, and where it remained until returning to India in November 1944. On its return to India the Division was disbanded. One brigade, the 26th, was sent to Egypt when the Eighth Army withdrew to El Alamein, and served for a while with the 50th Division. This same brigade returned to India in July 1944, ahead of the Division, and by the end of the year was serving in Burma.

This formation's badge was the head of a Deccan tiger in black and yellow on a square black background.

7th Indian Division?

Known as the 'Golden Arrow' Division. A yellow arrow on a black square or circle was the badge of the 7th Indian Division. The badge was chosen to indicate the direction of the line of advance to the protection of the North-West Frontier of India, which the Division was raised to protect; but all its fighting took place in the north-east. This formation saw much hard fighting in the Arakan, and was cut off for sixteen days in the Ngakyedauk pass, where it formed the famous 'box' at Sinzweya and held off all the Japanese attacks, stopping the enemy advance towards India.

This formation later formed part of the Fourteenth Army in the advance into Burma. Crossing the Irrawaddy on 14th February 1945, it established at Nyanugu a bridgehead which enabled the 17th Indian Division to make their dash to Meiktila, the capture of which by the latter formation and 255th Indian Armoured Brigade caused the Japanese resistance in North Burma to crumble. The 7th Division later took part in the hard fighting which drove the Japanese from Myingyan and Yenangyaung. In September 1945, it was flown to Siam where it concentrated and disarmed over 113,000 Japanese troops. In April 1946, the Division arrived in Malaya where it remained till the end of the year, when it returned to India.

brigade moved to Syria and one to Egypt. This latter brigade suffered heavy losses at El Alamein and was disbanded in September 1942. The remainder of the Division again concentrated in 'Paiforce'. After a short spell of training in Syria during mid-1943, the Division embarked for Italy, landed at Taranto in September 1943, and formed part of Eighth Army in the advance up the Adriatic Coast. It crashed through the German defences on the Trigno and Sangro Rivers, and spent the winter in the line between Ortona and Orsogna. The Division played a big part in the final breaking of the enemy's defences at Cassino in May 1944, and it the pursuit northwards to the Gothic Line, where again it was heavily engaged in the high Apennines. In December 1944, the Division checked the German counter-offensive in the Serchio Valley, and was later in the van of Eighth Army's attack across the Senior River when the final and decisive Allied offensive was launched in the Po valley. The Division returned to India in July 1945.

Three yellow clover-shaped leaves on long stems on a dull red background was the badge of the 8th Indian Division, the stems were set to form a 'V' for Victory, with an 'I' for India in the apex. The central clover leaf was of the four leafed variety—for luck. The original Divisional badge was taken from the armorial bearings of the G.O.C., Major-General C.O. Harvey, C.B., C.B.E., C.V.O., M.C., who commanded the formation in Paiforce. It was a 'Garb' (sheaf of wheat and trefoil (a three-lobed leaf)) above the motto 'Carpe diem', set on a black background, but this was later changed to the three yellow clover-shaped leaves on on long stems on a dull red background.

8th Indian Division?

Formed in October 1940, this Division moved to Iraq in June and July 1941. It took part in the operations in Persia in 1941, advancing through Khoramshah to Ahwaz. Thereafter, the Division served in 'Paiforce' until June 1942, when one

9th Indian Division.

The 9th Indian Division embarked for Singapore in 1940 and formed part of our forces in Malaya at the time of the Japanese invasion.

The division was located in the Eastern Coastal Area of the Peninsula when the

Japanese attacked.

It took part in the hard fighting, and suffered heavy casualties in the withdrawal down the mainland to Singapore Island, where it linked up with the 11th Indian Division, and was lost when the Command was forced to capitulate at Singapore in February 1942.

The divisional badge was a nine-pointed star, in royal blue, set on a black circle.

10th Indian Division.
This formation was raised in January 1941, at Ahmednagar. It arrived in the Persian Gulf in the late spring of that year and took part in the defence of Habbaniyah and later in the capture of Baghdad. The Division also saw action Persia, one column occupying Teheran. It joined the Eighth Army in Libya in 1941, moving from Iraq to Cyrenaica in fourteen days, and took part in the hard fighting when Rommel attempted to break through into Egypt. The formation was then withdrawn to Cyprus. The Division next saw action in Italy, where it arrived in March 1944. It went first to Ortona, then to the Tiber basin and the Central Apennines, and back to the Adriatic coast in October to form part of the Eighth Army in the final operations in the Po Valley in April and May 1945.

The badge of the 10th Indian Division was a black square, on it two diagonal bands of dark pink or red and blue, forming a diagonal cross.

11th Indian Division.
The 11th Indian Division formed part of our forces in Malaya at the time of the Japanese invasion. The Division was, at the outset of the brief ten weeks

campaign, located in the north of the Malay Peninsula on the Thailand border, and was the first formation in action in North Kedah against the Japanese when they launched their attack on 8th December 1941. The formation saw much hard fighting and sustained heavy casualties in the withdrawal through Malaya, the two British battalions of the Division, the 1st Leicesters and the 2nd East Surreys being amalamated and designated 'The British Battalion'. The Division was finally compelled to withdraw to Singapore Island where following the increasing intensity of the Japanese assaults, the Command capitulated.

The badge of the 11th Indian Division was an eleven-spoked wheel on a yellow or gold background. The badge was retained whilst the Division was in captivity, and at Changi the entrance to the P.o.W. camp was decorated with the badge to which was added in 'dog Latin' the motto, 'Qui Ultime Melior Ridet' ('He who laughs last, laughs best'). This for a considerable time was accepted by the Japanese with all solemnity as the divisional motto without realizing the purport, and the fact that it had been added for their discomfort.

12th Indian Division.
This Division also served in Persia and Iraq. Its badge was a Persian lion outlined in blue set on a yellow background.

14th Indian Division.
The Division was formed in India, and in May 1942, served in the Eastern Army, taking part in the hard-fought campaign in the Arakan, before the formation of the Fourteenth Army, taking part in the operations in the Mayu Peninsula before being forced to withdraw when Maundu and Buthidaung were evacuated. In May 1943, the Division was moved back from the Arakan to Central Command, India, assuming the role of a training formation. The Divisional badge depicted a mountain range in black—the centre peak being Takatu, a 10,000 ft peak overlooking Quetta—set in a white frame on a dark background, the white frame taking the form of a 'Q' to link the formation with Quetta, where the Division was raised in May 1942, by Major-General H.H. Rich.

17th Indian Division.
Raised in Ahmednagar in the spring of 1941, this Division, under the command of Major-General J.G. Smythe, V.C., less one brigade, moved to Burma in November 1941. The Division was in action against the Japanese in Burma and Assam, with a few short breaks for reorganization and training, from January 1942, until the Japanese surrender in August 1945, and fought against the Japanese for a longer period than any other British or Indian formation.

The 17th saw much hard fighting in the Chin Hills and in the Tiddim and Imphal areas. It crossed the Irrawaddy in February 1945, and, after bitter fighting, captured Meiktila in March—a victory which led to the destruction of the Japanese forces in Burma. The Division was twice reported by the

Japanese to have been annihilated but, in spite of this, played a major part in the Fourteenth Army's victorious campaign in Burma.

The divisional badge was a black cat on a khaki square background. This badge was adopted in 1943, and replaced a dark blue square which had been introduced in 1942.

19th Indian Division.
Known from its formation badge—a yellow dagger held in a clenched hand on red background—as the 'Dagger Division', this formation served with the Fourteenth Army in Burma under the command of Major-General T. Wynford Rees, C.B., C.I.E., D.S.O., M.C., and in the fighting which led to its liberation. It was the 19th Indian Division which, after severe fighting, eventually established the Irrawaddy bridgehead at Kyaukmyaung which enabled them to drive through and capture Mandalay, where they raised the Union Jack over Fort Dufferin on 20th March 1945.

20th Indian Division.
An Indian sword, a tulwar, in silver, raised aloft by clenched hand set on a black circle, was the badge of the 20th Indian Division. The sign was chosen to symbolize the 'swift and deadly execution' of the Japanese armies. The Division was raised in Bangalore on the 1st of April 1942, by General Sir Douglas Gracey, K.C.I.E., C.B., C.B.E., M.C., who commanded the formation through its training in Ceylon and its active service in Assam, Burma and Indo-China, until it was disbanded in April-May 1946.

The Division distinguished itself
in the Burma campaign, particularly
during the defence of the Imphal plain
in the spring and early summer of 1944,
and in the breaching of the Irrawaddy
line a year later. In September 1946,
the Division moved to French Indo-
China where it concentrated and disarmed 70,000 Japanese.

21st Indian Division.
This designation was temporarily given
to the H.Q. of the 44th Indian Armoured
Division when the formation ceased to
operate in an armoured role on moving
into Assam in May 1944.
The badge of the 44th Indian
Armoured Division was a charging
buffalo[5] and the badge chosen for the
21st Indian Division to link with this
was a buffalo's head in white, with red
horns, set on a blue background. This
badge was subsequently retained, on the
splitting up of the formation, by the
268th Lorried Infantry Brigade.[6]

23rd Indian Division.
A red fighting cock on a light yellow
circle was the badge of the Division
which was designed by the G.O.C. Major
General R.A. Savory C.B., D.S.O., M.C.
It was intended as being symbolic to
both British and Indian troops and,
in the case of the latter, without
giving offence to either Muslim or
Hindu. In 1942 the Division covered
the withdrawal of General Alexander's
army through Imphal and later fought
with distinction round Shenam, Palel
and Tamu during the Japanese offensive
against Imphal in 1944.
In 1945 the Division took part in

Operation 'Zipper', landing in Malaya
in September. In the same month it
moved to Java where its main task was
the evacuation of internees and the
restoration of law and order during
the Indonesian disturbances.

25th Indian Division.
The 25th Indian Division's badge was
a black ace of spades set on a green
background. The Division was formed
in Southern India in August 1942, under
the command of Major-General
H.L. Davies, C.B.E., D.S.O., M.C. Under
the command of the 15th Indian Corps
the Division first saw action in the
Arakan in March 1944, where it
fought with distinction in 1944 and
1945, notably at Kangaw, which was
one of the fiercest fought battles of the
entire Arakan and Burma campaigns.
The Division formed part of the
Fourteenth Army in the hard jungle
fighting which led to the liberation
of Burma. In January 1945, the Division
took part in the first large-scale
amphibious operation in South-East
Asia, which ended in the liberation
of Akyab when the formation was
ferried across the four-mile-wide
Mayu estuary to land on the northern
beaches of Akyab Island. In the course
of combined operations during the
weeks that followed, the Division
occupied Myebon and Ru-Ywa.

26th Indian Division.
This Division was raised in April 1942,
and moved into the Arakan in the
winter of 1942. It first saw action in
January 1943, in the Kalapinzin valley

and south of the Maungdaw-Buthidaung road. The Division fought its way to the relief of the 7th Indian Division in their 'box' at Sinzwya. The formation took part in the amphibious operations. down the Burma coast in support of the main Fourteenth Army offensive through Mandalay, Meiktila and down the Irrawaddy. The Division was allotted the task of the capture of Rangoon by sea. Troops landed ten miles south of the city on 2nd May 1945, and captured Rangoon before the arrival of the main body of the Fourteenth Army advancing southwards from Pegu. After the capture of Rangoon the Division returned to India as part of 34 Corps, but subsequently served in the Netherlands East Indies.

The formation badge was a yellow and black Royal Bengal tiger stepping out of a blue triangle set on a black triangular background, and from this badge the formation became known as the 'Tiger Head' Division. The triangle was taken from the Greek letter Delta for it was in the Hoogli Delta that the Division was raised from the H.Q. Presidency and Assam District.

39th Indian Division.
An Indian tulwar in white, held aloft in a clenched brown hand on a dark green circle, was the 39th Indian Division's badge. Originally designated 1st Burma Infantry Division, composed of the 1st and 2nd Burma Brigades and an Indian brigade, this formation was known as 'Burdiv' and took part in the withdrawal from Burma in 1942. Whilst in India it was redesignated 39th Indian Division, and in 1943 became a training formation.

31st Indian Armoured Division.
A black elephant on a green background was the badge of the 31st Indian Armoured Division, which was raised in India in 1941 and later saw service in Iraq, Syria and Egypt. It was redesignated 1st Indian Armoured Division in the latter part of 1945, and returned to India early in 1946.

42nd Indian Armoured Division.
This Division was raised in 1941. Its badge was a rhinoceros head in grey, picked out in black on a red circle; below the head the motto, 'Laro Aur Larte Raho' ('Strike, and keep on striking'). The Division was amalgamated in May 1943, with the 43rd Indian Armoured Division to form the 44th Indian Armoured Division.

44th Indian Armoured Division.
This Division was raised in Secunderabad in January 1943, by the amalgamation of the 42nd and 43rd Armoured Divisions. In April 1944, it was announced that the formation was to be converted into an Airborne Division, and the Armoured and Lorried Infantry Brigades to become independent brigades.
Before the change was made the Divisional H.Q. was hurriedly moved to

command certain detached brigades of the lines of communication. The H.Q., then redesignated 21st Indian Division,[8] concentrated at Jorhat in May 1944, with the task of controlling operations in the Silchar area and lines of communication in rear of 33 Indian Corps. As the advance progressed along the Imphal road the Division moved to Kohima and became responsible for the security of the communications between Dinapur and 33 Corps.

The Division was then split up to become 255th Indian Tank Brigade; 268th Lorried Infantry Brigade and the nucleus of 44th Indian Airborne Division.

The Divisional badge was a charging buffalo, in black, with red horns, hooves and eyes, below an inscription in Urdu— 'Laro Aur Larte Raho' ('Strike, and Keep on Striking'). The design was on a white background within a black circular border.

This badge was subsequently retained by 255th Indian Tank Brigade[9]

44th Indian Airborne Division.
Raised in May 1944, from elements of the 44th Indian Armoured Division. The 50th Parachute Brigade of the Division was in action at Imphal in 1944 and again in May 1945, when it made an airborne landing south of Rangoon in support of the 26th Indian Division.

The badge of this Division was the same as that worn by the British airborne divisions, the well-known Pegasus, with the addition of the word 'India' in pale blue below the hooves.

INDIAN ARMOURED
AND TANK BRIGADES

2nd Indian Armoured Brigade.
A white Fleur-de-lis on a scarlet square background.

3rd Indian Armoured Brigade.[1]
A small replica of the badge of the Fourteenth Army, set on a square yellow background.

3rd Indian Motor Brigade.
This Brigade was formed from the prewar 2nd (Sialkot) Cavalry Brigade of three Indian cavalry regiments, and wore as its badge a red horseshoe on a black circle. The Brigade moved overseas to Egypt in January 1941, and in April suffered heavy casualties at Mechile, when it sacrificed itself, thereby gaining time for Tobruk to be occupied. One regiment went into Tobruk with the Australians, where it remained for almost the whole period of the siege. The remainder of the Brigade was

stationed in Egypt and Syria for a year before returning to the Desert in time to meet Rommel's attack in May 1942. Near Bir Hacheim the Brigade took the first blow from the enemy and again suffered heavy losses. The Brigade was then withdrawn to Egypt and, ultimately to Iraq, where it joined the 31st Indian Armoured Division. In January 1943, the cavalry regiments returned to India and infantry battalions took their place. In February 1943, the Brigade was renumbered and redesignated the 43rd Lorried Infantry Brigade.[2]

50th Indian Tank Brigade.
A clenched fist in white on a black circle was the badge of this Indian Tank Brigade. This Brigade originally formed part of the Indian Expeditionary Force and later 33 Indian Corps. In November 1944, the Brigade was moved to the Arakan and took part in the hard fighting following the seaborne landings carried out under 15 Indian Corps. In March 1945, the Brigade was withdrawn to India to prepare for the assault on Malaya under 34 Indian Corps.

251st Indian Tank Brigade.
This Brigade was formed in 1942 and initially employed in the defence of Southern India under command of 33 Indian Corps. The formation was broken up in the latter part of 1943, personnel going to provide reinforcements for the Chindits. The Brigade badge was officially described as

'the forequarters of a tiger rampant with white eyes, teeth and claws, on a red background'.

254th Indian Tank Brigade.
This Brigade was raised at Risalpur in April 1941, as the armoured brigade of the 32nd Indian Armoured Division. Its original designation was the 4th Indian Armoured Brigade. This was changed to 254th Indian Armoured Brigade at the end of the year.

In May 1943, the Brigade moved to Ranchi and in October part of the formation moved into the Arakan, going ashore on the beaches from landing craft. The Brigade distinguished itself in the subsequent operations. In October 1944, the formation moved into the Imphal area and, under command of the 7th Indian Division, advanced down the Kabaw valley on the Tamu—Kalewa—Gangaw—Pauk axis, crossing the Irrawaddy in mid-February 1945, when it made its first contact with the Japanese. Eleven days after the establishment of the bridgehead, it assisted the 17th Indian Division in annihilating the Meiktila garrison after some of the severest fighting of the Burma campaign, and later advanced 300 miles in thirty days from Meiktali to Hiegu, thirty miles north of Rangoon, capturing Toungoo and Pegu en route.

The Brigade's badge was a geometrical design in black set on a red inverted triangle, the design representing tank tracks and three drops of blood, significant of the Brigade motto, 'Blood on the Tracks'.

255th Indian Tank Brigade.
A charging buffalo, black body with red eyes, hooves and horns, set on a blue triangular background, was the badge of this formation, which originally formed part of the 44th Indian Armoured Division. The Brigade's badge was a modified version of the Divisional sign which was retained when the Armoured Division ceased to exist. Shortly after the disbandment of the Division, this Brigade was despatched to Burma where it took part in the final operations of the Fourteenth Army. After the capture of Rangoon the Brigade was allotted to 15 Indian Corps for operations in Malaya.

INDIAN INFANTRY BRIGADES

52nd Indian Infantry Brigade.
A black design of a castle, mural crown and leaves flanked by two fish in green on a white background. This badge was adopted from the old Moghul crest of Bhopal State, where the Brigade was located at the time of its adoption. This Brigade was made up of British units, and its role was that of a training formation for training reinforcements for British units in Burma in jungle warfare.

38th Indian Infantry Brigade.
A crane bird, with red head, neck and legs, and a blue body.

43rd Indian Lorried Infantry Brigade.
This Brigade was formed in Iraq in January 1943, as the Lorried Infantry Brigade of the 31st Indian Armoured Division. The Brigade was detached from its parent formation and dispatched to Italy, where it joined the 1st British Armoured Division prior to the Eighth Army's attack on the Gothic Line in August 1944. Later the Brigade became a Corps and Army Troops formation, serving with the 10th Indian Division, the 2nd New Zealand Division, the 56th Division, and the Polish Corps in the Po Valley. It adopted the badge of two crossed kukris in white on a dark green background, denoting the unusual brigade formation of three Gurkha battalions.

60th Indian Infantry Brigade.
Two crossed lances with red and white pennants, surmounted by a bugle horn. in white, the whole on a black square, was this Brigade's badge, which was chosen when the formation was in Iraq as a motorized brigade and composed of two former Indian cavalry regiments (represented by the lances), and one rifle regiment (the 5th Frontier Force Rifles), represented by the stringed bugle.

72nd Indian Infantry Brigade.
A red circle on a square black background was the badge of this Brigade, which was composed of the 10th Bn. The Gloucestershire Regiment, the 9th Bn. The Royal Sussex Regiment

and the 6th Bn. The South Wales
Borderers. The Brigade was formed
from the 267th Armoured Brigade in
March 1943, when the 43rd Indian
Armoured Division was broken up.
It had been composed of three British
battalions which had arrived in India
in July 1942, and had been converted
to armoured regiments to form the
267th Brigade. In March 1943, when
the 32nd and 43rd Armoured Divisions
were amalgamated, the Brigade was
reconverted to infantry. The Brigade
subsequently formed part of the
36th Division with the 29th Infantry
Brigade. The badge of the 29th was
a white circle on a black background
and this, linked with the red circle
of the 72nd, became the Divisional badge?

109th Indian Infantry Brigade.
This was an Independent Brigade which
formed part of the Fourteenth Army in
Burma. For some time it was located at
Aigal, in the hills south of Silchar, with
the object of providing some degree of
protection to the right flank of 4 Corps.
It took nearly three weeks to reach the
brigade from Corps Headquarters through
jungle tracks. The Brigade adopted its
own badge, which was a representation
of the goad used by a mahout to urge
on his elephant. This was a good-natured
'dig' at 4th Corps Headquarters, whose
badge was a charging elephant, and
whom owing to the difficulties of
communication they had, it was said
to press for their requirements.

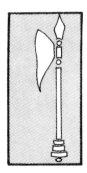

116th Indian Infantry Brigade.
An Indian battleaxe in yellow on a
royal blue rectangular background within
a narrow yellow border. The badge was
also worn with the battleaxe in black
on a khaki background with a narrow
black border. This Brigade reoccupied
the Andaman Isles when the Japanese
occupation troops surrendered.

150th Indian Infantry Brigade.
A vertical bayonet, point uppermost, in
yellow set on a black shield was the
badge of this Brigade, which was raised
in May 1944, to train Indian units in
jungle warfare. In December 1945, the
Brigade was moved to Hong Kong.

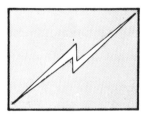

155th Indian Infantry Brigade.
A yellow lightning flash set on a royal
blue or black oblong background.

268th Indian Infantry Brigade.
Originally forming part of the 44th
Indian Armoured Division, this was an
independent all-Indian infantry brigade
and formed part of 33 Indian Corps
with the Fourteenth Army in Assam
and Burma, serving under the command
of 21st Indian Division in the maintenance of communications between
Dinapur and 33 Corps. After the
battle of Kohima this Brigade, under the
command of Brigadier M.G. Dyer, D.S.O.,
was employed, until the end of operations
in Burma, in an independent role under
33 Corps. The composition of the

Brigade changed continually. At the end of 1945 this Brigade was selected as the Indian element of B.C.O.F. and was moved to Japan early in 1946.

Its badge was a buffalo's head in white with red horns set on a square blue background.[3]

Lushai Brigade.
A buffalo's head in white, set in the apex of a 'V'—for Victory— on a red background, was the badge of this formation which served in Burma with the Fourteenth Army, and saw much hard fighting in the jungle-covered hill country between Manipur State and the Arakan, through which the Brigade advanced to capture Gangaw.

The Brigade was formed in March 1945, and was in continuous action against the Japanese until January 1945. In clearing the west side of the Chindwin the Brigade materially assisted the 33 Corps advance on Tiddim and Kalemyo.

Indian Contingent in U.K.
This Indian unit's badge was made up of five-pointed star, the star of the Order of the Star of India set on a circular band bearing the legend 'Heaven's light our guide' in light and dark blue. Surrounding the badge was a circle of golden flames. The whole design was set on a light blue square background.

This contingent was originally 'Force K.6', four mule companies and administrative units, which sailed from India and landed in France during December

1939. These companies served on the Belgian frontier with 1 and 2 Corps, and in the Maginot Line with 51st Highland Division. When France fell one company was captured but the others were transferred to England, where the title was changed to 'The Indian Contingent'. Until returning to India in January 1944, the contingent was engaged largely in training with British formations for mountain and arctic warfare.

Indian Units—British Commonwealth Occupation Force (Japan).
On joining the British and Indian Division ('Brindiv') in Japan in September 1945, the 268th Indian Infantry Brigade[4] ceased to wear their war-time badge and adopted the Star of India in gold on blue background. This badge was worn below the 'Brindiv' Union Jack on the left arm, with the B.C.O.F. badge on the right.[5] The wearing of this Star of India badge was confined to the Brigade H.Q. and the three infantry battalions—the 5th/1st Punjab Regiment, the 1st/5th Maratta Light Infantry and the 2nd/5th Royal Gurkha Rifles.

Military Adviser-In-Chief— Indian State Forces.
A white five-pointed star set on a background evenly divided top half light blue-grey, lower half dark blue.

INDIAN STATE FORCES

The Indian State forces played their part in the active defence of India, and most of the units adopted a distinctive formation sign in addition to their recognized badges.

Bahawalpur State Forces.
A white pelican on a black shield, was the formation badge of the Bahawalpur State Forces, pelicans being the supporters in the coat of arms of Bahawalpur State, which is also the cap-badge of the State Forces.

Cooch Behar State Forces.
A shield, divided into three vertical bars, red, yellow and green, the edges in black. On the red bar is a white ring, on the central yellow bar a white trident, and on the green bar a white five-pointed star.

Jaipur State Forces.
A full sun—yellow in colour—on a circular red background, was the badge of the Jaipur State Forces. The sun denotes the lineage of the ruling house of Jaipur, which claims descent from Surya Vansh, the Solar Dynasty.

EAST AND WEST AFRICAN FORMATIONS

East African Expeditionary Force (E.A.E.F.).
A double horned rhinoceros in black on a white circular background within a black circle was the badge of the H.Q. of the East African Expeditionary Force which served under South-East Asia Command in Burma with the Fourteenth Army. The double horned rhinoceros is a species found only in East Africa and common to the territories from which the units of the Force were recruited.

West African Expeditionary Force.
The badge of the R.W.A.F.F. (Royal West African Frontier Force)' in yellow, outlined in black, set on a green circle was the distinguishing badge of the West African Expeditionary Force.

11th (African) Division.
This Division was formed in 1940 in

East Africa and was composed of the 22nd (East African) and the 23rd (Nigerian) Brigades. It formed part of the force responsible for the defence of Kenya and later formed part of Lieut.-General Sir Alan Cunningham's force which advanced into Italian Somaliland and Abyssinia, in the campaign which broke the Italian armies under the Duke of Aosta. The Division took part in the operations which led to the capture of Harar and Addis Ababa and in the final rounding up of the broken Italian forces at the conclusion of the campaign. A black ace of clubs on a white square was the formation badge.

12th (African) Division.
Raised in East Africa in 1940, the Division comprised the 21st (East African), 24th (Gold Coast) and 25th (East African) Brigades. The 1st South African Brigade joined the Division for the first advance into Italian territory to El Wak in December 1940. The formation formed part of Lieut.-General Sir Alan Cunningham's force which drove the Italians from Somaliland and advanced into Abyssinia, routing the Italians at Jelib and Wadara, breaking through the Juba line on to Hara and Addis Ababa, and taking part in the final rounding up of the scattered Italian army. A kudu in white on a square black background was the Divisional badge.

11th (East African) Division.
The head of a double horned rhinoceros was the badge adopted by the 11th (East African) Division. This formation served with the Fourteenth Army in

Burma, taking part in the hard jungle fighting which led to the liberation of Burma. Originally the rhino's head in brown was set on a buff oval background, but this was later changed to a black head on a red oval. The Division was composed of the 21st, 25th and 26th (East African) Brigades made up of battalions of the King's African Rifles (from Kenya, Uganda, Nyassaland and Tanganika) and the 1st Bn. The Northern Rhodesia Regiment.

22nd (East African) Brigade.
An elephant in white on a black dircular background was the badge adopted by this brigade. It formed part of the 11th (African) Division in the conquest of Italian East Africa and Abyssinia and later served in Madagascar and Ceylon and with the 11th (East African) Division in Burma with the Fourteenth Army.

28th (East African) Brigade.
The panga is to the African askari what the kukri is to the Gurkha, and was carried by every man of the King's African Rifles in the 28th (East African) Brigade, so the formation adopted as their badge an upright panga, white blade and black hilt set on a red shield within a black border. The formation formed part of the Fourteenth Army in S.E.A.C., as an Independent Brigade, and the red shield was chosen to conform in colour, shape and size to that of the Fourteenth Army, so matching the Army badge which was worn on the right arm whilst the Brigade badge was worn on the left.

81st (West African) Division.
The 81st (West African) Division, the first Division ever to have been formed from units of the West African Frontier Force, chose as their badge a black tarantula spider on a yellow circle. In the folklore of the West African tribes (equivalent to Aesop's Fables) it is the spider who comes out on top at the end of the tales. This Division, which was under the command of Major-General C.G. Woolner, C.B., M.C., formed part of the Fourteenth Army in the hardfought campaign which liberated Burma. It was made up of troops of each of the four West African colonies, was assembled in Nigeria in March 1943, and was dispatched to India in August 1943. One brigade was taken to form part of General Orde Wingate's Special Force and was trained in long-range penetration. In December 1943, the Division crossed the hills into the Kaladan valley and operated on the left flank of the main advance in the Arakan, being the first large formation to be supplied wholly by air. In the following year it again advanced down the Kaladan and took part in the successful assault on Myohaung.

82nd (West African) Division.
Two spears, crossed on a native carrier's head band, set on a yellow shield was the distinguishing badge of the 82nd (West African) Division. It was dispatched to India in July 1944, and served in S.E.A.C. as part of the Fourteenth Army, joining the 81st (West African) Division in the assault on Myohaung and in the victorious advance through Burma to the liberation of Mandalay and Rangoon.

COMBINED OPERATIONS, COMMANDO, AND BEACH FORMATIONS

R.A.F. air cover. Then Dieppe, and finally the invasions of Sicily, Italy and the greatest combined operation of all time, the landings in Normandy on 6th June 1944.

Combined Operations Headquarters.
This familiar badge incorporated emblems of the three Services: in red, on a dark blue circle, a naval anchor; the tommy-gun and the R.A.F. albatross were linked in the sign symbolic of close co-operation which welded the combined forces of the three Services into the efficient organization which controlled and organized all combined operations. It was in 1940 that the need for such specially trained units became necessary, and selected independent companies were formed to carry out raids into enemy-occupied territory. These were the Special Service Troops, made up of Independent Companies, which were later designated Commandos—the name becoming a household word in consequence of their daring and spectacular exploits at the same when Britain stood alone in Europe. Raids commenced on a small scale, but under the direction of the late Admiral of the Fleet Lord Keyes, (who became the first Director of Combined Operations at the newly formed Combined Operations Head-quarters C.O.H.Q.), the size, nature and scope of the Commandos' tasks were increased. Lord Keyes was succeeded in 1941 by Captain (later Admiral) Lord Louis Mountbatten, G.C.V.O., C.B., D.S.O., and the work went on. From the French coast the Commandos' activities moved to Scandinavia, and thence all over the world wherever the enemy presented a vital target in a coastal area. The Lofoten Islands, Spitzbergen, Vaagso, Maaloy, Bruneval, St. Nazaire, Crete, the Libyan coast, the Channel Islands, Diego Suarez, Arakan, Rangoon, Singapore, all saw the Commandos on their beaches coming ashore from their landing-craft under the protection of the Navy and with

Beach Groups.
The fouled anchor in red on a pale blue background within a red circle was the badge of the Beach Groups. These groups were composed of specialist units of the Army, Navy, and R.A.F. formed in a complete amphibious formation. The naval element was made up of R.N. Signals and R.N. Commandos; the R.A.F. provided a balloon barrage section for the defence of the beaches and specialists who prepared the way for the R.A.F.'s airstrips; the Army provided an infantry battalion for the seizing of the beach and the defence of the beachhead perimeter, Royal Engineer Field Companies, Mechanical Equipment Platoons, a Stores Section and Transportation units, R.A.S.C. general transport companies with D.U.K.W.'s, a D.I.D. and Petrol supply unit, an R.A.M.C. unit, C.M.P. traffic control, and an R.E.M.E. Recovery Section and Pioneer Companies.

Beach groups first operated in the landings in Sicily. On 6th June 1944, D Day, on the Normandy beaches beach-group troops landed with the assault troops and distinguished themselves in the establishment and maintenance of the beachhead.

Indian Beach Groups.
Beach Groups which operated under South-East Asia Command wore a different badge. This took the form of a red sword and wings, and dark blue sea on a pale blue background within a red circle. These groups were also employed, in Burma, in an air-supply role.

No. 1 Commando.
A green and black salamander passing through red and yellow flames, an allusion to Commandos 'living in fire', the design on an oval patch, was No. 1 Commando's badge.

No. 2 Commando.
A Commando dagger in silver, hilt uppermost flanked by a silver letter 'S' on each side of the hilt, on a black background.

22nd Beach Brigade.
This Brigade adopted a black and white penguin on a khaki background as its formation badge. The penguin was chosen when it was decided that a flight of communication aircraft would not be included in the Brigade's order of battle—for the penguin, although amphibious, does not fly.

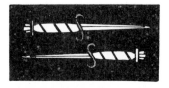

H.Q. Special Service Brigade.
Two silver Commando daggers set horizontally, with the hilt of each dagger in the shape of a letter 'S' in red, against a black rectangular background was the S.S. Brigade's badge.

Commando Brigades. A red, unsheathed dagger, blade pointing upwards, set on a black background was the badge of the Commando Brigades? The dagger being the weapon of the Commandos.

ROYAL MARINE FORMATIONS

Mobile Naval Base Defence Organization.
The function of the M.N.B.D.O. was to
provide the Fleet with a base in any
theatre of operations, on an island or on
the mainland coast, and defend it after
its establishment. The M.N.B.D.O. was
about 8,000 strong and composed of
an H.Q. and Landing and Maintenance
Group and a Land Defence Force,
including Anti-Aircraft and Coast
Defence Gunners. The Landing and
Maintenance Group was made up of
skilled technicians and was responsible
for the collection and landing of
stores and the construction of wharves,
jetties, roadways and accommodation.
Workshop and signal units were included
in the organization, together with all
types of administrative personnel.

The 1st M.N.B.D.O. was raised early
in 1940. During the Battle of Britain its
Anti-Aircraft and Searchlight Batteries
were in action in A.D.G.B., whilst other
units assisted in mounting and manning
Coast Defence Batteries on the East and
South-East Coasts.

The 1st M.N.B.D.O. embarked for the
Mediterranean early in 1941 to be
employed with the Fleet, and after the
evacuation from Greece it was employed
in providing a naval base in Crete. Only
part of the force was landed and this
element took part in the stubborn
defence of Canea and Suda Bay against
the German airborne invasion. The
M.N.B.D.O. lost over 1,000 all ranks in
the hard fighting and the subsequent
evacuation from Crete, the Marines
being among the last to leave the island;
the survivors returned to Egypt, where
the organization was re-formed for
service in the Middle East, taking part
in the defence of the Canal Zone. It
later served in Syria and took part
in the seaborne landings at Tobruk.
In June 1943, the formation moved

to Ceylon, where it was re-formed into
two brigade groups. One served in India,
the other remaining in Ceylon, detach-
ments from which served in the Maldive
Islands. The anti-aircraft element of the
Brigade in India later served with 33rd
Corps. This Royal Marine formation's
badge was circular; on it were five diagonal
stripes, blue, yellow, green, red and blue,
and in the case of the sign of the 2nd
M.N.B.D.O. a polar bear was superimposed. The Polar Bear was the badge
of Iceland Force [and the 49th (West
Riding) Division] of which 2nd
M.N.B.D.O. formed part in May-June
1940.

Royal Marine Division.
Neptune's trident in yellow, set on a
scarlet background of an inverted
isosceles triangle with a circular base,
was the badge of the Royal Marine
Division. When this formation was
disbanded the badge continued to be
worn by the 116th (Royal Marine)
Independent Infantry Brigade.

116th (Royal Marine) Infantry Brigade.
This Brigade was raised in 1945 and was
composed of the 27th, 28th and 30th
Battalions Royal Marines. Under the
command of Brigadier C.F. Phillips, the
Brigade served with 21st Army Group
in North-Western Europe, going into
action on the Lower Maas and later
taking part in the advance into Germany
to Oldenburg. The Brigade wore the
badge of the former Royal Marine
Division (see above).

117th (Royal Marine) Infantry Brigade.
This Brigade was also formed in 1945
from Royal Marine boat crews, retrained
for land service to meet the shortage of
infantry. The badge adopted by the
Brigade was a Naval fouled anchor in
yellow on a red circle set in the centre
of a yellow eight-pointed star; the design
set on a khaki background. The badge
was based on the Royal Marine cap-
badge, 1770-75. The yellow represented
the brass and the red the traditional
colour of the Infantry.

**Amphibian Support Regiment,
Royal Marines.**
A yellow anchor, set on an inverted red
equilateral triangle (with a narrow yellow
edge on the two sides meeting at the
apex), superimposed on a dark blue
shield, was the badge borne by this
Royal Marine unit, which was one of
the lesser-known units which came about
in the development of the technique in
combined operations. The Regiment
mobilized at Aldershot in February 1945.
It had been formed as a result of investi-
gations into the Dieppe operation. The
Regiment went into action on D Day
in Normandy. It was moved to India
later in 1945, and it would have taken
part in the operations planned to take
place in Malaya. The unit, however, did
not see action, although it took part in
a few minor operations in Java in an
infantry role. In April 1946, it returned
to the United Kingdom and was
attached to the School of Combined
Operations in North Devon.

Royal Marine Siege Regiment.
A bursting grenade with red flames set on
a khaki background.

Royal Marine Engineers.
A yellow seven-flamed grenade, set on
a red fouled anchor, set on a dark blue
shield.

Royal Marines Training Centre.
This R.M. Training Centre wore a
distinctive badge of a yellow sea-horse
set in a royal blue circle against the background of an inverted red triangle, the
base of which was curved.

SPECIAL FORCES

'V' Force.
This force came into being during the withdrawal from Burma, and was made up of local dispersed troops—in the early days, mainly Kachins. In 1943-44 it operated in the no-man's-land on the right flank of the Tiddim Road in the almost impenetrable hills around Haka and Falam. Its primary task was intelligence and the upkeep of local morale.

When operations recommenced in 1944, after the monsoon season, 'V' force operated in advance of the Lushai Brigade in the hill country between Manipur State and the Arakan. In much the same way as it grew up so did the force 'fade out' as the Fourteenth Army advanced leaving behind the dense jungle-covered hills which lie between the Chindwin river and the Arakan coast.

The 'V' force badge was two crossed daggers—the blades forming a 'V'—a letter 'V' superimposed on the hilts which rested on a scroll on which was inscribed the word 'Force'. The design was in white, picked out in black, set on a circular light green background.

'R' Force.
This was a force of mixed arms which formed part of 21st Army Group and

was allotted a special operational role under the direct command of Field-Marshal Montgomery's H.Q. The badge of the force was a white capital 'R' on a black shield. The G.H.Q. troops, R.E., which formed the Sapper element of this force wore a white 'R' on blue square.

Force 135
(Channel Islands Liberation Force).
This force, which was assembled for the liberation of the Channel Islands, wore as its badge the Arms of Jersey and Guernsey, three yellow lions set on a red shield. The three lions on a red field were part of the coat of arms of Richard I, who was also Duke of Normandy, the Channel Islands being originally incorporated in that Dukedom.

First Special Service Force.
Comprised two U.S. battalions, one Canadian battalion (1st Canadian Special Service Battalion) and an S. and T. company. This force was trained in parachute, ski, beach assault, and other infantry roles, including the use of all forms of allied and enemy small arms and M.T. All equipment, including uniforms, was American. The force, after training in U.S. and Canada, proceeded to Italy and came under command of

Fifth Army in December 1943. It served
with great distinction at the first Anzio
landing and subsequent fighting; and also
served in the invasion of Southern France;
and was then disbanded. The force never
wore any badge but its own—a red arrow
(or spear) head; on it, in white, the
words 'Canada—USA'.

**G.R.E.F. (General Reserve Engineering
Force).**
When the withdrawal from Burma commenced in the spring of 1942, there was
practically no military engineering
organization or resources in Assam.
Engineer units; Military engineering
services; Public Works department staffs
and Civil engineering firms' resources
were rapidly collected together and
played a major part in the operations.
With the turn of the tide it was necessary
to reorganize this Engineer Force which
had been hurriedly raised in emergency,
and it was decided to form an Engineer
Task Force to support our forces on
the north-eastern frontier of India. A
headquarters was formed at Shillong
in May 1943, and the organization was
designated General Reserve Engineering
Force (G.R.E.F.) under the command
of G.H.Q. India. In October 1943, the
force was placed under command of
Fourteenth Army and moved forward
into Burma.
      The distinguishing badge of G.R.E.F.
was a five-pointed yellow star, the
letters 'G.F.' in dark green, in the
centre, the star set on a dark green circle.

DISTRICTS (U.K.)

The Districts
The Districts of the Home Commands were reorganized on several occasions and the detail of some of the badges as follows does not refer to those worn at the final reorganization.

London District.
A mural crown in gold, with a sword in red pointing upwards through the centre, the whole set against a dark blue background, was the badge adopted by London District. The sword was taken from the Arms of the City of London and the mural crown from above the shield in the arms of the London County Council.

Northumbrian District (Northern Command).
Formerly 9th Corps District, Northumbrian District came into existence in 1942. Its badge was the St. Oswald's shield of Northumbria, six yellow and and red vertical bars set in a shield on a blue background. The shield was a copy of the badge used by the Northumberland County Council. St. Oswald, the first Christian King of Northumbria in the seventh century, who, legend has it, used to come out of battle with his golden shield streaked with blood. The badge was also worn by the Northumberland Battalions of the Home Guard.[2]

The District covered at one period the counties of Northumberland and Durham and the North Riding of Yorkshire, but the latter subsequently became a separate District.

West Riding District (Northern Command) East and West Riding District.
A hanging Golden Fleece enclosed within a ring set on a green diamond was the badge of this District of Northern Command. The fleece, indicative of the area of the West and East Ridings of Yorkshire, was abstracted from the Arms of the City of Leeds, where the District H.Q. was established.

North Riding District (Northern Command).
This District's area included the important training area of the Yorkshire wolds, and of Catterick. Its badge, adopted from the arms of the North Riding County Council, was a red cross on a white shield, above it a dark blue bar on which were superimposed three white Yorkshire roses.

**North Midland District
(Northern Command).**
The figure of Robin Hood, in Lincoln
green, with brown cap feather, gloves,
belt, pouch and boots, with his longbow
in black, set against a light green background was the appropriate badge of
North Midland District, which included
Sherwood Forest within its boundaries,
whilst the Headquarters of the District
was in Nottinghamshire and the County
Regiment, the Sherwood Foresters.

**East Riding and Lincs District
(Northern Command).**
A golden eagle on a square black background was this Distict's badge, and
vehicle marking. The badge was adopted
from the device used by the East Riding
County Council—a blue eagle on gold—
before the grant of arms in 1945. The
eagle was taken from the arms of the
ancient kingdom of Mercia.

**North Wales District
Midland West District
(Western Command).**[3]
The Prince of Wales's feathers, in red,
on a dark green circle, was the badge of
North Wales district, which was raised,
with its H.Q. at Shrewsbury, consisted

of the six counties of North Wales,
Anglesey, Caernarvan, Denbigh, Flint,
Montgomery and Merioneth, and the
border county of Shropshire. The
district was redesignated Midland West
District in 1944 when part of the former
West Lancashire District was absorbed
into its boundaries.

**South Wales District
(Western Command).**[3]
The heraldic red dragon of Wales set on
a bright green background was the
national badge adopted by South
Wales District, which had its Headquarters at Abergavenny.

**West Lancashire District
(Western Command).**
The red rose of Lancaster formed the
basis and background of this District's
badge. In the centre of the large rose
were the emblems of the Cheshire
Regiment (the acorn and oak leaf),
Lancashire (the Tudor rose), and
Staffordshire (the knot), these counties
being within the District's boundaries.
The District was disbanded in 1944 and
absorbed into the adjacent Districts of
Western Command.

Brigade which served in the Western Desert with the Eighth Army taking part in the sweep into Tunisia. It later served in North-Western Europe.

23rd Armoured Brigade.
A black liver bird, in its beak an olive branch set on a white square or circular background was the badge of this Armoured Brigade, which was composed of the 40th, 46th and 50th Royal Tank Regiments, and the 11th Bn. 60th Rifles (K.R.R.C.). The badge was chosen to link the formation's association with Liverpool, where the Brigade was raised. The Brigade originally wore the badge of the 8th Armoured Division.

The Brigade saw considerable service in the Middle East and in the Mediterranean, taking part in the battle of El Alamein with 51st (Highland) Division and the advance across the Western Desert to Tunisia. The Brigade then moved to Malta and thence to Sicily and Italy, taking part in the Salerno landing—one regiment also took part in the Anzio landing. Withdrawn in 1943 to Egypt, the Brigade rejoined the Eighth Army in Italy later in the year.

The 23rd Armoured was the first formation to move to Greece, where it was engaged in the fighting following the E.L.A.S. rising. The Brigade remained in Greece until it was disbanded in May 1946.

25th Armoured Engineer Brigade.
Originally designated 25th Assault Brigade R.E., this Brigade was formed, on the disbandment of the 25th Tank

Brigade, early in 1945 at Viterbo, the Italian Parachute Depot just north of Rome. It was composed of the 1st Assault Regiment R.A.C./R.E. (originally the 'Scorpion Regiment'), which later became 1st Armoured Engineer Regiment R.E.; the Divisional Engineers of the 1st Armoured Division, which became the 2nd Armoured Engineer Regiment; and the 51st Royal Tank Regiment with a squadron of 'Crocodiles' and two of 'Flails'. The Brigade was equipped on similar lines to the Armoured Engineer Brigade of the 79th Armoured Division in North-Western Europe with A.Vs.R.E. and special assault Engineer equipment.

The Brigade's badge was composed of the familiar diabolo sign of the Tank Brigades, in black, set on a red shield, divided vertically by two royal blue bars (the R.E. Colours).

27th Armoured Brigade.
A yellow and white sea-horse set on a saxe blue shield was this formation's badge. The Brigade formed part of 21st Army Group with the British Liberation Army in North-West Europe.

32nd Army Tank Brigade.
A white Marguerite, with a pale green centre, stalk and leaf set on a black square, was the badge adopted by this Brigade, which formed part of our forces in the Middle East.

33rd Armoured Brigade.
This Brigade's badge varied from the triangular badges of other armoured formations inasmuch as the triangles were equilateral, the top triangle being green and the lower one black. The Brigade formed part of the armoured force of 21st Army Group.

35th Armoured Brigade.
Similar in design to the badge of the 33rd Armoured Brigade, the colours of the triangles of the 35th Brigade were brown at the top, and green at the bottom.

34th Armoured Brigade.
A mailed fist clenching a spiked mace in white, picked out in black, superimposed on a red shield divided diagonally by a yellow band, was the 34th Armoured Brigade's badge. The Brigade served in North-West Europe with 21st Army Group.

The same pattern of formation badge was adopted by the following Army Tank and Armoured Brigades. In each case the design was a diabolo or two isosceles triangles, one inverted above the other, the apices meeting. The colours of the triangles varied in each case.

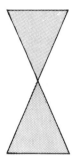

21st Army Tank Brigade.[3]
Colour of triangles: Yellow.

23rd Army Tank Brigade.
Colour of triangles: Green.

24th Army Tank Brigade.
Colour of triangles: Blue.

25th Army Tank Brigade.
Colour of triangles: Black. A white maple leaf was added to the centre of the upper triangle to commemorate this Brigade's service with the 1st Canadian Infantry Division in Italy. This Brigade was disbanded early in 1945, part of it being incorporated into the then newly-raised 25th Assault Brigade R.E. (later the 25th Armoured Engineer Brigade). The black diabolo of the Brigade's sign being included in the badge of the new formation.[4]

31st Independent Armoured Brigade.
Colour of triangles—pale green.

Lancs and Border District
North-Western District
(Western Command).
This District's badge also featured the
red rose of Lancaster set on a dark green
background within yellow interwined
chains, representing the two borders,
Scotland and Wales, which formed the
Northern and South-Western boundaries
of the District. The District covered the
counties of Westmorland and Cumber-
land and part of Lancashire. In 1944
it was redesignated North-Western
District and absorbed part of West
Lancs District—the counties of
Lancashire and Cheshire—on its
disbandment.

Hants and Dorset District
Aldershot and Hants District
(Southern Command).
The District badge, which came into use
in 1943, depicted a white winged figure
of Victory, set on a saxe blue background representing sea and sky, before
her the white points of the Needles.
It was in this District's area that a high
proportion of the D Day concentrations
were assembled, and it was from the
District's South Coast ports that the
invasion fleet set sail in June 1944. On
the reorganization of Southern Command
consequent upon the disbandment of
South-Eastern Command in 1944, the
area was redesignated Aldershot and
Hants District and its boundaries were
altered to include the former Aldershot
Command, but lost the territory within
the county of Dorset.

Salisbury Plain District
(Southern Command).
The Great Cromlech of Stonehenge, in
red, set against a yellow background and
green grass base, within a black and red
circle was appropriately chosen as the
badge of Salisbury Plain District, which
had its Headquarters at Bulford. The
District's area originally covered the
county of Wiltshire, but on the
reorganization of Southern Command
in 1944 took in the county of Dorset
and was redesignated Wilts and Dorset
District. The badge was designed in the
spring of 1944, by Captain Walter Clark,
F.R.I.B.A., R.E., then serving on the
staff of the District H.Q. The design of
the Cromlech is correct in outline and
proportion. The dominating colour, red,
was chosen for its striking qualities.

South-Western District
(Southern Command).
This area was, until 1943, known as
8 Corps District, but was redesignated
South-Western District on the withdrawal
of H.Q. 8 Corps to train for its operational
role with 21st Army Group. South-
Western District retained the original
8 Corps District badge—a black
Francolin partridge, in flight, set upon
a white oval. The District comprised the
counties of Devon, Cornwall and
Somerset and part of Gloucestershire.
The District Badge was adopted in 1940
when 8 Corps District was commanded
by General Sir Harold E. Franklyn, K.C.B.,
D.S.O., M.C., the Francolin Partridge
being chosen as a pun on the name of
the Corps Commander.

**South Midland District
(Southern Command).**
A yellow bell set on a dark blue background was this District's badge. The sign was chosen to associate the District H.Q. with Oxford, where it was located, the bell depicted in the badge representing 'Great Tom' of Christ Church, Oxford. South Midland District's area covered the counties of Oxfordshire and Berkshire and part of Gloucestershire.

**East Kent District
(South-Eastern Command).
Home Counties District
(Eastern Command).**
A shield, on which was depicted Dover Castle above the white cliffs, was the appropriate and distinctive badge of East Kent District. The colouring of the sign was white, black, grey, and light and dark blue. The District was redesignated, in 1946, Home Counties District and formed part of Eastern Command.

**North Kent and Surrey District
(South Eastern Command).**
The White Horse of Kent, as it appeared in the cap badge of the Royal West Kent Regiment,[5] was the badge adopted by North Kent and Surrey District. The horse was set on a green oval-shaped background within a narrow white border. This badge was adopted in 1941; previously the District's badge was a white horse's head on a green circular background within a narrow white border.

**Sussex and Surrey District
(South-Eastern Command).**
The head of a black wolf, with open mouth showing a bright red tongue, set in a pale green/blue oval within a black border, was the badge of this District, which was formed to administer the area of South-Eastern Command vacated by Canadian Corps District on its assumption of a field force role. The badge was adopted to commemorate the association of the area with 1st Canadian Corps which maintained a striking force known by the code name

'Woolf force'. A British static element was attached to the Canadian Corps which, when disbanded, was replaced, by Sussex and Surrey District with its Headquarters at Haywards Heath.

Canadian Corps District (South-Eastern Command).
This District, which subsequently became Sussex and Surrey District, was the static District of South-Eastern Command allotted to the Canadian Corps. Its badge was a Sussex martlet set on a green circle, the martlet being taken from the shield of the Arms of the West Sussex Council[6] which also formed the centre of the badge of the Sussex Yeomanry.

2 Corps District (Eastern Command).
Two seaxes, from the arms of the County of Essex, in blue, with yellow hilts set on a black shield within a yellow border was the badge of this Corps District which was located in Essex prior to the formation of Essex and Suffolk District of Eastern Command.

Essex and Suffolk District
East Anglian District
(Eastern Command).
The badge of Essex and Suffolk District was a shield divided horizontally; in the upper half a castle—adopted from the badge of the Suffolk Regiment—on a light blue background; in the lower against a red background, the three seaxes of the arms of Essex.

On the reorganization of Eastern Command in 1944, this District ceased to exist and a newly created District designated East Anglian assumed this badge, the colours being changed to a black design on a yellow shield.

Norfolk and Cambridge District (Eastern Command).
Members of the coats of arms of the East Anglian cities, Norwich and Cambridge, and of the county of Norfolk, set in quarters on a shield in black and white, was the badge adopted by Norfolk and Cambridge District, castles being featured in the arms of Cambridge and Norwich, Tudor Roses in the Cambridge arms and a lion passant guardant in the Arms of the City of Norwich.

Central Midland District
East Central District
(Eastern Command).
The distinctive badge of Central Midland
District subsequently redesignated East
Central District, depicted a helmet,—
similar to a Burganet or Burgonette— as
worn by Cromwell's 'Ironsides', superimposed on crossed cavalry swords and
an upright pike, set on a red rectangular
background. This design was chosen as
the District boundaries included the
battlefields of some of the major
engagements of the Civil War.

The District covered the counties
of Hertfordshire, Bedfordshire,
Huntingdonshire, Northamptonshire
and Buckinghamshire. These five
counties can be described as the centre
of Cromwell's County. Huntingdonshire
was his home county and he raised his
original cavalry regiment, the famous
Ironsides, mainly in Huntingdon and
Hertfordshire. These two counties,
together with Buckinghamshire, formed
part of what was known as the Eastern
Association of Counties, whilst Bedfordshire and Northamptonshire formed part
of the Midland Association. Buckingham
and Northampton were both 'border'
counties and saw much of the fighting
in the Civil War.

The District badge was chosen for this
reason. The Cromwellian helmet representing that spirit and discipline based on
highest moral qualities, which Cromwell
inspired. The Cromwellian pike pushed
forward with the swords on either flank
ready to protect or strike representing
the tactical skill at arms, individual and
collective, which he imbued and which
he taught can only be attained by hard
unremitting training. The scarlet background being the traditional colour of
the British Army uniform.

The original badge of Central Midland
District was similar to that of the Guards
Armoured Division, a black and white
eye on a white ground within a black
circle.

East Scotland District
West Scotland District
(Scottish Command).
In 1939 H.Q. Scottish Command ordered
that all static formations and troops
should carry for identification purposes
a white St. Andrew's Cross on a coloured
field. The Colour chosen for the Edinburgh
Area (which in 1941 became Lothian and
Border District and, in 1944, East Scotland
District) was green. The Scottish Lion
rampant was then superimposed on the
St. Andrew's Cross on the green field.

Both East and West Scotland Districts
had similar signs, and both incorporated
the same basic pattern as set by H.Q.
Scottish Command—the lion rampant of
Scotland in gold. In the West Scotland
District badge the lion was superimposed
on a white St. Andrew's cross on a red
background, and in the case of East
Scotland District the badge was identical
but for the colour of the background,
which was dark green.

North Highland District
(Scottish Command).
The heraldic lion rampant of Scotland,
in gold, as it appeared on the H.Q.
Scottish Command badge was also the
sign of North Highland District, which
had its H.Q. at Inverness. The lion was
superimposed on a diagonally divided
background of purple and green. The
Colours of the Highland Brigade, the
green and purple being the colours of
the heather on the mountains. This
District was redesignated 'Highland
District' on 1st January 1946.

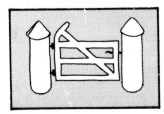

Northern Ireland District.

The initial letters of Northern Ireland District, being N.I.D., formed the word 'nid', French for nest, hence the nest lodged on two black boughs on a dark green background being adopted as the District's sign, and, with a white bird to stress the nest in the design. Northern Ireland District had been, for many years, the Senior formation in Ulster. With the considerable increase in the number of troops in Northern Ireland in 1940 a higher formation was established and designated H.Q. British Troops Northern Ireland. This formation was senior to the District H.Q. and was jokingly referred to as the 'Cuckoo in the Nest'—hence the bird in the nest in the N.I.D. formation sign. H.Q. British Troops in Northern Ireland and H.Q. Northern Ireland District were amalgamated in May 1943, and the N.I.D. badge was changed to the sign of the Irish gate, similar in design to that previously used by B.T.N.I. ; in the case of the District badge, the gate was white and the background emerald green.

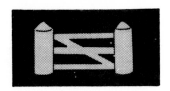

British Troops in Northern Ireland (B.T.N.I.).

A typical North Irish three-barred gate between two stone posts, so familiar to the troops in Northern Ireland, was adopted as the badge of B.T.N.I. on the original badge. The gate was red set on a black oblong background, to denote command colours of red and black. It was adopted in 1940. On 9th May 1943, on the amalgamation of H.Q. B.T.N.I. and H.Q. Northern Ireland District the badge was changed to a white gate and posts on an emerald green background as being more appropriate and natural colours.

Orkney and Shetland Defences.

The military garrison of the Orkneys and Shetlands, known as 'Osdef', was composed mainly of Anti-Aircraft and Coast Defence Gunners and Infantry and adopted as its badge the naval fouled anchor in red on a dark blue background denoting its close association with the naval base at Scapa Flow.

OVERSEAS FORCE AND GARRISON HEADQUARTERS

Malta Force.

All formations in Malta incorporated the Maltese Cross in their distinguishing badge. Command Headquarters adopted the cross in white set on an evenly divided gackground of Command colours, red, black, red, whilst the Malta Infantry Brigade (later the 231st Infantry Brigade) wore a white Maltese Cross on a red shield.[1]

Field Defences—Malta.

A Maltese cross, the arms each divided evenly into silver and red, the badge on a square black background was the distinguishing sign of the troops of Malta's field defences.

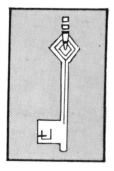

Gibraltar Garrison.

The appropriate badge of the Fortress Headquarters was the Gibraltar 'Key to the Mediterranean' which figures in the Rock's coat of arms. The badge was a yellow key upright, on a scarlet rectangle. The R.A. units of the garrison wore this badge on a diagonally-divided background of red and blue.[2]

Faeroe Islands Force.

These North Atlantic Islands were occupied by British forces in 1940 as a preventive measure against German aggression and the possible establishment of a hostile base which would threaten our sea communications. The Force H.Q. was at Thorshaven, and the original garrison was made up of the Lovat Scouts, Royal Artillery, Coast Defence and Heavy and Light A.A. Batteries, and R.E. lines of communication and Works Units.

The badge of the Faeroe Islands Force depicted a 'Tjaldur' (an oyster catcher)— the national emblem of the Faeroes. The bird, in natural colours of black and white, stood on a black rock against a background of sea and sky in dark and light blue.

Iceland Force.

The well-known polar bear badge of Iceland Force was originally chosen as their badge by the first brigade of the 49th (West Riding) Division to land in Iceland in May 1940. Previous to this the 49th Division had worn the white rose of Yorkshire as their sign.[3] The white polar bear on the black background was subsequently adopted by the rest of the 49th Division when they disembarked in Iceland, and also by the Force H.Q. at Reykjavik and all the non-divisional British troops under command.

New Guinea Force.
This force was formed from 2 Australian Corps and its staff formed the operational and administrative Headquarters for all Australian troops in New Guinea. The formation was disbanded in 1944 and reformed as a Corps. Its badge was a parakeet's head above a boomerang.

Force 281 and Dodecanese District.
A leaping wild goat in red above three wavy blue lines set on a square white or khaki background was the badge of Dodecanese District which was originally designated Force 281.

This badge was chosen because the original Force Headquarter Staff was drawn mainly from personnel of the Mountain Warfare Training Centre which had as its badge a wild goat, and as Force 281 was designed to control an area composed largely of sea, the blue bars were added to the original badge.

Force 281 was formed on the 8th September 1944, and occupied Syme on the 25th December 1944, from where it moved to Rhodes after the surrender of the German Garrison in May 1945. During this time a number of islands were occupied, and raids carried out on other islands in the Dodecanese. After the German capitulation, Force 281 was redesignated Dodecanese District, carrying out internal security duties and civilian relief.

H.Q. Palestine and Transjordan.
An Arab dagger, white blade, black hilt, on a red square background was the distinguishing badge of H.Q. Palestine and Transjordan.

H.Q. Sudan and Eritrea.
In black silhouette on a white square background, a camel and rider, the badge of Sudan Defence Force, was adopted by H.Q. Sudan and Eritrea. This badge was the emblem of the S.D.F. from 1924 and was taken from the design on the postage stamps of the Sudan.

H.Q. British Troops Aden.
A white Arab dhow in full sail on a black square background was the badge of Aden District, which was adapted from the badge of the Colony.

H.Q. British Troops in Iraq.
The same badge as was formerly used by
'Paiforce'—a red elephant's head with
white tusks on a blue background—is
worn by H.Q. British Troops in Iraq.[5]

H.Q. Land Forces Hong Kong.
Established on the liberation of Hong
Kong, this H.Q. has adopted as its badge
a China dragon in gold set on a rectangular
background of Command colours, red,
black and red. The dragon was the same
design as that which was the badge of the
Hong Kong Regiment.

H.Q. British Troops in the Low Countries.
Formerly H.Q. lines of communication
21st Army Group,[6] this Headquarters
continued to wear its former badge; a
dark blue cross on a yellow shield. With
its Headquarters in Brussels it was the
Administrative H.Q. for all British
troops located in Belgium and Holland
after the cessation of hostilities in North-
Western Europe.

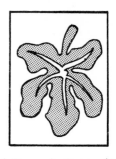

**H.Q. British Forces in Greece (B.F.I.G.).
H.Q. Land Forces, Greece.**
H.Q. 3 Corps on arrival in Greece assumed
command of all British land forces in that
country, the Headquarters being
redesignated accordingly. The formation
Headquarters continued to wear the
badge of the green fig leaf on a white
background, and this badge was retained
when the Headquarters was later renamed
British Forces in Greece.[7]

British Troops in Norway.
A Viking's galley with three wavy lines
below to denote the sea, and on the
horizon, the midnight sun, the whole
design in white on a pale blue background, was the badge of British Troops
in Norway. This force, which formed
part of the Allied Liberation Force
(American, Norwegian and British) under
the direction of S.H.A.E.F., was composed
of the 1st Airborne Division, commanded
by Major-General R.E. Urquhart, C.B.,
D.S.O., the Headquarters of the 50th
(Northumbrian) Division (which later
became H.Q. British Land Forces,
Norway), the 1st S.A.S. Brigade,
commanded by Brigadier J.M. Calvert,
D.S.O., the 303rd and 304th Infantry
Brigades and 88 Group, R.A.F., together
with Lines of communication units
withdrawn from 21st Army Group. The
Allied force landed in Norway on the
9th May, the 1st Airborne Division
going ashore at Oslo and Stavanger. The
task of this force was to control, disarm
and evacuate the German occupation
forces, to assist Allied prisoners of war
and displaced persons, and to help the

Norwegian authorities in the re-establishment of their power. A composite battalion of the Guards later joined the force and replaced the Airborne units.

Headquarters Allied Forces Northern Europe.
Established in Oslo after the liberation of Norway in May 1944, the H.Q. adopted a symbolic Viking ship in white with a red and white striped sail, set on a blue shield, as its formation badge.

British Troops in Egypt.
A scarlet pyramid and two palm trees on a white background was the badge of B.T.E. (British Troops in Egypt) and was worn by H.Q. B.T.E. and troops under command stationed in the Delta, the Canal Zone, Western Desert and in Cairo and not belonging to any formation having its own distinguishing badge.

British Troops in Siam.
A Siamese ceremonial dancer in black silhouette on a yellow background

within a narrow black border was the badge adopted by our forces which moved into Siam after the defeat of the Japanese.

Land Forces Adriatic (L.F.A.).
This force, which operated in Yugoslavia and in Albania, had its base at Bari in Italy. Its primary task was to aid the partisans of Marshal Tito's forces in Bosnia and Montenegro. After a year's successful activities the force was disbanded in June 1945. Its badge, which linked with the amphibious activities of the force, was a white winged horse—Pegasus—swimming, set on a dark blue oval background. The badge was symbolic of the airborne and amphibious activities of the force.

Transjordan Frontier Force.

This force wore one distinguishing badge of a black scorpion on a white background. The Transjordan Frontier Force was raised in Palestine in 1926 under the auspices of the Colonial Office. N.C.Os. and men of the Palestine Gendarmerie formed the cadre on which the force was built. The officers were British, and the men were of various nationalities—Arabs, Sudanese, Circassians and Jews.
    The force was originally horsed, but was subsequently partly mechanized. With its headquarters in Zarga, the force had two main tasks—internal security and guarding the frontiers of Transjordania.

The Arab Legion.
This was a Middle East force. Its badge
a falcon's head in white on a red square.
The badge, it was said, was chosen as
falconry is a favourite Arab sport in the
Desert.

The famous Arab Legion was established in Transjordan after the 1914-18 War
by Major Peake Pasha, who built up this
force in order to check the raiding
Bedouins and to maintain Transjordan's
frontiers.

Under the command of Brigadier
Glubb Pasha the Arab Legion served the
Allied cause during the 1939-45 War.

Among the most essential roles of the
Arab Legion is that of guarding the cross
country pipeline, achieved by means of
groups of men quartered in small forts.

OVERSEAS DISTRICTS AND L. of C. AREAS (EXCLUSIVE INDIA AND S.E.A.C.)

21st Army Group (G.H.Q. and L. of C. Troops).
The H.Q. 21st Army Group sign, minus the crusaders' swords—a blue cross on a red shield—was worn by all ranks of the 21st Army Group G.H.Q. troops and lines of communication formations and units not allotted to any lower formation which had its own distinguishing badge.

Headquarters L. of C. 21st Army Group.
Of similar design to the 21st Army Group G.H.Q. troops badge was that of the H.Q. Lines of Communication 21st Army Group and the L. of C. and Base Sub-Area H.Qs. This was a dark blue crusader's cross on a yellow shield and was worn by all ranks, and stencilled on the vehicles of the H.Qs. of the L. of C. and certain formations and units under direct command of those Headquarters—i.e., Chief Engineers (Works) and Cs.R.E. (Works), etc.

Netherlands District.
Originally designated West Holland District, this formation came into existence early in 1945 for service in B.L.A. as one of the Districts of 21st Army Group's L. of C. The District was formed to cover, initially, the liberated area of Holland from Walcheren and the Scheldt estuary and south of the Waal, but later assumed responsibility for the military administration and rehabilitation of the Netherlands following the German surrender in May 1945. It was then that the District was redesignated 'Netherlands' and its H.Q. was established at The Hague. The District's badge was a typical Dutch scene, a windmill, cottage, and a dyke by the banks of a canal, the design being in light blue on a white background within a blue circular border.

H.Q. L. of C. British Troops in North Africa.
Originally H.Q. L. of C. First Army, this formation adopted as its sign a gazelle which appeared in the design as 'Bambi' of the Walt Disney film. The gazelle was in black and white and was set on a green background. The formation was, whilst in North Africa, presented with a gazelle, which was adopted as its mascot.

Tripolitania District.
A Barbary pirate's galley in black, set on a square background of a white sky and blue sea, was the Tripolitania District's badge. The design was taken from the emblem of the city of Tripoli, as used by the Italian Colonial authorities during their regime. This was another administrative H.Q. set up when this area was occupied after the conquest of the Italian North African colonies.

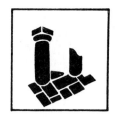

Cyrenaica District.
Two Greek pillars in black, one of which is broken, set on black pavings, representative of the ruins of ancient Carthage, set on a square white background, was Cyrenaica District's badge after its establishment as an administrative H.Q. of this conquered and occupied former Italian colony. The Headquarters was established in Benghazi on 7th February 1943, moving to Barce on 9th March. The badge, designed by the District Commander, Major-General A.L. Collier, C.B.E., M.C., was significant of 'the parts of Libya about Cyrene' (Acts, ch. 2, verse 10). Cyrene, where there are still magnificent Greek and Roman remains, was one of the most flourishing Greek Colonies, and was later of considerable importance in Roman times when many of its temples and public buildings were restored. The badge was subsequently changed, the design being in white on a black background. It was only used as a vehicle marking sign.

No. 15 Area, M.E.F. North Palestine District.
This Middle East administrative area had as its badge a blue dolphin on a square black background. At one period this area was designated 'Northern Area' and after the war became North Palestine District.

No. 16 Area M.E.F.
Located in the Alexandria Area, this District adopted as its badge a typical caique as used by the Egyptians. The craft was in white, on a black sea, against a dark blue sky.

No. 17 Area M.E.F.
This Area H.Q. was located in Cairo and had as its badge a black mosque flanked by two minarets set on a white background representing the Mohammed Ali Mosque within the citadel of Cairo, which as a fortress on the Muquattan Hills dominating the city has been long associated with its military history.[2]

No. 18 (Suez Canal) Area M.E.F.
Originally designated Canal Zone, and later Suez Canal Base Sub-Area, 18th Area, M.E.F. H.Q. adopted the appropriate badge of a yellow ground, representing the desert, across it a diagonal blue line for the canal, and on it a dhow with triangular sail.

North Levant District.
Originally the badge of the Ninth Army.[4] A charging elephant in red, on its back a small castle carrying a flag, set on a black circular background was the badge of North Levant District.

Tunisia District.
The badge was adopted following notification in a District Routine Order in June 1943, and it was used as a vehicle marking. Shortly after Tunisia District was absorbed into North Africa District and the badge discontinued. The badge took the form of the letters 'TD' in blue set in the white space of the archway of a Moorish building in blue.

Iraq Base and L. of C. Area.
An Arab sheathed knife in black, set on a white jagged-edged background on a dark green square, was the badge of this Base and L. of C. Area.

Cyprus District.
The badge of Cyprus, two red lions 'passant guardant' (taken from the Arms of Richard Coeur de Lion) on a white background.[3] The two lions also formed part of the heraldic arms of the Lucignian Kings of Cyprus, 1192-1489, and the badge of Cyprus District, which formed part of the Middle East Land Forces, was adopted from the Cyprus badge and comprised of a yellow lion on a green background.

No. 21 Area, M.E.F.
This Middle East Forces area badge was made up of a white crusader's sword, point uppermost, on a black shield, superimposed on the flag of St. George— a red cross on a white background. 21 Area was located in the Lydda District, reputed to be the place where St. George was buried, hence the adoption of the St. George's cross and the crusader's sword.

No. 88 Area M.E.F.
A red escallop shell on a yellow square was the badge adopted by this Middle East Administrative Area. The escallop shell had its origin during the crusades as an heraldic emblem, a 'charge' in arms.

No. 1 District C.M.F.
A husky dog, white head and with red ears and tongue set on a pale green circle was the badge of No. 1 District C.M.F. Formerly H.Q. Tunisia District the formation was moved to Sicily. The code name for the move was Operation 'Husky' hence the adoption, in Sicily, of the District's badge.

No. 2 District C.M.F.
Two white columns, typical of Roman architecture, set on a black background was the vehicle marking of No. 2 District C.M.F. in Italy, whilst the District's badge depicted a horizontal dagger from which, suspended by two links, hung

an anchor. The design was in black on a red background. This District at the conclusion of hostilities occupied one north-western area of Italy.

No. 3 District C.M.F.
The District Commander, Major-General A.L. Collier, C.B.E., M.C., was formerly G.O.C. Cyrenaica District, which had as its badge two columns representative of the ruins of ancient Cyrene.[5] When No. 3 District C.M.F. was established on 9th February 1944, at Castellammare di Stabia about twenty miles south of Napes, the Commander retained the architectural basis for the new badge and No. 3 District's badge became the three pillars of the Temple of Castor and Pollux in Rome, in white set on a black background, the pillars being identified with the Roman figure III and the District's number. The District H.Q. moved into Naples at the end of 1944.

No. 56 Area C.M.F.
A black torch, with a red flame—similar to that in the G.H.Q., C.M.F. badge—held in a white hand, set on a buff or yellow background was the badge of this area which was used as a vehicle sign and not worn by personnel.

North Caribbean Area.
The H.Q. of this area was located in Jamaica. Its badge was a sea-horse, in black picked out in white, above a red bar, set on a khaki background. This was changed to a black sea-horse on a yellow background. The tail of a sea horse is normally turned down, but for reasons of morale the badge was designed with the tail turned up.

South Caribbean Area.
With its H.Q. in Trinidad, this area administered the British troops and auxiliary forces in the South Caribbean. Its badge, adopted in November 1942, was composed of two crossed swords, a rapier and a cutlass, in black, set on a yellow background within a black border. The rapier representing the Spanish influence in the West Indies and the cutlass that of the Buccaneers.

Gold Coast Area.
An elephant and a palm tree, as appeared in the badge of the Colony (and on the Gambia Postage Stamps), in white on a black circle, was adopted as the badge of this Area H.Q.

Nigeria Area.
A crown bird in black on a white rectangular background.

Gambia Area.
A native craft in full sail in white set on a black circle within a white square was adopted as the badge of this Area H.Q., for the badge of the Colony was similar to that of the Gold Coast—an elephant and a palm tree.

Sierra Leone Area.
A lion and a palm tree in yellow on a black circle or rectangle. The palm tree was incorporated into the badge of the Colony.

INDIAN AND S.E.A.C. DISTRICTS AND L. of C. AREAS

101st (Bihar and Orissa) L. of C. Area.
A rampant unicorn in red on a yellow circular background, was the badge of this area which had its H.Q. at Jhansi.

105th (Madras) L. of C. Area.
Madras Area.
This L. of C. Area wore as its badge a golden phoenix, with outspread wings and a red eye, rising from red flames surmounted by a red seven-pointed corona. The design was set on a square black background. Originally designated Madras District, it was, in November 1942, renamed, for security reason, 105 L. of C. Area. On the 1st April 1946, it assumed the title of Madras Area. The following is an extract from Madras Area Orders dated 30th October 1946:

'The mythological story of the Phoenix varies as told by different authors. The salient points of the story are, however, similar. The bird was always male, and there was never more than one alive at any one time. It died by setting its nest on fire and burning itself alive; from the ashes another Phoenix was born. India is one of the countries in which the Phoenix is said to have lived. In July 1942, when the question of the Area sign was being considered, the Phoenix was thought appropriate because it indicated that the Madras District was determined to rise again to renewed heights of martial vigour and achievement for which, in times of stress, the Southern Indian peoples have won fame in the past.'
The sign was adopted in August 1942.

This badge was intended to represent the new warlike spirit of Madras rising from the ashes of the old Madras Army which, with the exception of the Madras Sappers and Miners, had been disbanded after the 1914-18 war.

106th L. of C. Area.
This Area adopted as its badge two battleaxes in red, crossed, and superimposed on a white circle on a black background. The Area covered the whole of Hyderabad State and the northern part of Madras Province, including Vizagapatam.

107th L. of C. Area.
The badge of this Area, which included the whole of Bombay Province, depicted 'The Gateway of India' at Bombay (where all the Viceroys landed on first entering the country) in black and white set on a red square.

108th (Bombay) L. of C. Area.
The first badge of this Area was a white swan set on a blue circular background (jokingly referred to as the 'Bombay Duck') which had been the badge of Bombay Fortress Area (later designated 'Bombay Defended Port Area'). When 107 L. of C. Area was disbanded, 108 L. of C. Area adopted the Gateway of India badge formerly used by 107 L. of C. Area.

109th (Bangalore) L. of C. Area.
A yellow palm tree on a red background.

110th (Poona) L. of C. Area.
Two Mahratta swords crossed below a circular shield. The design in black on a red square with a black border.

202nd (Assam) L. of C. Area.
A black arrow representing a Naga spear

pointing upwards through a blue wavy band, representing the River Bramaputra, on a white circle within a black border and set on a khaki square.

303rd (Bengal) L. of C. Area.
A round of .303 ammunition, the case in yellow, the bullet in white set diagonally on a red square.

404th (East Bengal) L. of C. Area.
A white paddy-bird on a red square. (The paddy-bird being symbolic of the East Bengal area.)

505 L. of C. District.
This district was formed in Chittagong, in March 1945, under the command of Major-General A.H.J. Snelling, C.B., C.B.E. At the end of the month the H.Q. flew to Shwebo and took over command of No. 551 Sub-Area at Kalewa, and later assumed command of No. 253 Sub-Area, Mandalay, and No. 553 Sub-Area at Myitkyina.

The H.Q. moved in May to Meiktila and assumed control of No. 445 Sub-Area at Magwe, and 552 Sub-Area at Myingyam.

The district's badge was composed of two strong arms holding a circle below the Roman figures 'XIV', the design was in black set on a red shield of similar pattern to that of H.Q. Fourteenth Army and was linked with the District's role—the support of the Army. The two arms and the circle together formed 'VOV' or '505'.

253 L. of C. Sub-Area.[1]
The rear view of an elephant in white on a khaki background. 253 L. of C. Sub-Area was the base for 4 Corps. The Corps badge was a charging elephant, hence the selection of the Sub-Area badge—the base of the Corps.

254 L. of C. Sub-Area.
This L. of C. Sub-Area, which operated in the Fourteenth Army in the Kohima area on the Dimapur—Imphal road, bore as its sign the same buffalo's head in white with red horns set on a square blue background as was worn by the 268th Indian Infantry Brigade.

Sind District.
A native craft in full sail in white on a maroon background.

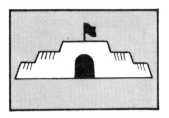

Peshawar District.
A white frontier fort on a red background. The badge represented Jamrud Fort at the entrance to the Khyber Pass.

Delhi District.
A leopard, in black and yellow, on a red background.

Rawalpindi District.
A white falcon on a square red background. The falcon being chosen because hawking was a popular sport among the people of the Northern Punjab.

Lahore District.
An old pattern cannon, in black, on a red background, was the badge of Lahore District. The badge was representative of the gun Zam-Zammah which stands outside the Lahore Museum, and is referred to in Rudyard Kipling's 'Kim'—'Who hold Zam Zammah, that 'fire-breathing dragon',

hold the Punjab; for the great green bronze piece is always first of the conqueror's loot'.

Waziristan District.
Two white crossed daggers on a red background. The daggers are of the traditional pattern carried by Waziri Pathans.

Nagpur District.
A black and yellow cobra on a red square edged in black was the badge of this District, which was renamed in 1946 and became Deccan Area, the badge undergoing a slight change, the tail of the cobra being changed to yellow.

KOHAT DISTRICT
A white dog-fish above three wavy white lines on a red background.

United Provinces Area.
Two blue-grey fish ('The Fishes of Oudh'), set on a red circular background, was the badge of the U.P. Area. Its H.Q. was in Lucknow. These fishes formed the supporters in the badge of the Rampur and Bohpal State forces, the Rampur Infantry and Bohpal Infantry, and was the insignia of the Nawabs (rulers) of Oudh.

Baluchistan District.
A head and horns of a Sind Ibex in white set on a red background. This animal is found in the mountains of Baluchistan.

Madras Defended Port Area.
Madras Fortress Area.
(164 L. of C. Sub-Area.)
Originally designated Madras Fortress Area, later as Madras Defended Port Area, this formation wore as its badge a yellow coconut palm tree and square black background.
   This badge was similar to that of the 109th (Bangalore) L. of C. Area. The Madras Defended Port Area badge differed in colour and slightly in design.

North Ceylon Administrative Area.
A vertical white directional arrow set on a shield divided, upper half red, the lower dark blue, was the North Ceylon Administrative Area's badge.

Colombo Sub-Area.
A square quartered patch. The top quarters red and green, the lower green and red—the L. of C. colours.

Trincomalee Fortress Area.
This Ceylonese Garrison adopted as its badge a head and antlers in black set on a yellow square or circular background.

H.Q. L. of C. S.E.A.C.
South Burma District.
A white flying stork, with red beak and legs set on a pale green rectangular background with a narrow white border, was the badge of this formation. This badge was originally designed for H.Q. L. of C.

Command S.E.A.C., which was formed in October 1944, to relieve H.Q. Fourteenth Army of the responsibility of the Lines of Communication from India up to the fighting line between Imphal and Maungdaw. One of the main functions of this H.Q. was the flying in of supplies to the Fourteenth Army, hence the adoption of the flying stork badge. (It was jokingly said that the badge was adopted as the formation was always 'carrying the baby'). In July 1945, this formation was moved to Rangoon and became South Burma District and, as such, was disbanded on the 31st December 1945.

No. 2 Area S.E.A.C. (Singapore).
Headquarters No. 2 Area was formed in S.E.A.C. in April 1945, as a planning staff for the reoccupation of Singapore and the establishment there of an advanced base. In June 1945, the formation moved from Calcutta to Kurunegala, Ceylon, where it combined with the offices of the Flag Officer (R.N.), Malaya, 77 Base R.A.F. and Civil Affairs. In August the staffs left Ceylon and No. 2 Area was established in Singapore with its headquarters in Fullerton Building in September. The area of responsibility included Singapore Island, the Dutch Riow Archipelago, and a major portion of Johore State. Towards the end of 1945 the designation was changed to Singapore District and the Johore Causeway became the northern boundary. The badge of No. 2 Area was a red figure '2' set on a black anchor on a blue circular background with a black border.

OCCUPATION FORCES

H.Q. British Army of the Rhine.

When H.Q. 21st Army Group was in August 1945, redesignated H.Q. British Army of the Rhine, the H.Q. 21st Army Group badge, two crusaders' swords in gold, set on a dark blue cross on a red shield, was retained by H.Q. B.A.O.R.

British Troops Berlin (B.T.B.).

Originally designated Berlin District (and later 'Area'), the designation, British Troops, Berlin, was adopted shortly after the occupation of the British Zone by the 7th Armoured Division and attached troops, for the Administrative H.Q. of the British sector. The formation badge was a black circle surrounded by a scarlet ring—symbolic of the encirclement of the city.

H.Q. British Troops in Austria.

The Headquarters of our occupational force in Austria adopted the badge of the Eighth Army, the golden cross set on a white shield on a dark blue background.

Vienna Area.

A white cross on a red shield was the badge adopted by the British Administrative Headquarters in internationally-controlled Vienna after the Allied occupation.

Control Commission for Germany.

The familiar blue cross on a scarlet shield of 21st Army Group was adopted as the badge of the Control Commission for Germany; the letters 'CCG', linked, in yellow, being superimposed on the cross.

This distinguishing badge was worn by all members, military and civil,[3] of the Control Commission for Germany and Military Government. Field-Marshal Viscount Montgomery, in his capacity as Commander-in-Chief, B.A.O.R., adopted the wearing of the Control Commission for Germany badge on his left sleeve, retaining the former 21st Army Group (now H.Q. British Army of the Rhine) badge on his right.

Allied Control Commission for Austria.
This Civil Affairs/Military Government formation set up for the control of Austria adopted as its badge that of the Eighth Army (and H.Q. British troops in Austria). The yellow Crusader's cross in a white shield on a dark blue background with the addition of a white scroll above the shield, upon it the letters 'A.C.A.' (Allied Control Austria) in blue.

British Commonwealth Occupation Force (Japan).
The British Commonwealth Occupation Force (Japan) was composed of 'Brindiv' (British Indian Division), made up of the 5th British Infantry Brigade (ex-2nd-Division), and the 268th Indian Brigade together with the 34th Australian Infantry Brigade and the 9th New Zealand Brigade. The 5th Brigade[4] was composed of the 2nd Bn. The Dorsetshire Regiment, the 1st Bn. The Queen's Own Cameron Highlanders, and the 2nd Bn. The Royal Welch Fusiliers. The 268th Indian Brigade[5] was composed of

the 5th/1st Punjab Regiment, the 1st/5th Mahratta Light Infantry, and the 2nd/5th Royal Gurkha Regiment. The Division was originally raised in September 1945, as Force 153, later redesignated 'Brindjap'. It joined B.C.O.F. in Japan in March 1946, as 'Brindiv', commanded by Major-General D. Tennant Cowan, C.B., C.B.E., D.S.O., M.C., who had commanded the 17th Indian Division from 1942-45.

The badge of H.Q. B.C.O.F. was the Imperial Crown in gold and red, set above a dark blue scroll, outlined and backed in red, on which was the legend in white 'British Commonwealth Forces'. The design was set on a dark blue background. The wearing of the badge was not confined to the H.Q. staff, it was worn also by all personnel, British, Indian, Australian and New Zealand, including the R.A.F. It was worn on the right sleeve by all troops of 'Brindiv' with the Divisional badge on the left.

The divisional badge of 'Brindiv' was a small Union Jack (1½in, x 2½in.) worn on the left sleeve above the brigade badges. All vehicles of 'Brindiv' bore both the Divisional and B.C.O.F. badges.

ARMOURED AND TANK BRIGADES

1st Armoured Brigade Group.
A red stencilled tiger's head, on a white background, was the distinguishing badge of this formation, which served in the Middle East.

6th Guards Tank Brigade.
The badge of this Tank Brigade was a golden sword, point uppermost, set in the centre of a white shield and super-imposed on a diagonal band in House-hold Brigade colours—equal bars of blue, red, blue. Originally part of the Guards Armoured Division, this Brigade subsequently became an independent tank brigade in North-West Europe with 21st Army Group.

2nd Armoured Brigade.
This Brigade continued to wear the white rhinoceros on the black oval of the 1st Armoured Division' when the Division was broken up after the break through the Gothic Line in Italy.

7th Armoured Brigade.
Another of the armoured formations of . the M.E.F. which adopted the jerboa—the desert rat— as its badge. The 7th Armoured Brigade's rat was light green set within a red circle on a circular white background. The Brigade served in the M.E.F. as part of the 7th Armoured Division. It was withdrawn from the Desert and sent to Burma in 1942. It was here that its badge was adopted. The same desert rat as it had worn with the Division in the desert but changed to green and nicknamed the 'Jungle Rat'. After the withdrawal to the Arakan, the Brigade joined Paiforce. May 1944, saw the formation in Italy where it fought at Pescara, in the operations which broke the Gothic Line and finally in the Po Valley campaign.

4th Armoured Brigade.
A jerboa (desert rat) in black on a white square background. The Brigade served in the Middle East with the Eighth Army and in North-West Euorpe as part of 21st Army Group.

8th Armoured Brigade.
Of similar design to the badge of the 10th Armoured Division, a fox's mask was the badge of this Armoured Brigade, the 8th Brigade's sign being a reddish-brown fox mask on a yellow circle, with a narrow brown border. The Brigade served in the Western Desert with the Eighth Army and formed part of 21st Army Group, serving in North-West Europe and the occupation forces in Germany.

9th Armoured Brigade.
The Brigade served in the Middle East and later in Italy. With the Eighth Army at El Alamein the formation was the Armoured Brigade of the 2nd New Zealand Division. The formation badge was appropriate, for the Brigade was composed of one regular cavalry regiment (the 3rd King's Hussars) and two yeomanry cavalry regiments (the Royal Wiltshire and the Warwickshire Yeomanry). A white horse on a square or semi-circular bright green background was the Brigade's badge.

16th Armoured Brigade.
The two triangles common to most Tank Brigades feature in this badge. They were dark blue, set on a yellow circle, behind the triangles was a red

devil. The Brigade served in North Africa and in Italy.

20th Armoured Brigade.
The armour-clad head of a knight's charger in white on a black square background was this Brigade's badge. This Brigade served with Home Forces in 1942 and was disbanded the following year.

21st Army Tank Brigade.
Originally this formation wore the usual Tank Brigade 'diabolo' in yellow,[2] but the badge subsequently adopted was a black diabolo superimposed on a vertically divided shield of Royal Armoured Corps colours of yellow and red. This formation served in Italy.

22nd Armoured Brigade.
A stag's head in red was the badge of this

33rd Army Tank Brigade.
Colour of triangles—Green (top), black
(bottom).

35th Army Tank Brigade.
Colour of triangles—Brown (top), green
(bottom).

36th Tank Brigade.
Colour of triangles: Red (top), black
(bottom).

INDEPENDENT INFANTRY BRIGADES AND BRIGADE GROUPS

1st Independent Guards Brigade Group.
A white figure '1', set in the centre of an oblong divided horizontally into three bands, blue, red and blue, the colours of the Household Brigade. This Brigade served in North Africa and Italy.

5th Infantry Brigade.
Originally forming part of the 2nd Division and composed of the 2nd Bn. Dorset Regiment, 1st Bn. the Queen's own Cameron Highlanders and (from 1940-1945), the 7th Bn. the Worcestershire Regiment. This Brigade retained the 2nd Division's badge when it joined B.C.O.F. (Japan), with the 2nd Bn. Royal Welch Fusiliers, who had replaced the Worcesters in 1945.

When the Dorsets were ordered to take over public duties in Tokyo in June 1946, they were instructed to wear the B.C.O.F. sign as they were the B.C.O.F. Guard Battalion for the time being. This led to the fashion of the two brigades of 'Brindiv' wearing three formation badges—the B.C.O.F. badge on the right arm, the Union Jack of 'Brindiv' on the left arm, with their brigade badge below the 'Brindiv' badge.

24th Independent Guards Brigade Group.
An heraldic pinion (wing) in the form of a crest in red, set on a dark blue background. This formation served in North Africa and Italy.

29th Independent Brigade Group.
A plain white ring set on a khaki or black background. The white ring was, it was said, intended to be the 'O' of General Oliver Leese's name, for he was the first commander of the formation. The Brigade took part in the operations in Madagascar in April 1942. Moving later to India, it subsequently formed part of the 36th Division with the 72nd Brigade. The 72nd's badge was a red circle in a black background, and this, linked with the white circle of the 29th, became the Divisional badge.[1]

31st Independent Brigade Group.
A demi bull rampant in red rising from a coronet, on a dark blue background

was adopted by this brigade as its badge and said to have been taken from the crest of the arms of the Brigade Commander. This formation later became the 1st Air Landing Brigade.

32nd Independent Guards Brigade.
An eight-pointed star, composed of eight diamonds, four red and four blue in alternate colours (the Houshold Brigade Colours). This was the badge of the Brigade which subsequently formed part of the Guards Armoured Division.

33rd Guards Brigade.
A sword bayonet point uppermost, set on a rectangle divided horizontally into three bands of the Household Brigade colours, blue, red, and blue.

36th Independent Infantry Brigade.
Formed of Battalions of The Buffs (Royal East Kent Regiment) and the Queen's Own Royal West Kent Regiment it was appropriate for the badge of this Brigade to be a Kentish cob nut with green shell and yellow nut on a khaki background. This

Brigade formed part of the 12th Division[2] in the B.E.F., where it saw hard fighting following the German break-through to the Channel Ports. Cut off from the Division, the Brigade served for a time with the 23rd and 50th Divisions and with 'Petreforce'. Coming into contact with a German armoured formation near Albert, it was heavily engaged and but few survivors eventually returned to England. Reorganized in U.K., the Brigade later saw service in North Africa with the First Army and afterwards in Italy.

37th Independent Brigade Group.
A black clock face on a grey background, the hands pointing to seven minutes past three, 0307 hours, a link-up of the Brigade number, '37'. The background of the badge, the grey diamond, was chosen of 12th Division of which it originally formed part in the B.E.F. The Brigade subsequently served in North Africa.

38th Infantry Brigade.
Composed of Irish Regiments, this formation of the 78th Division wore a Brigade flash of a cut-out green shamrock. When at one time the Brigade formed part of the 1st Division, (1941-2) a white spearhead[3] was superimposed on the centre of the shamrock.

I

56th Independent Infantry Brigade.
A yellow sphinx set on a black circle within a yellow square. The 56th was one of the independent brigades of 21st Army Group, landing in Normandy on D Day. The Brigade subsequently served with First Canadian Army and the 49th and 59th Divisions and formed part of B.A.O.R. The choice of the sphinx badge was made because it was a feature of the Cap Badges of the three Regiments of the Brigade—the South Wales Borderers; the Gloucestershire Regiment and the Essex Regiment.

Brigade number. Green is the Regimental Colour of the Durham Light Infantry—two battalions of which formed part of the Brigade, and red that of the Tyneside Scottish, the Brigade's third Battalion (originally a battalion of the D.L.I.). This Brigade saw service in Iceland and later in North West Europe.

71st Independent Infantry Brigade.
The red and white roses of Lancashire and Yorkshire, set on a black oblong background was chosen as the Brigade's badge as it was composed of the 7th Bn. The King's Own Royal Regiment (Lancaster) and the 8th and 9th Bns. The York and Lancaster Regiment.

61st Independent Infantry Brigade.
Composed of the 2nd, 7th and 10th Battalions of the Rifle Brigade, this Brigade, which served in the C.M.F., wore a black and white stringed rifle bugle, surmounted by a crown, and with the figures '95'—the Rifle Brigade's former Regimental Number, superimposed on the bugle cords. The design set on a square divided diagonally into the Rifle Brigade colours of green and black.

72nd Independant Infantry Brigade.
A six-pointed white star on a square red background. The 'lone star' of an independent brigade. The Brigade saw service in India and Burma.

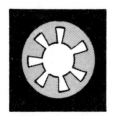

70th Independent Infantry Brigade.
A capstan-like design with seven 'spokes' in red, set on a green circle on a square black background. The seven spokes and the central 'O' forming the '70' of the

73rd Independent Infantry Brigade.
This Independent Infantry Brigade wore the badge of the Devon and Cornwall County Division. The Arms of Cornwall, fifteen gold bezants on a black shield with a gold border, superimposed on the sword

Excalibur, white blade, yellow hilt, set on a dark blue rectangular background.

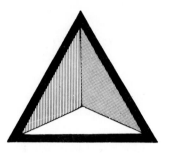

115th Independent Infantry Brigade.
Two unsheathed crossed swords in black on a scarlet shield. This Brigade formed part of 21st Army Group, and its badge was adapted from the 21 Army Group badge.

204th Independent Infantry Brigade.
A pyramid, composed of three inner triangles incorporating the colours of the regimental facings of the three battalions of the Brigade within a blue border. Grey (7th Bn. Leicestershire Regiment), Salmon buff (7th Bn. South Lancashire Regiment), Green (12th Bn. Sherwood Foresters).

148th Independent Infantry Brigade.
The letters 'NM' in black and joined together, set on a khaki background was this brigade's badge. Allotted a training role, the formation subsequently became the pre-O.C.T.U. training establishment, located in South-Eastern Command.

206th Independent Infantry Brigade.
A chessman, the king, in black on a red background.

162nd Independent Infantry Brigade.
This Brigade retained the badge of the 54th (East Anglian) Division[5] its parent formation, when it became one of the Independent Brigade Groups of 21st Army Group.

212th Independent Infantry Brigade.
A red tulip with a green stem and leaf set on a white rectangular background. Originally the badge of the Lincolnshire County Division[6] this badge was subsequently adopted by the 212th Infantry Brigade.

214th Independent Infantry Brigade.
A Viking's winged helmet in red on a blue
background.

218th Independent Infantry Brigade.
A yellow torch, with a red flame, set on
a black diamond background.

219th Independent Infantry Brigade.
A white phoenix, rising from red flames,
in its beak a white torch with red flame,
set on a dark blue background within
a white circle.

223rd Independent Infantry Brigade.
The three seaxes of the arms of the
county of Essex in blue set on a red
square background, the same badge as
worn by the Essex County Division? The
badge being adopted from the Arms of
the County Council of Essex, 'Gules,
three seaxes fesswise in pale argent,
pomels and hilts or pointed to the
sinister and cutting edges upwards', on
15th July 1932.

231st Independent Infantry Brigade.
A white Maltese cross on a scarlet shield
was this formation's badge. The Brigade
had several titles, and was known at
different times as the Malta Infantry
Brigade, the Southern Infantry Brigade,
1st (Malta) Infantry Brigade, 231st
Infantry Brigade, and finally the 231
(Malta) Independent Brigade Group.
It was made up of the three Regular
battalions which formed part of the
garrison of 'George Cross Island': the
2nd Bn. The Devonshire Regiment, the
1st Bn. The Hampshire Regiment, and the
1st Bn. The Dorsetshire Regiment. It was
pure coincidence that these happened
to be three South-West England county
regiments from adjoining counties. This
Brigade stood ready to oppose any
attempts at an Italian invasion during
the long months when the island was
in a stage of siege, withstanding the
combined air attacks of the Italians
and the Luftwaffe, during the ordeal
of constant bombing and famine. The
successes in North Africa of the First

and Eighth Armies raised the siege of Malta, and in April 1943, the Brigade was withdrawn from Malta to Egypt, where it underwent special training and became an Independent Brigade Group. The Brigade took part in the invasion of Sicily and saw much hard fighting from the beaches across the island to the Straits of Messina. The Brigade also took part in the landings on the toe of Italy on the Pizzo beaches and in the left hook attack up the coast of Italy. Joining 50th (Northumbrian) Division, the Brigade returned to U.K. in 1943. In June the following year the formations made their third assault landing, in Normandy, on D Day, and took part in the operations in N.W. Europe until the end of 1944.

301st Infantry Brigade.
Two crossed cannons, and a cannonball in dark blue on a square red background. The Brigade was made up of converted Coast Artillery Units, hence the choice of the cannon to associate the formation with its R.A. origin, the red background being the traditional infantry colour, and the red and the blue also being the R.A. colours.

303rd Infantry Brigade.
A white hart's head on a divided background, top half red, the lower blue. The hart's head was taken from the Arms of the Borough of Eastbourne, associating the Brigade's connections with the town. It was formed from an Anti-Aircraft Brigade and its three battalions were formed from Searchlight Regiments R.A.

The Brigade, under the command of Brigadier H.G. Smith, C.B., O.B.E., M.C., T.D., formed part of the British force which participated in the liberation of Norway in May 1945.

304th Independent Infantry Brigade.
This Brigade, formed from an A.A. Brigade, was composed of three infantry battalions which had been converted from Searchlight Regiments R.A. Its badge was designed to represent three searchlight beams, which were in red on a blue background. This formation, commanded by Brigadier F.W. Saunders, D.S.O., formed part of the Allied Land Forces, Norway, and took part in the liberation of that country in May 1945.

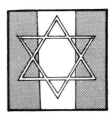

Jewish Brigade Group.
This Brigade Group was formed in Palestine and saw service in Italy and in North-Western Europe. Its badge was the yellow star of David set on a rectangular background divided vertically into three bands, two light blue and a central white band.

MISCELLANEOUS BADGES

G.H.Q. Liaison Regiment.
The 'P' of this badge stood for 'Phantom' the code name of the G.H.Q. Liaison Regiment of 21st Army Group. This unit had a special role in keeping G.H.Q. in touch with every development in operations.

'The Phantoms' operated in the forward areas, patrols moving in armoured vehicles, and radioing information to G.H.Q. about allied troops movements and general battle progress. The Regiment was recognized as the 'eyes and ears of the Commanding General'. By VE Day the G.H.Q. Liaison Regiment in North-Western Europe totalled about 105 officers and 800 men.

Indian Field Broadcasting Units.
Indian Field Broadcasting Units were formed by the 'I' Branch of G.H.Q. Fourteenth Army in February 1943, and before the monsoon of that year the first experimental I.F.B.U. had seen service in the Arakan. The experiment was successful and during the operations in 1943-44 five I.F.B.Us. were employed on the Fourteenth Army front.

I.F.B.Us. were propaganda units and were employed against enemy and inhabitants of Enemy Occupied Territories. During their short existence they met with considerable success, and on three occaision during the Jap attack on the Imphal Plain (April—July 1944) they were successful in making the Japs show the white flag.

The badge was a deer's head in yellow with black eyes and outlines set on a dark blue circular background.

Army Film and Photographic Service.
Army Film and Photographic Units wore the appropriate badge of a camera, in white, flanked by the initial letters 'A.F.P.U.' in red, set against a black background. This service was established under the control of the Director of Public Relations at the War Office, and sections served in all overseas theatres, whilst an Army Film and Photographic Centre was formed in U.K.

The overseas sections were composed of operational cameramen, developers, camera mechanics and administrative personnel. The sections were responsible for filming the battle sequences from which the Home Centre made the films 'Desert Victory', 'Tunisian Victory', 'True Glory', 'Burma Victory', and many other official documentary films.

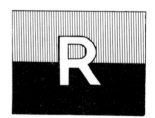

Transportation Directorates (India).
The staff of the Directorate of Railways wore a white letter 'R' on a square background top half green, lower half red. The Staff of the Director of Docks wore a white letter 'P' set on a square background, top half red and lower half yellow.

**British Military Headquarters in
the Balkans.**
The head of a phoenix in blue, bearing in
its beak the torch of liberty, rising from
red flames. The design, on a white oval
background, was also used by the staff
of the Allied Liaison H.Q. in Greece,
Albania and Yugoslavia.

Political Warfare Executive, M.E.F.
The special badge of this branch of
G.H.Q., M.E.F., was a peewit in black
and white set on a light blue diamond
background with a red border. The
peewit being a play on the abbreviation
P.W.E. This organization was an off-
shoot of the Political Intelligence
Department of the Foreign Office and
was responsible for propaganda in the
field by radio, leaflets, etc.

ROYAL ARTILLERY

Newfoundland Units R.A.
These units wore as their distinguishing
badge the head of a caribou, in gold, set
on a red oval background.

Coast Artillery Units.
A muzzle-loading gun and a stack of
cannon balls in black on a circular background divided in red and blue was the
badge of the Coastal Artillery Fire
Commands, Regiments and Batteries.
This badge was used as a vehicle marking.

Anti-Aircraft School (India).
The A.A. School (India) located at
Karachi wore as its badge (designed by
Colonel E.F. Carne Commander 1943-45)
the letters 'AA' in yellow on a five-pointed
star which was divided vertically red and
blue contrasting with diamond shape
background of the same colours in reverse
—the Star of India on Royal Artillery
Colours.

The badge was worn on the Pugaree
of the Wolesley helmet which although
generally superseded by the Slouch hat
in India continued to be worn in the
area of N.W. Army India, including
Karachi, in hot weather.

The Coast Artillery School.
The Coast Artillery School formerly at
Shoeburyness was re-established in the
war years at Llandudno, moving later
to the Citadel, Plymouth. Its badge
was a 'Hong Kong' target in black and
white on blue wavy lines (for the sea)
set in a circle.

**Anti-Aircraft and Coast Defence
Units R.A. (C.M.F.).**
During the operations in Italy, it was
decided that a special badge should be
given to the A.A. and Coast Regiments
R.A. of the C.M.F. The badge chosen
was two white capital letters 'AA',
conjoined, set on an evenly divided
background of red and blue, the
Gunner colours.

Maritime Anti-Aircraft Artillery.
The Maritime A.A. Gunners wore a red
fouled anchor with a white rope, set on
a black square background. Originally the
letters 'AA' (Anti-Aircraft) in white
appeared one either side of the anchor,
but these were subsequently changed
to 'RA' (Royal Artillery). The Maritime
A.A. Artillery came into being in 1941,
being formed from the Light A.A.

Defence of Coastal Shipping organization
which had been set up in 1940, and from
volunteers of Anti-Aircraft Command.
The Maritime A.A. Artillery consisted of
gun crews, each a separate unit, allotted
to the Royal Naval D.E.M.S. (Defensively
Equipped Merchant Shipping) organization.
The gun crews served in troop-ships,
tankers, and Merchant Navy craft of all
types, and were armed with 40mm
Bofors guns or, in the case of smaller
coastal craft, with Bren and Lewis light
automatics. The crews formed part of
Home-based Maritime Anti-Aircraft
Regiments and Batteries at Liverpool,
London, Glasgow, Leith, Newcastle,
Cardiff and other U.K. ports, and also
at Cape Town, Alexandria, Halifax
(Nova Scotia), Madras, Bombay,
Colombo, and other naval stations
around the 'seven seas'. The Maritime
A.A. gunners set up a fine record
during the Battle of the Atlantic and
in the dogged maintenance of our
convoy routes around the world.

1 Corps Artillery.[1]
The white spearhead badge of 1 Corps
was worn by the Corps Artillery set
on a diamond-shaped background of
Gunner colours, red and dark blue.

1st Division R.A.[2]
The white triangle badge of 1st Division
was worn by the Divisional Artillery
set on a diamond patch vertically
divided into Gunner colours of red and
royal blue.

6th Army Group R.A.
This A.G.R.A. was one of the few that
adopted a badge of its own—the majority
of Army Group formations wore the
badge of the higher command. The 6th
A.G.R.A., commanded by Brigadier
J.St.C. Holbrook, C.B.E., M.C., however,
wore the sixth sign of the Zodiac in
silver on a black background. White
paint, instead of silver, was used for
vehicle markings. The badge was worn
on the left shoulder, with the Eighth
Army badge on the right.

This A.G.R.A. was raised in Egypt
in April 1943. It took part in the Sicily
landing and saw much hard fighting in
the campaign in Italy.

74th Field Regiment, Royal Artillery.[3]
Although not a formation badge as such,
and worn only by one Regiment it is

worthy of mention for this unique badge was that it was an amalgam of the badges of the 49th and 50th Divisions; it was worn by 74th Field Regiment R.A., when it came from 50th Division under command of 49th Division on the break up of 50th Division in November 1944. 74th Field Regiment were ordered to take down the 50th Division badge and wear that of 49th Division, but the Regiment, proud of its association with the Northumbrian Division since 1908 appealed against the loss of their "TTs" Badge and so a compromise was reached by adding the "TTs" (of the 50th Division) to the Polar Bear badge of the 49th Division.

R.A. Units, Gibraltar Garrison.[5]
The R.A. Units of Gibraltar Garrison wore the yellow key badge of the Garrison H.Q., set in a rectanbular background divided diagonally into the Gunner colours of red and royal blue. A.A. units wore the plain red background with a yellow letter 'A' on either side of the key.

H.Q. R.A. and Mobile Artillery, Malta.
A dark blue Maltese cross with red edges —the R.A. colours—set on a square black background was the badge of the Royal Artillery H.Q. in Malta, and was also worn by the mobile artillery units under command.

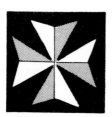

Heavy A.A. Brigade R.A. Malta.[4]
The Heavy A.A. Brigade of Malta's A.A. Defences wore a Maltese cross divided into dark blue and gold with red edges set on a black square.

Light A.A. Brigade, R.A., Malta.
A Maltese Cross as above divided into dark blue and gold with narrow white edges set on a black square was worn by the L.A.A. Brigade.

ROYAL ENGINEERS

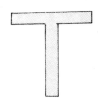

R.E. Depot.
The R.E. Depot was moved in 1941 from Chatham to Halifax, Yorks, where it occupied the pre-war Regimental Depot of the Duke of Wellington's Regiment. The permanent staff of the R.E. Depot wore below the shoulder title the Sapper red and royal blue flash set on a dark blue background, edged with red.

Transportation Training Centre R.E.
The Royal Engineers' Transportation Training Centre at Longmoor, Hants, adopted as its badge the cross-section of a railway line. This was in royal blue on a red background, with a narrow royal blue border, the R.E. colours. Longmoor Camp was the 'home' of R.E. Railway troops since the early 1900s and here ran the training railroad 'the Longmoor Military Railway'.

Tunnelling Companies R.E.
The Tunnelling Companies of the Royal Engineers wore a distinctive shoulder badge in addition to any formation sign. It was a plain red letter 'T'. Tunnelling Companies were employed in the B.E.F. in 1939-40, and in U.K. and M.E.F., but their main work was in Gibraltar where they were engaged in the improvement and expansion of the defences of 'The Rock'.

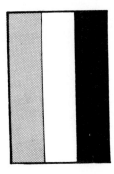

Chemical Warfare Groups R.E.
These Groups, each comprising a Headquarters and three C.W. Companies, were raised in 1939 and 1940 and wore a distinguishing flash below the shoulder titles, a rectangle evenly divided into three vertical strips of green, yellow and red. The Groups were converted into G.H.Q. Troops Engineers in 1942-43.

Airfield Construction Groups.
The Airfield Construction Groups were composed of Royal Engineer Road Construction Companies and Pioneer Corps Companies. Their circular badge,

divided into three segments, incorporated
their colours: the red and blue of the
Sappers, and the red and green of the
Pioneers. The white or pale blue geometrical design set in the centre of the badge
was representative of the airstrips they
constructed. Their task was that of
rapid airfield construction for
fighter strips in the forward areas.

8th G.H.Q. Troops Engineers.
Formed in 1940, as 8th Chemical Warfare Group R.E., this formation was
converted into G.H.Q. Troops Engineers
in 1943 and formed part of the Beach
Group which established the Normandy
Beach head on D Day 6th June 1944.
This formation wore the badge of the
Beach Groups, the fouled anchor in red
on a pale blue background within a red
circle, and continued to wear it when
later it assumed a normal G.H.Q. Troops
role in 21st Army Group and later in
B.A.O.R.

1st Corps Troops Engineers.[1]
The white spearhead badge of 1 Corps
was worn by the Corps Troops
Engineers on a background of R.E.
colours, red and blue set diagonally
on a diamond shaped background.

8th Army Troops Engineers.
Originally the Edinburgh Fortress
Engineers, a First Line T.A. Unit, and
converted to Corps Troops Engineers
in 1940, the formation became the
Eighth Army Troops Engineers whilst
in the M.E.F. The Unit had its own
badge which was worn in North Africa
and in Italy, and finally by the unit's
two representatives in the Victory
Parade in London.

The central badge was that of the
original Submarine Miners, formerly
a branch of the R.E. before it became
a Royal Naval unit. The Edinburgh
Fortress R.E. were formed as a volunteer
unit from a former Submarine Miner
Company.

The badge was in red, set on a background of R.E. colours, red and blue.
When the design was chosen, instructions
issued laid down that all Scottish units
should have a tartan background. Not
having a tartan of its own, the unit
selected a portion of the Mackenzie
tartan, which although predominantly
green, has a dark blue background
and stripes of both red and white. The
background to the old Submarine
Miner badge was therefore chosen and
that portion of the tartan which has
two red stripes on a blue background.
This linked with the R.E. Corps Colours
and the tartan of the C.R.E. at the
time—Lieut. Colonel W.H. Mackenzie,
M.B.E., T.D.

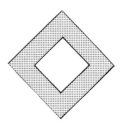

42nd Armoured Engineer Regiment.
Originally the Divisional Engineers of
the 42nd (East Lancashire) Division, and

subsequently the 42nd Armoured Division, this Regiment converted into an Assault Regiment R.E. (later redesignated Armoured Engineers), retaining the 42nd Divisional badge, a small white diamond within a red diamond. The Regiment served in North-West Europe with the Armoured Engineer Brigade of the 79th Armoured Division.

Madras Sappers and Miners.
The head of a Madrassi Sapper in black silhouette on a grey background within a black circle was the badge adopted by the Madras Sapper and Miner groups.

ROYAL SIGNALS

Air Formation Signals.
White wings set on a dark blue triangle within a white border was the distinguishing sign of the Air Formation Signals. The vehicle marking was, however, a black aeroplane silhouette set on a background of the Royal Signals colours of white and blue. Some units wore their number in the centre of the triangle.

1st Divisional Signals.
The Royal Signals units of the 1st Division wore a dark blue diamond, with the Divisional badge, a white equilateral triangle in the upper half,¹ thereby incorporating the Divisional sign with the Royal Signals colours of dark blue and white.

Indian Air Formation Signals.
A scarlet five-pointed star and an aeroplane set on a diamond shaped patch which was divided vertically into the Royal Signals colours of blue and white, was the badge adopted by the Indian Air Formation Signals with the Fourteenth Army.

ROYAL ARMOURED CORPS

R.A.C. Training Centre B.A.O.R.
A tank in white, similar to that in the
badge of the R.T.R. (Royal Tank
Regiment) set in the centre of crossed
lances, also in white, emblematic of the
cavalry regiments now incorporated in
the Royal Armoured Corps, the design
superimposed on the blue crusader's
cross on the red shield badge of the
21st Army Group G.H.Q. and L. of C.
troops was the badge adopted by the
Royal Armoured Corps Training Centre
of the Rhine Army.

No. 1 Armoured Replacement Group
C.M.F.
This Group was composed of R.A.C.
Forward Delivery Squadrons and supplied
A.F.Vs. and personnel to all armoured
formations under British Command in
Italy. The sign of this group was the head
of Mars, in black, a tank blown from his
(white) tongue. The design on a divided
background of R.A.C. colours—top yellow,
and lower half red.

Air Despatch Group, R.A.S.C.
A yellow aircraft, a Dakota, on a royal
blue square was the badge of this
R.A.S.C. organization which was first
formed in April 1944, and held in
readiness to carry out maintenance by
air for any formation that might be cut
off during the invasion of the Continent.
By July of that year, it had expanded
to a strength of over 5,000 and was
responsible for air supply and maintenance of all formations including airborne and S.A.S.

The task of the Air Despatch Group,
R.A.S.C. was twofold: a) Maintenance
by Air and b) Supply by Air. The first
task involved a large number of men
trained as 'Air Despatchers' flying in
aircraft of Transport Command, R.A.F.,
and dropping ammunition, petrol and
supplies by parachute, the second task
involved the transport of supplies to
airfields and loading those which were
to land on the Continent.

The Air Despatch Group carried out
maintenance by air in the operations in
North-Western Europe and dropped
supplies to our troops in the Falaise
Gap; at Arnhem; and on Walcheren,
when troops were cut off owing to
weather conditions which made sea
communication impossible.

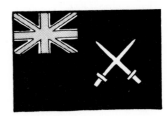

War Department Fleet.
The W.D. Fleet is an R.A.S.C. organiza-
tion composed of Water Transport
Companies, Motor Boat Companies, and
Boat Stores Depots (for the provision
of Marine Stores to the Army). The
Motor Boat Companies were divided
into Harbour, Ambulance and Fast
Launch Companies and also Oil Barge,
Coaster, Floating Workshops, and Fire
Boat Companies. The R.A.S.C. Ensign

of the W.D. Fleet was a Blue Ensign, on
it the crossed swords of the Army badge,
and was worn as the shoulder badge of
the R.A.S.C. personnel of the Army's
own fleet which saw service in Iceland;
in the expedition to Spitzbergen; in
West and North Africa, the Middle East,
the Far East and North-West Europe.

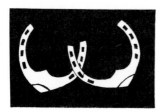

H.Q. Pack Transport Group, C.M.F.
Formed in North Africa as the administrative H.Q. for the Pack Transport
Companies raised in Algeria and Tunisia.
This unit adopted as their badge, two
white horseshoes on a black background
—of similar design to the Divisional sign
of the 2nd Cavalry Division of the
1914-18 War.
    This Pack Transport Group served
in the North African and Sicilian
Campaigns and also in Italy.

ROYAL ARMY SERVICE CORPS

R.A.S.C. Unit Badges.
The R.A.S.C. made a feature of unit
badges. These, however, were used
primarily as vehicle marking signs, and
were not worn by the personnel, who
wore their Army, Corps, Divisional,
Brigade or L. of C. formation badges.

The value of the unit-distinguishing
badges on vehicles was proved at times
when forward and maintenance routes
were packed with convoys; at the same
time they fostered an esprit de corps
among the many varied companies and
units of the R.A.S.C.—from the General
Transport Columns to the D.I.Ds. The
choice of the signs gave ample scope to
the ingenuity of designers—unlike the
approved formation badge there was
a touch of informality, and opportunity
for the humorous artist, in the selection
of the unit vehicle marking. Some units
adhered to formality and heraldic design
and association with the formation badge;
others made a point of linking their sign
with their function, i.e., the predominance
of the horseshoe in the signs of the Pack
Transport Companies, and the jerricans
of the Petrol Depots and Filling Centres,
whilst a third category specialized in the
lighter vein, with adoptions of Walt
Disney's characters and other animals
and figures which became their mascots.

The following are but a few examples
of the many R.A.S.C. unit signs which
were seen on mudguards and tailboards
of the lorries which drove by; in dust,
rain or snow; through desert, jungle,
mountains, and the rubble of the battlefields, on the forward routes to Victory.

840 General Transport Company.
This unit served with the C.M.F. The
unit sign 'The Toddler' was selected
owing to the youth of personnel on its
arrival in Italy.

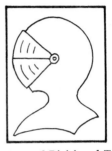

**No. 277 Armoured Divisional Transport
Company.**
This unit served in Tunisia with the 6th
Armoured Division and adopted as its
sign the knight's helmet which linked
up with the Divisional badge of the
mailed fist. The unit subsequently served
in Italy.

No. 236 Bridge Company.
A representation of Tower Bridge was
appropriately chosen as this unit's sign.
The company served in Paiforce, the
Middle East, and in Italy, where it
transported bridging equipment for the
assault crossings of the Reno, Senio, Po
and Adige rivers.

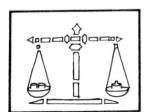

No. 14 C.R.A.S.C.
This unit served in the Middle East and
later in Italy at Salerno, under the
Command of 10 Corps, and on the
Italian L. of C. The unit sign, emblematic
of the 'Balanced Ration', was a pair of
evenly balanced scales.

K

No. 534 Tank Transporter Company.
The unit sign was emblematic of its role
and depicted the wings of Mercury
bearing aloft a tank—signifying speed
of delivery of armour into battle. The
unit served in North Africa and in Italy.

No. 9 Military Petrol Filling Centre.
This unit which served in Tunisia with
the First Army and in Italy with the
Eighth Army, chose the appropriate
sign of a robot-like petrol pump in the
act of filling a jerrican.

No. 558 Water Tank Company.
A soda water siphon—quick delivery of
water—was the sign chosen by this
company which served in the Western
Desert and in Italy with the Eighth Army.

No. 36 Detail Issue Depot.
The D.I.D. was one of the R.A.S.C. units
of the B.E.F. in France, 1930-40. It next
saw service in the M.E.F. and formed part
of 10 Corps in the Western Desert. The
unit went ashore at Salerno on D Day and
continued to serve with 10 Corps through
the Italian campaign.
  The appropriate unit sign was a teapot,
to indicate one of the commodities
supplied by the D.I.D.

No. 234 Petrol Depot.
The familiar jerrican was the unit sign
of this Petrol Depot which took part
in the Sicily landing under command
of the 1st Canadian Division and later
served throughout the campaign in Italy.

No. 25 Field Bakery.
This unit served in the Middle East, in
the Western Desert and in Italy. The unit
sign was the 'cheerful baker'.

TRAINING ESTABLISHMENTS AND ADMINISTRATIVE UNITS

British Reinforcement Training Centre (India).
A white bulldog (the British Bulldog), set on a yellow star (the Star of India) on a red square background, was the badge of the organization set up for the training of British reinforcements in India.

Royal Armoured Corps Depot (India).
A black letter 'D' on a square equally divided vertically, right half yellow, left half red, the Royal Armoured Corps colours.

B.A.O.R. Training Centre.
The Rhine Army Training Centre, located at Sennelager, adopted as its badge the badge of 21st Army Group G.H.Q. and L. of C. troops, with the addition of the torch of learning (as was used as a road sign in U.K. to denote a school) in yellow set on the vertical of the blue Crusader's cross on a red shield.

Special Training Centre, Lochailort.
A golden eagle on a black and white quartered shield set on a black background.

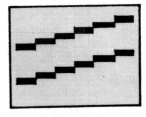

G.H.Q. 2nd Echelon C.M.F.
Two rows of red rectangles set in echelon diagonally on a blue background was the badge of G.H.Q. 2nd Echelon C.M.F.

163rd Infantry O.C.T.U. (Artists' Rifles).
This O.C.T.U. was formed in 1939 from the Artists' Rifles, which had, in 1937, become an officer-producing unit of the Territorial Army. The Artists' Rifles were raised in 1860 as the 38th Middlesex (Artists) Rifle Volunteers. In 1908 the Regiment was redesignated the 28th (County of London) the London Bn. Regiment (Artists' Rifles), and during the 1914-18 war served in France and Flanders with the 47th (London) and 63rd (Royal Naval) Divisions. From formation the Artists wore the cap-badge designed by Wyon, Queen Victoria's Medallist, of the heads of Mars and Minerva, and the badge was retained by this O.C.T.U., the design being in white on a green background.

HOME GUARD UNITS

All Home Guard units wore the shoulder title—HOME GUARD—in yellow on a khaki background, and below this a khaki patch bearing distinguishing black letters to denote their county, e.g., LON (London); BHM (Birmingham); BRX (Berkshire); EL (East Lancs); LEI (Leicester); WAR (Warwickshire); KT (Kent); SY (Surrey), etc., and below this the battalion number in black figures on khaki.[1]

Few units of the Home Guard adopted any distinctive badges. There were, however, exceptions: the Lincolnshire and Cornwall Home Guard Battalions had their own badges.

In addition to these, the Home Guard A.A. units, which operated in Anti-Aircraft Command, manning Heavy A.A. Search-light and Rocket Batteries, wore the distinguishing Anti-Aircraft Command badge, whilst the Northumberland battalions wore the badge of the Northumbrian District.

A distinctive badge was worn by 'special companies' composed of volunteers trained by Royal Engineers in demolition, and in destuction of A.F.V.s. There units were trained to operate behind enemy lines in the disruption of their Lines of Communication. The badge of their companies was a red dormouse (silent and stealthy) on an oblong khaki background.

8th Bn. Cornwall Home Guard.
This was the battalion recruited in the Lizard area of Cornwall, which appropriately adopted as its badge a green lizard with black markings set on a black rectangle.

9th Bn. Cornwall Home Guard.
This Battalion wore an adaptation of the shield of the arms of the Duchy of Cornwall (which is fifteen gold bezants on a black shield with a gold border). In the Home Guard badge the shield was outlined in white, the bezants in white and with a white figure '9' superimposed. The whole design set on a bright green background.

Lincolnshire Home Guard.
The Lincoln Imp, in lincoln green, picked out in brown and set on a brown background, was the distinctive badge of the Lincolnshire Home Guard units.

12th Bn. Cornwall Home Guard.
Raised in the Land's End area of the Duchy, this Battalion adopted a badge which depicted in black the rugged coast and the Land's End lighthouse. This design was set on a scarlet background within a black border.

In addition[2] to the foregoing Battalion badges were:

Cornwall Home Guard Battalions

1st   Three Clarions (or Clarichords) (The rest of a lance) in yellow on a red shield—the arms of the Grenville family.

2nd   A knight's helmet in light blue, surmounted by a yellow coronet on a dark blue background.

3rd   A Castle in outline and in yellow (Launceston Castle) on a red shield superimposed on a larger blue shield.

4th   A brown camel on a yellow square —a play on the association between the battalion area (Wadebridge) and the River Camel.

5th   A red cross outlined in black border, adapted from the arms of St. Austell.

6th   The arms of the Dutchy of Cornwall, surmounted by the figure '6', on a black square.

7th   A black eagle and the figure '7' on a inverted yellow triangle.

10th   An Elizabethian Ship above two fishes in red on a black background, adapted from the arms of the City of Truro.

11th   A black sea-bird with red beak and claws on a yellow square.

13th   A red horseshoe (for luck) enclosing the battalion number '13' also in red set on a green square.

14th   An upraised sword in black arising from the tower of a castle in red, set on a khaki background, with the Battalion number in Roman numerals (XIV) set on the tower.

AMERICAN FORMATIONS

The wearing of formation badges was
also adopted by the American Army.
Coloured patches and badges were
introduced in the American Expeditionary Force on the Western Front in 1918[1]
and were reintroduced when the United
States forces mobilized in 1941. Designated, in 1918, as 'Shoulder Patches' and
'Divisional Insignia', the official designation 'Shoulder Sleeve Insignia' was
subsequently adopted in the late war.
Many of the badges of the U.S. formations became familiar in the U.K. with
the arrival of the American forces. Over
two hundred different 'Shoulder Insignia'
were adopted by the U.S. Army between
1941 and 1946. The following badges
are, therefore, but a few of those which
distinguished the American forces which
saw action in the hard-fought battles
in the Pacific, in North Africa, Italy,
France and Germany. The majority of
the badges now described belonged to
formations which served in the U.K., or
fought alongside British troops in
North Africa, the Mediterranean and
in North-Western Europe.

European Theatre of Operations.
An oval badge with a dark blue background; on it a fork of red lightning,
picked out in yellow, pointing downwards, breaking a chain symbolic of
occupied Europe, on the lightning the
dark blue five-pointed star on a white
background of the Army Service Forces.
This was the insignia of the Administrative
H.Q. of the American Forces in the U.K.
—E.T.O.U.S.A. (European Theatre of
Operations United States Army).

Persian Gulf Service Command.
The badge of the H.Q. of the U.S. forces
in the Persian Gulf area which had as
its primary task the movement of Lease-
Lend supplies to Russia, was a red Arab
dagger outlined in white, and a white
seven-pointed star set on a light green
shield with a dark green border.

U.S. Army Forces in the Middle East.
On a background shaped like the entrance
to a mosque, a white-five-pointed star on
red, above two white and two blue wavy
bands. This was the distinguishing shoulder
insignia of the personnel of the United
States Forces in the Middle East.

12th Army Group.
Composed of the First, Third and Ninth
U.S. Armies, this formation served in the
European Theatre of Operations—France
and Germany. Its inisignia was diamond-
shaped, with the top point of the diamond

squared off; within a black border the colouring was red and blue divided by a white band.

First American Army.
A black letter 'A' on an olive drab background was the insignia of the First American Army which fought in Normandy, liberated Paris and was the first U.S. Army to cross the Rhine.

Third American Army.
A white letter 'A' within a red circle set on a blue circular background was the badge of the Third American Army which served in North-Western Europe, exploiting the break out of the Normandy beach-head and fighting through France and into Germany.

Fifth American Army.
A dark blue Moorish archway on a red background, the letter 'A' and the figure '5' in white superimposed on the blue, was the 5th American Army's insignia. The 5th served in North Africa: it landed at Salerno, was the first formation to enter Rome when it fell to the Allies; and as part of the 15th Army Group took part in the final operations in Northern Italy, ending in the German capitulation.

Ninth American Army.
A white letter 'A' surrounded by a white clover leaf design set on a red nonagonal background was the 9th Army's shoulder insignia. This formation landed in Normandy in June 1944, captured Brest, after the break out of the beachhead, broke through the Siegfried Line to Aachen; fought through the Northern Ruhr and advanced to the Elbe in the final stages of the campaign in North-West Europe.

XVIII Airborne Corps.
A blue dragon's head on white within a blue border was the badge of this Airborne Corps which landed in Normandy on D Day and later took part in the Airborne operations in the crossing of the Rhine.

17th Airborne Division.
A yellow eagle's claw on a black circular background, above the circle the word 'Airborne' in yellow on a black background distinguished the 17th American Airborne Division, which saw action in the Ardennes and took part in the Airborne operations in the Rhine crossing.

82nd Airborne Division.
The white letters 'AA' in a dark blue circle on a red square surmounted by the word 'Airborne' in white on a blue background was the badge of the 82nd U.S. Airborne Division which saw action in Sicily, Italy, in Normandy on D Day, at Nijmegen, and in the Ardennes.

1st Division.
A red figure '1' on an olive drab shield-shaped background was the insignia of the 1st American Division which served in Algeria, Tunisia, in the invasion of Sicily, went ashore on 'Omaha Beach' in Normandy on D Day; took part in the hard fighting in the Ardennes and in the advance into Germany.

101st Airborne Division.
Known as the 'Screaming Eagle' Division. This formation badge was well known in England, where the Division was trained. It took part in the air invasion of Normandy and later won fame in its stubborn defence of Bastogne in the Ardennes. The Division insignia was an eagle's head in white with a yellow beak set on a black shield, above it the word 'Airborne' in yellow on a black background.

2nd Division.
Known as the 'Indian Head' Division from its insignia, the head of a Red Indian with feathered head-dress set on a white five-pointed star on a black shield; this division served in England before taking part in the invasion of Normandy. Their formation took part in the hard fighting in Normandy, in Brittany, in the 'Battle of the Bulge' in the Ardennes, and the drive into Germany.

3rd Division.
The 3rd U.S. Division insignia was a square evenly divided by dark blue and

white diagonals. The Division took part in the invasion of Sicily and the hard fighting in the Salerno beach-head and at the crossing of the Volturno. It formed part of the force which landed in the South of France, driving northwards to Strassbourg and Colmar and deep into Germany, being the first U.S. troops to reach Munich and Berchtesgaden.

29th Division.
This Division wore as its badge a circular design of dark blue and grey, the colours of the Union and Confederate armies. The formation took part in the D Day landings in Normandy and in the advance into Germany, seeing hard fighting at Aachen and in the Ruhr.

5th Division.
A red diamond was the insignia of the 5th American Division. The formation served in Northern Ireland and took part in the invasion of North-Western Europe. The Division was present at hard-fought battles in the Ardennes in January 1945. It was part of the American force which liberated Luxembourg and then drove on into Germany.

34th Division.
This formation was known from its insignia as the 'Red Bull' Division, its badge was a red bull's head on a black background. The Division served in Tunisia and in Italy, at Salerno, the Volturno, at Cassino and Anzio and in the final campaign in the Po Valley.

28th Division.
Known as the 'Keystone' Division, the 28th Division wore as their insignia a red patch shaped like a key-stone. The Division served in Normandy, took part in the liberation of Paris and in the hard fighting in the Ardennes and in the Colmar pocket.

42nd Division.
Known as the 'Rainbow' Division, its insignia was a rainbow-shaped badge of red, yellow and blue. The Division served in North-West Europe and took part in the advance into Germany.

45th Division.
Known as the 'Thunderbird' Division from its badge, a yellow bird on a red background, this division served in Sicily and Italy, in the invasion of Southern France and the advance northwards into Germany.

66th Division.
The black panther on a yellow circle within a red circle, the formation insignia, gave it the name of the 'Black Panther' Division, which served in France, in Normandy and at Lorient and St. Nazaire.

75th Division.
A blue '7' and a red '5' on a diagonally divided background of red, white and blue, was the 75th American Infantry Division insignia. The Division saw action in the 'Battle of the Bulge' and in the drive into Germany.

85th Division.
This formation was known as the 'Custer Division' and its insignia was the letters 'CD' in red on an olive drab circular. The Division served in Italy with the 15th Army Group, taking part in the liberation of Rome and in the Po Valley campaign.

87th Division.
A yellow acorn on a green circle was the insignia of the 87th Infantry Division which served in the Ardennes and in Germany.

The American Armoured Divisions.
There were fourteen U.S. Armoured Divisions, each wearing the same shoulder insignia, a triangle evenly divided into three portions of yellow (at the top) and blue and red (at the base); superimposed on this background was a black tank, across it a flash of red lightning. The number of the Division was superimposed in black on the yellow portion of the badge. The insignia illustrated above is that of the 2nd ('Hell on Wheels') American Armoured Division which served in Tunisia, Sicily, Italy, Normandy, Belgium and Germany.

Tank Destroyer Units.
These units were attached to all American
Armoured and Infantry Divisions. Their
distinctive insignia depicted a black
panther crushing in its jaws a tank. The
design was in black, red and white on
a yellow circle with a black border.

Army Service Forces.
This badge was worn by the administrative
personnel which provided the services and
supplies for all U.S. Army units. It was a
dark blue five-pointed star on a white
background within a red scalloped border.

U.S. ARMY AIR FORCES

The insignia illustrated above was the
Headquarters badge of the American
Army Air Forces, a white five-pointed
star, a red circle in the centre, and two
golden wings, the design set on a blue
circular background. This insignia
formed the basis for all other U.S.
Army Air Force badges.

Ninth U.S. Air Force.
Also stationed in England. The distinguishing insignia of the 9th Air Force
was a red '9' on a golden circle below
the white five-pointed star with central
red circle flanked with white wings. The
design was on a blue shield.

Eighth U.S. Air Force.
A golden '8', the white five-pointed star
with central red circle, and golden wings
set on a blue circular background was the
insignia of the Eighth Air Force which
was located in England, taking part in
the bomber offensive against Germany
and occupied Europe.

ALLIED CONTINGENTS AND FORMATIONS (EXCLUSIVE U.S.A.)

Formation badges were also adopted by the Allied contingents which were raised and equipped in Britain and the Empire. The following are but a few of the many badges adopted by the Belgians, Free French Forces, Dutch, Czechoslovak, Greek, and Polish formations which served under British command during the operations which culminated in the liberation of their homelands.

BELGIUM

1st Independent Belgian Brigade Group.
This formation formed part of 21st Army Group and took part in the landings in Normandy and the liberation of its own homeland. The formation was raised, trained and equipped in the U.K.; its badge was a lion's head in yellow, set on a red inverted triangle with a black centre. The Belgian title of this formation was the Brigade Piron.

2nd Independent Belgian Brigade Group.
The Belgian lion rampant in gold above a green shamrock superimposed on a red

letter 'Y' within a black shield was this formation's badge.

4th Belgian Infantry Brigade.
A black shield; on it a yellow grenade picked out in black, a black letter 'S' in the centre; in the right hand corner of the shield a small triangle equally divided into blue and red; in the left hand corner a small green shamrock. This was the badge of the 4th (Steentraete) Infantry Brigade.

5th Belgian Infantry Brigade.
A dark green shield; on it a narrow inner border of yellow; two chevrons in yellow conjoined in the centre; superimposed on the lower part of the chevrons a white hunting bugle from which was suspended a green shamrock. This badge was worn by the 5th (Merckem) Infantry Brigade.

CZECHOSLOVAKIA

6th Belgian Infantry Brigade.
The badge of the 6th (Deynze) Infantry
Brigade may well be described as a truly
allied badge. It was composed of a white
shield with a red border. Within the shield
was the rampant lion of Flanders in
yellow, the white spearhead on a scarlet
diamond of 1 Corps;[2] the badge of First
Canadian Army, a horizontal diamond in
red equally divided by a central dark blue
band, and a green shamrock. This was
one of the Belgian formations which
served in Holland and Germany with
the Canadian Army and with 1 Corps.

**Czech Independent Armoured
Brigade Group.**
Formed and trained in England, this
Czech formation took part in the
operations in North-West Europe as part
of 21st Army Group, landing in Normandy
in June 1944. It was the Czech Brigade
which surrounded and held the German
pocket of resistance at Dunkirk when
the Nazi garrison was isolated by the
swift coastal advance of the Canadian
Army. The formation's badge was a red
cross on a pale blue shield, with the
white lion rampant of Bohemia superimposed on the cross.

FRANCE

Belgian Congo Brigade.
The yellow five-pointed star of the
Congo, set on a square cobalt blue back-
ground, was the badge of the Belgian
Colonial formation.

Belgian Army Infantry School.
The badge of the Belgian Army Infantry
School at Tervueren, near Brussels, was
a red triangle—on it was the Belgian crown
in yellow above two crossed rifles in black,
set above a yellow rising sun.

Free French Forces.
A red cross of Lorraine, on a blue back-
ground, was the badge of the Free French
Forces which fought alongside their
British Allies in North Africa, in Libya
at Bir Hakim, and in the invasion of
North-West Europe and the liberation
of France itself.

1st French Army.
The badge worn by all members of the
First French Army, who fought in the
operations in Germany and Austria, from
the Rhine to the Danube, was a shield
divided vertically into red and green,
with a yellow mace superimposed thereon.
At the base of the shield pale and dark
blue wavy lines, to indicate the two
rivers, Rhine and Danube, which appear
in yellow letters on the dark blue background.

1st Division.
The badge of the 1st Division of the French
French Army (1944-46) was a yellow
shield, a black lion rampant thereon
with red eye, tongue and claws.

4th Moroccan Division.
This French Colonial formation, 4ème
Division Marocaine de Montagne, was
trained and equipped as a Mountain
Division. Its badge (1943-46) was a

double Moroccan Star in green on a red
square.
The Mohamaden crescent and star in
white on a green square, with the French
tricolour superimposed on the crescent,
formed a vehicle marking used on troop-
carrying and supply vehicles of the First
Army, operated by French colonial
troops, in Algeria and Tunisia in 1943.

GREECE

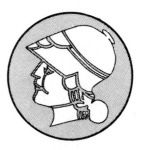

1st Greek Independent Brigade.
The head of Athena, in white, set on a
blue circular background, was adopted
by this Greek formation in the Middle
East.

2nd Greek Independent Brigade.
The badge of this Brigade was identical
with that of the 1st Greek Brigade except
that it was set on a diamond-shaped background.

3rd (Greek) Mountain Brigade.
The same badge was worn by this Brigade,
but on a square background. The Brigade
was formed and fought in Italy. It was
known as the 'Rimini Brigade' in
commemoration of the part it played
in the attack on that town.

NETHERLANDS

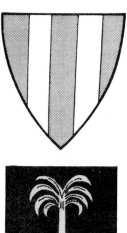

Royal Netherlands Brigade.
The Royal Netherlands Brigade (Princess Irene's) wore as their badge the royal lion of the House of Orange above a scroll, on it the word 'NEDERLAND'. This Brigade formed part of the Allied contingents of 21st Army Group and took part in the liberation of Holland. This badge was also worn by all Netherlands troops, in addition to other formation badges. When the Royal Netherlands Army was re-formed in Holland, the inscription 'NEDERLAND' was replaced by the motto of the House of Orange, 'JE MAINTIENDRAI'.

2nd Netherlands Division.
A shield divided vertically into five bars, red at the edges and in the centre, and two yellow between the red was the distinguishing badge of the Netherlands 2nd Division when it was raised in 1946. The badge was subsequently changed, the Division adopting a green palm tree on a dark blue shield—the coat of arms of Jan Pieterszoon Coen, one of the first Governors-General of the Netherlands East Indies (1617-1629).

1st Netherlands Division.
A white sword with yellow hilt set in the centre of a wreath of green leaves, the hilt flanked with the letters 'E' and 'M' in white, the whole design on a scarlet shield is the badge of the 1st Netherlands Division. The letters 'E' and 'M' stand for 'Expeditionair Macht' (Expeditionary Force). This badge was worn after the liberation of Holland in May 1945, by all those who volunteered for service against the Japanese in the Dutch East Indies. The shield is in the shape of the native weapon shield of Batavia.

**Royal Netherlands Army
(Garrison Troops) (Overseas).**
The distinguishing badge of the independent battalions and garrison troops serving in Java, Sumatra and other islands of the Netherlands East Indies was a dark green shield with a white sword flanked by the letters 'BT' (Bewakings Troepen—Garrison Troops)—in red, with a spray of green

leaves on either side of the hilt of the sword.

BRAZIL

Royal Netherlands Army (Garrison Troops) (Holland).
Garrison troops in Holland wore as a distinguishing badge a white archer, standing between two white frontier posts set on a red shield.

NORWAY

Norwegian Brigade.
Raised in the United Kingdom, this Norwegian Formation was attached to the 52nd (Lowland) Division—the Mountain Division. All Norwegian troops serving with the Allies wore a small replica of their National flag on the upper arm of their sleeves below the shoulder title 'Nörge', but, in addition, this Brigade wore a distinguishing badge depicting the North Cape, in white, the midnight sun in yellow, set on a black square background with a khaki border.

Brazilian Expeditionary Force.
The Brazilian Expeditionary Force was composed of the 1st Brazilian Infantry Division, one Base Section and one Reserve Personnel Section. Arriving in Italy on 16th July 1944, it was immediately incorporated in the American Fifth Army. Together with the Ninth Corps it took part in the 'Gothic Line' campaign in the Apennines, taking part in the capture of Monte Castelo, in the 1945 spring offensive, and in the conquest of the Po Valley.

The Division was composed of: the 1st, 6th and 11th Infantry Regiments, the 1st, 2nd, 3rd and 4th Artillery Regiments, 1st Reconnaissance Battalion, 1st Engineer Corps, 1st Radio Transmitter Company, and the 1st Hospital Unit.

The 6th Infantry Regiment distinguished themselves in the taking of Monte Prano in the Serckio Valley, also in the conquest of Castel Nuevo in the Reno Valley, whilst the 11th Regiment achieved distinction in the conquest of Montese in the Panaro Valley.

The Division wore a khaki shield bearing, in white, the word 'Brazil'.

POLAND

At the outbreak of war in 1939 the
Polish Army was the sixth largest
amongst those of the United Nations.
After the overrunning of Poland by
German and Russian forces in Sept.
1939 the Polish Army was reorganized
in France under General Sikorski and
elements of this force reached Great
Britain after the fall of France.

In July 1941, after the invasion of
Russia by Germany, a Polish Army was
formed in the U.S.S.R., and a part of
that Army, under General Anders, was
transferred to the Middle East where
it served under British Command.

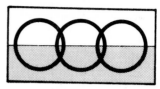

Polish L. of C. Units in the Middle East.
When 2nd Polish Corps took over the
original badge of H.Q. Polish Army in
the East, the Lines of Communications
units of that formation adopted a
distinctive badge of three linked circles
in black set on a rectangular background
evenly divided, top half white and lower
half red. This badge was only used as a
vehicle marking. A badge for wear on
the sleeve by L. of C. units, three linked
grey circles on a green background, was
later introduced but was never worn for
the new H.Q. Polish Army in the East.
badge was adopted.

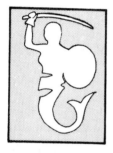

H.Q. Polish Army in the East.
A white (or silver/pale grey) 'Syrena' or
mermaid with shield and upraised sword
on a red background was the badge of
the Headquarters of the Polish Forces
in the Middle East. This badge was based
on the device of the arms of the City of
Warsaw. This Headquarters was raised
in the Middle East on 17th August 1941,
and its distinguishing badge adopted on
31st December 1942. This badge was
later taken into use by 2nd Polish Corps
when it was formed in July 1943, and
the H.Q. of the Polish Army adopted as
its formation sign the Arms of the City
of Cracow, three red towers on a blue
shield with a white eagle superimposed
on the centre tower. When used as a
vehicle marking the three red towers
were painted on a white rectangle.

In July 1944, this Headquarters
became H.Q. 3rd Polish Corps and on
30th December 1944, was redesignated
H.Q. Polish forces in the Middle East.

1st Polish Corps.
Raised in Scotland in the Summer of
1940, the title of this formation was
authorized on 21st December of that
year. During the threat of invasion in
1940-41 the Corps was responsible for
the defence of the Scottish coastal area
from Rosyth to Montrose. The formation
badge, worn only on the left sleeve, was
adopted in April 1942, and consisted of
the red and white flag of Poland superimposed on the Union Jack, the figure 'I'
in black on the white half of the Polish
flag and a red shield with a Polish eagle
thereon superimposed on the corner of
both flags. The badge was set on a khaki
background.

badge, shoulder titles, and N.C.O. chevrons.

2nd Polish Corps.

The 'Sirena' or Mermaid, armed with a sword, taken from the Coat of Arms of the City of Warsaw, in white, on a red shield with a white border was the badge of General Anders 2nd Polish Corps which formed part of the Allied armies in the Middle East and in Italy.[3] The badge, originally worn by the H.Q. of the Polish Armies in the Middle East, typified the fighting spirit of the people of Warsaw who on several occasions during the last centuries of Poland's history rose in arms against the invader, and it was adopted by the 2nd Polish Corps with a vow to show themselves worthy of the capital's great tradition.

The Base H.Q. of this Corps, raised in Italy in July 1944, wore a similar formation badge. The shield, however, was blue instead of red.

This badge was worn by a number of Household Cavalrymen. During the war, the Household Cavalry was formed into two regiments, the 1st and 2nd Houshold Cavalry Regiments, each having an equal complement of the Life Guards and Royal Horse Guards. The 1st Regiment served in the Middle East and in Italy. In July and August 1944, the Regiment was placed under command of 2 Polish Corps, forming part of a Polish Armoured Car Brigade. In recognition of their services in action with this formation, General Anders gave permission for all serving members of the 1st Household Cavalry Regiment to wear the badge of the 2 Polish Corps. This did not apply to the members of the 2nd Household Cavalry Regiment, at that time serving with the Guards Armoured Division in Normandy and the badge was therefore only seen worn by a limited number of the Life Guards and The Blues. The badge was worn on the lower half of the battledress sleeve, above the cuff, This position had no particular significance, but in any other position it would have created difficulties with placing it among the regiment's own formation

1st Polish Army Corps.

A winged wheel in white on a black background was used as a vehicle marking for all units of the Corps. Its use was discontinuedaafter 1943. In September 1944, H.Q. Polish Forces in Great Britain adopted a distinguishing vehicle marking, a combination of the Polish and Scottish national emblems, the White Eagle of Poland on red, and the Scottish Lion Rampant in red on a yellow background, set within a white and khaki border.

1st Polish Armoured Division.

Raised, trained and equipped in Scotland in February 1942, this formation formed part of 21st Army Group and took part in the invasion of Europe, landing in Normandy and taking part in the hard fighting in the Falaise Gap. The Brigade badge, adopted in August 1942, was in black set on a yellow circle on a khaki rectangular background represented the helmet and falcon wings of the Polish cavalry which, under the leadership of King John Sobeike, relieved Vienna in 1683 from the Turks.

In 1683, armed with long lances and heavy swords, these cavalrymen wore on their backs, stiff leathered wings intended to frighten the enemy's horses with their rustle.

2nd (Warsaw) Armoured Division.
Formed from the 2nd Polish Armoured Brigade the Division was finally, in June 1945, designated the 2nd (Warsaw) Armoured Division, this formation served with the 2nd Polish Corps in Italy.

Among the many exploits of the Polish cavalry from the fourteenth to the eighteenth centuries, great fame was won by what was called the 'Armoured Hussars'. It was appropriate, therefore, that this Armoured Division should have adopted as its badge a mailed arm and hand grasping a raised sword with the traditional wings of the Polish Cavalry rising from the shoulder. This design of the arm, sword and wing being in three shades of grey on a Gothic-window-shaped khaki background. The same design when used as a vehicle marking was in black on a white ground.

4th Polish Infantry Division.
A black and white grenade with red and white flames set on a khaki background was the badge of this formation, which was raised in September 1943, from the 2nd (Grenadier) Armoured Division. It was renamed the Grenadier Infantry Division in May 1944, and finally in February 1945, reorganized and redesignated the 4th Infantry Division.

3rd Carpathian Division.
This Division was raised at Qastina in Palestine in May 1942, from the Independent Carpathian Rifle Brigade. This brigade had been raised in 1940 in Syria, was the first Polish formation to see action in the Western Desert and had distinguished itself at Tobruk and Gazala in 1941. The Division joined the Eighth Army in Italy in 1943, taking part in the crossing of the Sangro, and the operations at Cassino, on the Adriatic coast, in the Apennines and at Bologna. The Divisional badge, adopted in December 1942, was a green fir tree on an equally divided background; top half white, and lower half red. The green fir tree (swierk) was adopted to represent the forest-covered Carpathian Mountains, Poland's natural Southern Boundary.

5th Kresowa Infantry Division.
Raised in Russia, at Tatishchevo and Jalal Abad, by order of the C.-in-C. Polish forces in U.S.S.R., in August 1941, and named 'Kresowa' by order of Supreme Command and Minister of National Defence in June 1943, the Division was reorganized at Khanagin in Iraq in October 1942, the Division trained in Paiforce and in Palestine. It landed in Italy in February 1944, and formed part of the Eighth Army in the Italian campaign. A brown bison (Zubr) on a yellow shield with a brown border was the Division's badge. The bison, once common, but now almost exinct

in Europe, was chosen as this beast lived in reservations in the Bialowieza Forest, the Polish National Park near Wilno, on the eastern border of Poland.

7th Polish Division.
A red griffin (Gryf) on a white background was the badge of this formation. The griffin was taken from the arms of the North-Western Polish town of Torun (the birthplace of the great astronomer, Mikolaj Copernicus) in the Province of Pomorze (Lowlands).

Throughout Polish history, Torun, under repeated onslaughts of the enemy, had always stood firm and many an assault was broken against its walls and towers. The Torun Griffin (Gryf) was adopted by the 7th Polish Division as the majority of its members were recruited from those coming from Poland's Western provinces. This formation was a training Division in the Middle East and later was moved to Italy as a training and reinforcement holding formation of 2nd Polish Corps.

Polish Parachute Brigade.
The Brigade, raised in Scotland, took part in the Battle of Arnhem in September 1944. Its badge (used only as a vehicle marking) was a white diving eagle set on an azure blue background, symbolic of the role of the Brigade.

6th (Lvov) Polish Infantry Division.
A Polish lion rampant in white set on a shield, divided diagonally into red and blue. In the lion's fore-paws is a wheel within which is a mailed arm and upraised sword. This symbolical lion was adopted from the main emblem in the Coat of Arms of the City of Lvov, the staunchest Polish bastion in the East of Poland and the only city to be awarded the highest decoration (The 'Virtuti Militari'). The Division was disbanded in the Middle East in March 1943 and its Infantry incorporated into the 5th Kresowa Infantry Division.

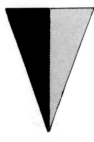

2nd Polish Army Tank Brigade.
This formation wore, in its time, three different badges. When raised it formed part of the 6th Polish Division and as such wore the badge of the formation. When the Division was disbanded in March 1943, the Brigade adopted the sign of the pre-war Polish Army Armoured Corps, an inverted isosceles triangle divided vertically into black and orange. Later this was changed to that of a black knight's helmet with visor and plume set on a yellow square.

2nd Polish Armoured Brigade.
Formed from the 2nd Polish Army Tank
Brigade in January 1944 the formation
continued to wear the black knight's
helmet badge inherited from the 2nd
Polish Armoured Division and adopted
the winged arm and sword badge.

YUGOSLAVIA

14th Wielkopolska Armoured Brigade.
This Brigade was raised in the Middle
East and Italy towards the end of the
war, and although it joined the 2nd
Polish Corps in Italy, it did not see
action. Its badge was a black panther
set on a Gothic window-shaped dark
yellow background.

Royal Yugoslav Forces.
Yugoslav troops serving in the Middle
East wore as a distinguishing badge the
double-headed eagle of Serbia in white
set on a royal blue shield.

16th Polish Armoured Brigade.
A black dragon, picked out in white and
set on an orange oval, was this distinctive
badge of this armoured formation, which
was raised in Scotland in 1940 as the
16th Polish Army Tank Brigade. In the
autumn of 1943, when most of the
personnel had been posted to the 1st
Polish Armoured Division, it became
a cadre formation and remained in
Scotland until the end of the war.

ITALY (CO-BELLIGERENT FORMATIONS)

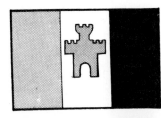

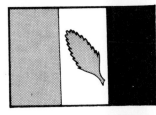

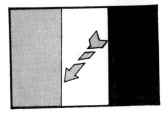

Italian Formations.

During the latter stages of the operations in the Italian campaign, Italian troops served with the Allied Armies under command of the 15th Army Group. Three Groups, the equivalent formations of Divisions, formed part of the Eighth Army. These were designated: The Cremona Group (under the command of 5 Corps), the Frimili Group (10 Corps), and the Folgore Group (13 Corps). These groups took part in the break out of the Apennines into the Po Valley; the liberation of Bologna; and the advance into Northern Italy which led to the German capitulation.

The Italian formations all wore as their badge a patch in the colours of the Italian flag, green, white and red, in each case a different emblem in bright blue set in the centre of the white portion. The Cremona Group an ear of wheat, the Frimili Group a castle gateway, and the Folgore Group a lightning flash. Other Groups serving with the Allied Armies included the Piceno Group, a Roman arch, and Legnano Group (the representation of a statue from that in one of the main squares of the town from which the group took its name).

Introduction

1. It is interesting to note that in Scott-ish Command, proposed formation badges were submitted to the Lord Lyon King-of-Arms (in Edinburgh) for revision. (The phraseology officially employed was that they had been 'perfected' by the Lord Lyon.) This ensured that provisional ideas were given technical correctness and the best effect. During the 1939-45 war the Albany Herald acted in liaison between H.Q. Scottish Command and the Lord Lyon
2. Caria — the South-west area of Turkey around Ephesus
3. Formation signs in the form of col-oured shapes were introduced during the U.S. Civil War (1861-5) and cloth patches in the shapes of a circle, a diamond, a star and differing forms of cross were worn on the forward-sloping tops of the kepis of the Army of the Potomac (in 1863). In the latter part of the nineteenth century, it became practice in the British Army to wear cloth patches of regimental colours on the right side of the pugaree of hel-mets when on foreign service — partic-ularly in India
4. Re-formed in 1939
5. Army Council Instructions Nos. 1118 and 1553 of 1940
6. Army Council Instruction No. 2587 of 1941
7. Formed, as part of the peacetime Establishment of the Army, at Aldershot in 1902
8. Army Council Instruction No. 872 of September 1948
9. Words of Constantine's vision, from Eusebius' *Life of Constantine*, i, 28

Higher Formations

1. The war-time badge of Home Forces reappeared in 1956 when it was adopted as the badge of H.Q. Land Forces, United Kingdom
2. G.H.Q. M.E.F. was redesignated Middle East Land Forces (M.E.L.F.) in 1946, and a badge for wear on uniform was adopted — a yellow camel on a shield evenly divided horizontally, the top red and the bottom blue
3. See also British Army of the Rhine, page 121

Home Commands

1. A demi-tiger rampant was the crest of the arms of the first Army Commander (Lieut.-General Sir Bernard Paget), and he chose the tiger badge because South-Eastern Army would — in the event of an invasion — "fight like tigers"

Overseas Commands

1. See also 21 Indian Corps, page 75
2. See also Ninth Army, page 24, and the British Troops in Iraq, page 108
3. See also Malta, page 106, and 231st Infantry Brigade, page 132
4. The R.W.A.F.F. then comprised the Nigeria Regiment, the Sierra Leone Batt-alion, and the Gambia Company

The Armies

1. In the programme the badge was referred to as the 'First Army Sign'
2. See British Troops in Austria, page 121
3. See North Levant District, page 113

British Corps

1. 1 Corps Troops Engineers wore the white spearhead on a background of R.E. colours, see page 140, and the Corps Artillery wore the spearhead on a diamond of R.A. colours, see page 137; 1 Corps badge was incorporated into that of one of the Belgian formations which served under its command — the 6th Brigade, see page 158
2. The formation badge of 1 Corps has the distinction of being flown, on a flag, on Mount Everest. Lord Hunt, C.B.E., D.S O., was serving as Colonel G.S., H.Q. 1 Corps, when appointed to the leadership of the Everest Expedition. On his return he presented the flag to the Officers' Mess of the Corps
3. See also H.Q. Land Forces, Greece and British Forces in Greece, page 108
4. Sometimes with a narrow black border
5. See also 253 L. of C. Sub-area, page 118
6. So far as the writer has been able to trace, 7 Corps never had a formation badge
7. The Francolin partridge was a pun on the name of the Corps Commander, Lieut.-General H.E. Franklyn, C.B., D.S.O.
8. See also South-Western District, page 101
9. Major-General R.P. Pakenham-Walsh
10. Rudyard Kipling's 'Tree Song', which refers to the early days of Kent and Sussex
11. From 1945 until 1954 this Corps badge was retained by the British element, Trieste Force
12. See also Cyprus District, page 113

British Armoured Divisions

1. Who was later killed in action in Normandy while serving with the Welsh Guards
2. See also 2nd Armoured Brigade, page 123
3. See 6th Armoured Division, page 33
4. When the 6th Armoured Division was

re-formed in 1950 on B.A.O.R., the mailed
fist badge was readopted
5. When the 11th Armoured Division was
re-formed in B.A.O.R. in 1950, the
badge was readopted, and it was worn by
the Division until 1956 on its conversion
to an infantry division (the 4th)
6. See also 42nd (East Lancashire) Division, page 41, and 42nd Armoured Engineer Regiment, page 140

British Infantry Divisions

1. See also 1st Div. R.A., page 137,
and 1st Div. Signals, page 142
2. See also 1 Corps, page 27
3. See 5th Infantry Brigade, page 128
4. See also 70th Division, page 48
5. Designation taken from Army Council
Instruction No. 337/1940 (April 1940)
6. Designation taken from Army Council
Instruction No. 337/1940 (April 1940)
7. Designation taken from Army Council
Instruction No. 337/1940 (April 1940)
8. See pages 128 and 87 0
9. See also 42nd Armoured Division, page
35
10. See also 42nd Armoured Engineer
Regiment, page 140
11. When the territorial Army was re-
formed in 1947, the 44th Division
adopted the badge of Home Counties
District, which was superimposed on the
red oval to which a white border was added. This badge was worn until 1956
when a new badge, a gold trident on a red
oval, was adopted
12. It was said by Territorials of the 7th
(T.A.) Bn. The Queen's Regiment
(formerly the 24th Bn. The London
Regiment) which had its H.Q. in Brag-
anza Street (formerly New Street) Kennington, that the shape of the badge was
chosen to link with the Surrey County
Cricket Ground — Kennington Oval
13. Designation taken from Army Council
Instruction No. 337/1940 (April 1940)
14. See also Iceland Force, page 106
15. When the Territorial Army was re-
formed in 1947 the 50th Division (T.A.)
retained this badge
16. See page 137
17. On its re-formation in 1947 as a Territorial Army Division this formation badge
was retained
18. The 53rd Division retained this badge
when it was re-formed within the Territorial Army in 1947
19. See also 162nd Independent Infantry
Brigade, page 131
20. The Division was given the number
'56' in November 1940, thereby reverting
to the number it had borne from 1915 to
1936. Before 1915, it had from 1908
been designated '1st London (T.F.)'

and after 1936 'The London Division'
21. Designation taken from Army Council
Instruction No. 337/1940 (April 1940)
22. See also 6th Division, page 37

The Airborne Divisions

1. The badge is still worn by all ranks of
the Parachute Regiment, Regular and
T.A., and all ranks of supporting arms
serving in the airborne role

Anti-Aircraft Formations

1. During the 1914-18 War, a badge of
similar design but in different colours
(white on grey) was the sign of IX Corps
and was adopted by the Corps Commander, Lieut.-General Sir Alexander
Hamilton-Gordon
2. Which later became the School of
Anti-Aircraft Artillery at Manorbier, Pem-
brokeshire

Anti-aircraft Corps and Divisions

1. See H.Q. Anti-Aircraft Command,
page 52
2. The Shield of the Arms of Cadell of
Grange and Banton was emblazoned with
three oval buckles azure (blue) below a
stag's head couped

The County Divisions

1. See 73rd Independent Infantry Brigade,
page 130
2. See 223rd Independent Infantry Brigade, page 132
3. See 212th Independent Infantry Brigade, page 131
4. See page 100
5. See page 99

The Canadian Formations

1. Brigade Bars: during the 1914-18 war,
the Canadian Corps used geometrical
designs to distinguish the three brigades of
a Division. In the later years, the same
colours were worn by the Brigade Headquarters staffs, but bars were used as distinguishing insignia instead of the previous
geometrical designs. The bars were worn
above the formation patch as follows:
GREEN, 1st, 4th and 7th Canadian
Infantry Brigades, and 4th and 5th
Canadian Infantry Brigades. BLUE, 2nd,
5th and 8th Canadian Infantry Brigades;
RED, 3rd, 6th, 9th, 10th and 11th
Canadian Infantry Brigades.
2. The basic colour for the Armoured
Brigade patches was black, based on the
Canadian tank colour of the 1914-18 war.
Hence the adoption of the black bar set
on the red or blue diamonds of the 1st
and 2nd Canadian Corps

Australian Formations

1. See also New Guinea Force, page 107
2. Resulting from the defence of Tobruk. by the Division in 1941, it was sometimes said that the 'T' stood for Tobruk; in fact, the Division had in 1939 adopted the distinguishing 'colour patch' of the 4th Division of the A.I.F. of World War 1, changing the shape from a circle to a 'T'
3. See page 65

New Zealand Formations
1. This badge was later borne on the vehicles of the Royal Wiltshire Yeomanry, an honour granted to the Regiment by the New Zealand Division with which the Wiltshire Yeomanry served in the Western Desert and Italy

South African Divisions
1. The 4th and 5th South African Divisions were never formed as such. When the Inland Area and H.Q. Coastal Area were formed in 1942 as Major-General's commands, the two were regarded as the equivalents of Divisions. Accordingly, when the South African Armoured Division was dispatched to the Middle East in April 1943, it was designated the 6th South African Armoured Division

Indian Formations
1. See also Eastern Command (India), page 20
2. This badge was subsequently worn by a formation of the Pakistan Army
3. This badge was subsequently adopted by one of the formations of the Pakistan Army
4. This badge was subsequently worn by one of the formations of the Pakistan Army
5. See 44th Indian Armoured Division, page 83
6. See also 268th Indian Infantry Brigade, page 88
7. This badge was later worn by an Infantry Brigade of the Indian Army
8. See 21st Indian Division, page 82
9. See 255th Indian Tank Brigade, page 86

Indian Armoured and Tank Brigades
2. See page 87
3. See 44th Indian Armoured Division, page 83

Indian Infantry Brigades
1. Sometimes referred to as the 43rd Gurkha Lorried Infantry Brigade
2. See 36th Division, page 40
3. See also 21st Indian Division, page 82 and 254 L. of C. Sub-Area, page 118

4. See 268th Indian Infantry Brigade, page 88
5. See also B.C.O.F., page 122

The East and West African Formations
1. See also West Africa Command, page 21

Combined Operations, Commando and Beach Formations
1. The anchor is of the stockless pattern, instead of the old-style stocked anchor generally depicted on the badges
2. A similar badge is worn by Commandos of the Belgian Army, a white dagger on the same-shaped background, but with a narrow white border

The Districts
1. See page 59
2. See page 148
3. It is interesting to note that the two Welsh Districts of the Western Command adopted as their badges the Divisional signs carried during the 1914-18 war. During World War 1, the 38th (Welsh) Division which served on the Western Front adopted the Red Dragon of Wales, and the 53rd (Welsh) Division which formed part of our Forces in Palestine utilised the Prince of Wales' feathers
4. See also 8 Corps, page 28
5. The White Horse of Kent was also the badge of the West Kent Yeomanry and the Royal East Kent Yeomanry
6. The martlet is an heraldic bird, which resembles a martin, although it has no legs and two tufts of feathers which represent the legs

Overseas Force and Garrison Headquarters
1. See Malta Command, page 21; R.A. Units, Malta, page 138; 231st Infantry Brigade, page 132
2. See R.A. Units, Gibraltar, page 138
3. See also 49th (West Riding) Division. page 44
4. See also 2 Australian Corps, page 66
5. See Persia and Iraq Command, page 21
6. See H.Q. L. of C., 21st Army Group, page 111
7. See 3 Corps, page 27

Overseas Districts and L. of C. Areas
1. See also British Troops in the Low Countries, page 108
2. This badge, set on a shield, is also the badge of the Cyprus Regiment, which was raised in 1940
3. See also Force 135, page 97
4. See also Ninth Army, page 26
5. See also Cyrenaica District, page 112

Indian and S.E.A.C. District and L. of C. Areas
1. See also 4 Corps, page 28

Occupation Forces
1. See H.Q. 21st Army Group, page 24
2. See Eighth Army, page 24
3. When in uniform. Battledress blouse and trousers were worn by civilian members of the Control Commission for Germany. A green epaulette on the blouse bearing, in yellow, the words 'Civilian Military Government' (or in black the words 'Civilian Military Government'), was used.
4. See also 5th Infantry Brigade, page 128
5. See also page 88

The Armoured and Tank Brigades
1. See also 1st Armoured Division, page 32
2. See also page 126
3. See also page 124
4. See 25th Armoured Engineer Brigade, page 124

Independent Infantry Brigades and Brigade Groups
1. See also 36th Division, page 40
2. See 12th Division, page 38
3. See 1st Division, page 36
4. See page 58
5. See also 54th (East Anglian) Division, page 46
6. See Lincolnshire Country Division, page 59
7. See page 58

Royal Artillery Badges
1. See also 1 Corps, page 27
2. See also 1st Division, page 36
3. A Territorial Army Regiment with its H.Q. in South Shields, and composed of the 293rd (1st Durham), 294th (2nd

Durham) and the 195th (3rd Durham) Field Batteries R.A. (T.A.)
4. See also Malta, page 106
5. See Gibraltar Garrison, page 106 approved for the 81st U.S. Division in October 1918

Belgian Formations
1. The Shamrock appearing in these Belgian Army badges links the formations with Northern Ireland, where they were raised and trained
2. See 1 Corps, page 27

Polish Formations
1. See also 2 Polish Corps, page 163
2. Order issued by the Supreme Commander and War Minister, Polish Forces, 8th October 1940
3. The Corps was formed on 6th July 1943 (Order of the Polish Supreme Commander) dated 29th June 1943

Royal Engineer Badges
1. See 1 Corps, page 27

Royal Signals Badges
1. See 1st Division, page 36

Home Guard Units
1. The full list of Country Distinguishing letters is given in Appendix 4
2. *Military Heraldry Society Bulletin* No. 60, January 1966

American Formations
1. The first 'shoulder patch' was

LIST OF ABBREVIATIONS

A.A.	Anti-Aircraft
A.A.I.	Allied Armies in Italy
A.C.A.	Allied Control Austria
A.D.C.	Aide-de-Camp
A.D.G.B.	Air Defence of Great Britain
Adm.	Administration, or Administrative
A.F.H.Q.	Allied Force Headquarters (North Africa and Italy)
A.F.P.U.	Army Film and Photographic Unit(s)
A.F.V.	Armoured Fighting Vehicle
A.G.R.A.	Army Group Royal Artillery
A.L.F.S.E.A.	Allied Land Forces, South-East Asia
A.M.D.C.	Army Mechanized Demonstration Column
A.V.R.E.	Armoured Vehicle, Royal Engineers
B.A.O.R.	British Army of the Rhine
B.C.O.F.	British Commonwealth Occupational Force
Bde.	Brigade

B.E.F.	British Expeditionary Force
B.F.I.G.	British Forces in Greece
B.L.A.	British Liberation Army (21st Army Group)
Bn.	Battalion
B.N.A.F.	British North Africa Force
Brindiv	British/Indian Division (B.C.O.F.)
B.T.A.	British Troops in Austria
B.T.B.	British Troops in Berlin
B.T.E.	British Troops in Egypt
B.T.L.C.	British Troops in the Low Countries
B.T.N.I.	British Troops in Northern Ireland
C.A.P.F.	Canadian Army Pacific Force
C.B.	Companion of the Order of Bath
C.B.E.	Commander of the Order of the British Empire
C.C.G.	Control Commission for Germany
C.I.G.S.	Chief of the Imperial General Staff
C.M.F.	Central Mediterranean Force
C.M.P.	Corps of Military Police (now C.R.M.P.—Corps of Royal Military Police)
C.O.H.Q.	Combined Operations Headquarters
C.R.A.S.C.	Commander Royal Army Service Corps
C.R.E.	Commander Royal Engineers
C.V.O.	Commander of the Royal Victorian Order
C.W.	Chemical Warfare
D.E.M.S.	Defensively Equipped Merchant Shipping
D.I.D.	Detail Issue Depot (R.A.S.C.)
D.L.I.	Durham Light Infantry
D.M.I.	Director of Military Intelligence
Div.	Division
D.S.O.	Distinguished Service Order
E.T.O.U.S.A.	European Theatre of Operations United States Army
G.H.Q.	General Headquarters
G.O.C.	General Officer Commanding
G.R.E.F.	General Reserve Engineering Force
H.Q.	Headquarters
Ind.	Indian
Indep.	Independent
I.T.C.	Infantry Training Centre
K.B.E.	Knight Commander of the Order of the British Empire
K.C.B.	Knight Commander of the Order of the Bath
K.D.	Khaki Drill
K.R.R.C.	King's Royal Rifle Corps
K.S.L.I.	King's Shropshire Light Infantry
L. of C.	Lines of Communication
L.F.A.	Land Forces Adriatic
M.B.E.	Member of the Order of the British Empire
M.C.	Military Cross
M.E.F.	Middle East Forces
M.E.L.F.	Middle East Land Forces
M.T.	Mechanical Transport
N.W.E.F.	North-Western Expeditionary Force
N.Z.	New Zealand
N.Z.E.F.	New Zealand Expeditionary Force
O.B.E.	Officer of the Order of the British Empire
O.C.T.U.	Officer Cadet Training Unit
P.A.I.C.	Persia and Iraq Command
Paiforce	Persia and Iraq Force
P.T.C.	Primary Training Centre
P.o.W.	Prisoner of War
P.W.E.	Political Warfare Executive
R.A.	Royal Artillery
R.A.C.	Royal Armoured Corps
R.A.F.	Royal Air Force
R.A.M.C.	Royal Army Medical Corps
R.A.S.C.	Royal Army Service Corps

R.A.O.C.	Royal Army Ordnance Corps
R.B.	Rifle Brigade
R.E.	Royal Engineers
R.E.M.E.	Royal Electrical and Mechanical Engineers
R.T.R.	Royal Tank Regiment
S. & T.	Supply and Transport
S.A.	South Africa
S.A.C.S.E.A.	Supreme Allied Commander, South-East Asia
S.A.S.	Special Air Service
S.D.F.	Sudan Defence Force
S.E.A.C.	South-East Asia Command
S.H.A.E.F.	Supreme Headquarters Allied Expeditionary Force
S.O.R.E.	Staff Officer, Royal Engineers
T.A.	Territorial Army
T.D.	Territorial Decoration (Efficiency Decoration [Territorial])
T.F.	Territorial Force
U.K.	United Kingdom
U.S.	United States (of America)
VE Day	'Victory in Europe' Day (8th May 1945)

ARM OF SERVICE STRIPS

Introduced in 1940 as 'Arms of Service Distinguishing Marks',[1] these strips of coloured cloth were two inches in length and were worn below the formation badge on the sleeves of the battledress blouse. They were later designated 'Arm of Service Strips'.[2]

Arm of Service		*Colours*
Royal Armoured Corps		yellow/red
Royal Artillery		red/blue
Royal Engineers		blue/red
Royal Signals		blue/white
Infantry (except Rifle Regiments)		scarlet
Infantry (Rifle Regiments)		Rifle green
Royal Army Chaplains' Department		purple
Royal Army Service Corps		yellow/blue
Royal Army Medical Corps		dull cherry

[1] Army Council Instruction No. 1118/1940   [2] Army Council Instruction No. 2587/1941

Arm of Service	Colours
Royal Army Ordnance Corps	red/blue/red
Royal Electrical and Mechanical Engineers	red/yellow/blue
Corps of Royal Military Police [3]	red
Royal Army Pay Corps	yellow
Royal Army Educational Corps [3]	Cambridge blue
Royal Army Dental Corps [3]	green/white
Royal Pioneer Corps [3]	red/green
Intelligence Corps	green
Army Physical Training Corps	black/red/black
Army Catering Corps	grey/yellow

VEHICLE ARM OF SERVICE MARKINGS

Painted on front and rear mudguards and/or on tailboards of trucks and lorries.

Arm of Service	Colours
Headquarters of Formations	black
Headquarters R.A. and R.A. Units	red/blue
Headquarters R.E. and R.E. Units	cobalt blue

[3] The distinction 'Royal' was granted in November 1946.

Headquarters Royal Signals and Royal Signals Units	white/dark blue
Reconnaissance Regiments (R.A.C.)	green/blue
Lorried Infantry Battalions	green
Headquarters R.A.S.C. and R.A.S.C. Units	red/green
Headquarters R.A.O.C. and R.A.O.C. Units	blue/red/blue
Headquarters R.E.M.E. and R.E.M.E. Units	black/yellow/red

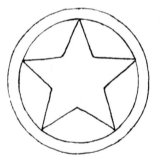

ALLIED VEHICLE MARKING

A white five-pointed star within a white circle, or the white star alone, was the universal Allied vehicle marking in the campaign in North Western Europe. This was painted on the top of all Allied vehicles to aid recognition by aircraft.

DESCRIPTIVE INDEX OF BRITISH AND COMMONWEALTH BADGES

ANIMALS

ALLIGATOR
White alligator and a white palm tree on a black background: 4th Australian Armoured Brigade **69**
BUFFALOS
Water buffalo in white above a white boomerang on a black background: 12th Australian Division **69**
Buffalo's head in white, with red horns, set on a blue square: 21st Indian Division **82** and 268th Lorried Infantry Brigade **88**
Buffalo, charging, in black, with red horns, hooves and eyes, set on a white circle below the inscription in black, 'Laro aur Larte Raho': 44th Indian Armoured Division **83**
Buffalo, charging, in black, with red horns, hooves and eyes, set on a blue triangle: 255th Indian Tank Brigade **86**
Buffalo's head in white set between the arms of a white 'V' on a red background: Lushai Brigade **89**
BEARS
White polar bear on black background: 49th (West Riding) Division **44** and Iceland Force **106**

White polar bear on a circular background divided evenly into five diagonal stripes—blue, yellow, green, red and blue: M.N.B.D.O. **95**

Koala bear in white on black background: 3rd Australian Division **67**

BULLS

Black bull, charging, red horns, eyes and hooves on a yellow background: 11th Armoured Division **35**

Bull's head with black and white markings, red and brown nostrils and red-tipped horns, set on a yellow background in an inverted equilateral triangle with a black border: 79th Armoured Division **35**

Charging bull in black and white on a black rectangle: 4th New Zealand Division **71**

BOARS

Black boar rampant in a white circle on a black square: 30 Corps **30**

Boar's head in white above a white boomerang on a black background: 5th Australian Division **68**

CAMELS

Camel, brown, on black square: G.H.Q., M.E.F. **14**

Camel, gold, on black square: G.H.Q., M.E.F. **14**

Camel and rider, in black silhouette on square white background: H.Q. Sudan and Eritrea **107**

CARIBOU

Caribou's head in yellow (gold) on a red oval: Newfoundland Units, R.A. **136**

CATS

Cat, black (Kilkenny), arched back, on orange square: 9 Corps **29**

Cat, black (Dick Whittington's), back view on red background: 56th (London) Division **47**

Cat, black, rear view, tail outlined in red, curled in shape of figure 9; aircraft silhouette in red on cat's back: 9th A.A. Division **56**

Cat, black, side view, back arched, on khaki background: 17th Indian Division **81**

DEER, etc.

Stag's head in red on white background: 22nd Armoured Brigade **124**

White hart's head on a rectangle divided, top half red, lower dark blue: 303rd Infantry Brigade **133**

Deer's head in yellow on a dark blue circle: Indian Field Broadcasting Units **134**

Black head and antlers on a yellow circle or square: Trincomalee Fortress Area **120**

Kudu, in white, on a black square: 12th (African) Division **91**

Springbok's head in light yellow, picked out in black and white, set on khaki: U.D.F. Repatriation Units **74**

DOGS

Bulldog in white on black background: H.Q. Eastern Command **17**

Bulldog in white, set above a white boomerang on a black background: 1 Australian Corps **66**

Greyhound in white, leaping over a boomerang in white, on a black background: 1st Australian Cavalry Division **67** and 1st Australian Motor Division **67**

Dingo (Australian) dog in white, above a boomerang in white, on a black background: Australian Imperial Forces Base, M.E.F. **65**

Head of a black Alsatian dog, open mouth showing bright red tongue set on a pale green oval with a black border: Sussex District **102**

Husky dog, white head, red ears and tongue, set on pale green circle: No. 1 District, C.M.F. **114**

White bulldog, set on a yellow five-pointed star, on a red square background: British Reinforcement Training Centre (India) **147**

DUCK

White duck on blue circle: 108 (Bombay) L. of C. Area **117**

DUCK-BILLED PLATYPUS

Duck-billed platypus in white above a white boomerang set on a black rectangle: 9th Australian Division **69**

ECHIDNA

White echidna above boomerang on black background: 4th Australian Division **67**

ELEPHANTS

Elephant's head, in yellow, on background evenly divided horizontally into red, black and red: Ceylon Army Command **20**

Elephant's head in red, with white tusks, on blue background: Persia and Iraq Command **21** and British Troops in Iraq **108**

Elephant in red, charging (on its back a small red castle), set on a black circle: H.Q. Ninth Army **24** and North Levant District **113**

Elephant in black on red background: 4 Corps **28**

Elephant in black on green background: 31st Indian Armoured Division **83**

Elephant in white, trunk raised, on a black circular background: 22nd (East African) Brigade **92**

Elephant and palm tree in white on a black circle: Gold Coast Area **115**

Elephant, rear view, in white on khaki background: 253 L. of C. Sub-Area **118**

FOXES

Fox's mask in red on a black (or yellow) circle: 10th Armoured Division **34**

Fox's mask in reddish brown on a yellow circle with a narrow brown border: 8th Armoured Brigade **124**

GAZELLE

Red leaping gazelle on a white circle in a red diamond with a narrow white border: 13 Corps **30** and H.Q. L. of C. British Troops in North Africa **111**

GOAT

Leaping goat in red, set above three wavy blue lines, on a white or khaki background: Dodecanese District Force 281 **107**

HOG

Black Hampshire hog on a white rectangular or semi-circular background: Hampshire County Division **58**

HORNET

Yellow hornet on a black background: 2nd Indian Division **77**

HORSES

Horse's head, heraldic, with flowing mane, in white on a square black background: Eastern Command (India) **21** and 21 Indian Corps **75**

Horse in white, set above a boomerang in white on a black background: 2nd Australian Army **65**

Knight's charger's head, armour-clad, in white on black background: 3rd Australian Army Tank **69**

Horse's head in white, within narrow white circle, set on a dark green circular background: North Kent and Surrey District **102**

Prancing white horse (the White Horse of Kent) on a dark green oval background: North Kent and Surrey District **102**

White horse on bright green square or semi-circular background. 9th Armoured Brigade **124**

Knight's charger's armoured-clad head in white on a black background: 20th Armoured Brigade **124**

IBEX

Ibex head in white on a red square: Baluchistan District **119**

KANGAROO

White kangaroo leaping over a white boomerang set on a black background: 6th Australian Division **68**

LEOPARD

A Leopard on a red background: Delhi District **118**

LIONS

Lion, heraldic, gold (or yellow) on circle divided top half dark blue, lower red: G.H.Q. Home Forces **14**

Lion, rampant (heraldic, Scottish), in gold on background divided into three bands—red, black, red: H.Q. Scottish Command **17**

Lion, rampant (heraldic, Scottish) in gold on red background: Scottish Command (other than H.Q. **17**

Lion, rampant (heraldic, Scottish) in gold on background divided into diagonals purple and green: North Highland District **104**

Lion, rampant (heraldic, Scottish) in gold superimposed on white St. Andrew's Cross on red background: West Scotland District **104**

Lion, rampant (heraldic, Scottish) in gold superimposed on white St. Andrew's Cross on dark green background: East Scotland District **104**

Lion, Assyrian, in gold on black background, or in white on light blue background. H.Q. Tenth Army **25**

Lion, Cyprus, in red on yellow background: 25 Corps **30**

Lion, rampant (heraldic, Scottish), in red in a yellow circle with a white border set on a black square: 15th (Scottish) Division **39**

Lion, Persian (scimitar in right paw), outlined in blue on yellow background: 12th Indian Division **80**

Lion and palm tree in yellow on black rectangle: Sierra Leone Area **115**

Lions, heraldic, in gold, three on a red shield: Force 135   **97**
Lion, Cyprus, in yellow on green background: Cyprus District   **113**
Lion's head, heraldic, in black outlined in white on a khaki background: 10th A.A. Division   **56**
LIZARD
Pale green lizard on black rectangle: 8th Bn. Cornwall Home Guard   **148**
PANDA
Head of a giant panda in black and white: 9th Armoured Division   **34**
PANTHER
Black leaping panther on a circle divided into three horizontal bands, red, white and red: 34 Indian Corps   **76**
RATS
Red desert rat (Jerboa) in a white circle on a red square: 7th Armoured Division   **33**
Red rat picked out in white on a black background: 7th Armoured Division   **33**
Black desert rate (Jerboa) on a white square: 4th Armoured Brigade   **123**
Green rat on a white circle within a red ring: 7th Armoured Brigade   **123**
RHINOCEROS
Standing rhino in white on a black oval: 1st Armoured Division   **32** and 2nd Armoured Brigade   **123**
Charging rhino in white on a black oval: 1st Armoured Division   **32**
Black rhino on a white circle: East African Expeditionary Force   **91**
Rhino's head in grey, picked out in black, on a red circle, with inscription in black 'Laro aur Larte Raho': 42nd Indian Armoured Division   **83**
Rhino's head in black on a red circle: 11th (East African) Division   **91**
SCORPIONS
Black scorpion on a white background: Transjordan Frontier Force   **109**
White scorpion on a black background: 2nd Australian Armoured Division   **66**
SALAMANDER
Green and black salamander passing through red and yellow flames: No. 1 Commando   **94**
SEA-HORSES
Black sea-horse, picked out in white above a red bar, set on a khaki rectangle: North Caribbean Area   **115**
Yellow and white sea-horse set on a saxe blue shield: 27th Armoured Brigade   **125**
Yellow sea-horse on a red circle on a royal blue inverted triangle: Royal Marines Training Establishment   **96**
SEA-LION
Black sea-lion balancing a globe on its nose; set on a yellow rectangle: 12th Army   **25**
SPIDER
Black tarantula spider on a yellow square or circle: 81st (West African) Division   **92**
TIGERS
Tiger's head in black, white, yellow and red on khaki circle: H.Q. South-Eastern Command   **17**
Tiger, in natural colours, stepping out of a blue triangle set on a black triangular background: 26th Indian Division   **82**
Tiger's head in black and yellow on square background: 6th Indian Division   **78**
Tiger's head and shoulders in yellow and black on a red square: 251st Indian Tank Brigade   **85**
Tiger's head in red on a white background: 1st Armoured Brigade Group   **123**

BIRDS

Bird in white seated on a nest on a black bough on a green background: Northern Ireland District   **105**
Cock in red on a khaki or light yellow circle: 23rd Indian Division   **82**
Crane bird with red head, neck and legs and a blue body: 38th Indian Infantry Brigade   **87**
Crown bird in black on white rectangular background: Nigeria Area   **115**
Black displayed German Eagle, picked out in yellow, a scarlet arrow thrust upward through its breast, set on a khaki background: 11th A.A. Division   **56**
Red eagle in flight, a red arrow through its breast, set on a bright blue background: 1 A.A. Corps   **53**
Eagle in red in flight on a dark blue background: 4th Indian Division   **77**
Eagle in gold, wings displayed, on a black background: East Riding and Lincs. District   **100**
Golden eagle on a black and white quartered shield on a black shield: Special Training Centre, Lochailort   **147**

Eaglet in white on a red square: Rawalpindi District **118**

Emu in white above a white boomerang, set on a black background: 8th Australian Division **68**

Falcon's head, in white, on a red square: Arab Legion **110**

Falcon, in white, on a red square: Rawalpindi District **118**

Kiwi in white on black background: 3rd New Zealand Division **71** and 6th New Zealand Division **72**

Kea's head in black and white on black background: 5th New Zealand Division **72**

Kookaburra in brown and white seated on a white boomerang on a black background: 7th Australian Division **68**

Liver bird in black on white square or circle: 23rd Armoured Brigade **125**

Macaw in blue on a red diamond with a dark blue oval: 48th (South Midland) Division **43**

Magpie on a black background: 3 Australian Corps **66**

Oyster catcher (Tjaldur), in black and white, standing on a black rock against background of dark blue sea and light blue sky: Faero Islands Force **106**

Paddy bird in white on a red square: 404th (East Bengal) L. of C. Area **117**

Pelican in white on a black shield: Bahawalpur State Forces, India **90**

Parakeet's head in white above a white boomerang on a black background: 2nd Australian Corps **66** and New Guinea Force **107**

Partridge, black, Francolin, in flight on a white oval: 8th Corps **28** and South-Western District **101**

Penguin above a white boomerang on a black background: 2nd Australian Division **67**

Penguin in black and white on a khaki background: 22nd Beach Brigade **94**

Peewit (plover) in black and white on a light blue diamond with a narrow red border: Political Warfare Executive, M.E.F. **135**

Stork in flight on green rectangular background: South Burma District **120**

Sussex martlet in black on a green circle: Canadian Corps District **103**

Swan in white above a white boomerang on a black background: First Australian Army **65**

FISH

Dogfish in white above three wavy white lines on a red square: Kohat District **119**

Dolphin in blue on a square black background: No. 15 Area M.E.F. **112**

Two blue-grey fish set on a red circle: Unit Provinces Area **119**

Red salmon on background of three wavy blue bands on a white background with a narrow red border: 2 Corps **27**

FLOWERS

White Tudor rose on blue (or green) background: 23rd Division **40**

Red (Lancashire) rose with green stalk and leaves on a khaki circle or square: 55th (West Lancashire) Division **46**

Red (Lancashire) rose set in a yellow entwined border on a dark green square: Lancs. and Border District **101** and North-Western District **101**

Red (Lancashire) rose and white (Yorkshire) rose on a black rectangle: 71st Independent Infantry Brigade **130**

Rose, thistle and shamrock, stalks entwined: 1st Air Landing Brigade **51**

Thistle flower on a stalk with two leaves in white (or silver) on a dark blue background: 9th (Scottish) Division **38**

Thistle flower on a stalk with two leaves in which, flanked either side, is the letter 'A' in white; set on a square blue background: 3rd A.A. Division **54**

Tulip in red, with light green leaves, set on white rectangle: Lincolnshire County Division **59** and 212th Independent Infantry Brigade **131**

White daisy, with pale green centre, stalk and leaf set on black rectangle: 32nd Army Tank Brigade **125**

FRUIT

Green apple on a royal blue diamond: Northern Command **17**

LEAVES

Three clover leaves and stems in yellow on a dull red background: 8th Indian Division **79**

Fig leaf in green on white square: 3 Corps **27** and H.Q. Land Forces, Greece **108** and H.Q. British Forces in Greece **108**

Fern leaf in white on black circle or square: 2nd New Zealand Division **71**

Maple leaf in gold (or yellow) on black circle with gold (or yellow) border: Canadian Military Headquarters **60**

Shamrock leaf in green: 38th Infantry Brigade **129**

NUTS

Acorn in brown on a white square: 40th Division **41**

Cob nut, green shell, yellow nut on a khaki background: 36th Independent Infantry Brigade **129**

TREES

Green oak tree (Sherwood oak), black branches and trunk, outlined in white on black square: 46th (North Midland) Division **42**

Black palm tree on white background: West African Command **21**

Palm tree in white on black background: 11th Australian Division **69**

Palm tree in yellow, outlined in black set above a yellow scroll with the black initials 'R.W.A.F.F.' on a green circle: West African Expeditionary Force **91**

Palm tree in yellow on a red square: 109 (Bangalore) L. of C. Area **117**

Three trees (oak, ash and thorn), green, with blank trunks on white oval set on a black rectangle: 12 Corps **30**

Yellow palm tree on black square: Madras Defended Port Area **119**

AEROPLANES

Black aircraft in silhouette, pierced by a red sword, on a light blue background with a black edge: 1st A.A. Division **54**

Black aircraft in silhouette, nose downwards, five red flames rising upwards from the wings and fuselage, the whole on a khaki background: 5th A.A. Division **55**

Black aircraft in silhouette, nose downwards, a red eight-pointed star superimposed on the fuselage, the whole on a sky blue square: 8th A.A. Division **56**

Red aircraft in silhouette below a red five-pointed star set on a diamond divided right half dark blue, left half white: Indian Air Formation Signals **142**

Yellow aircraft on a royal blue square: Air Despatch Group, R.A.S.C. **143**

ANCHORS

Naval fouled anchor in red on a pale blue circle with a red border: Beach Groups **93**

Anchor, a tommy-gun, and an albatross in red on a dark blue background: Combined Operations Headquarters **93**

Naval fouled anchor in red, set on dark blue shield, with yellow grenade superimposed on the anchor: Royal Marine Engineers **96**

Naval fouled anchor in yellow on a red circle set in the centre of a yellow eight-pointed star: 117th (Royal Marine) Infantry Brigade **96**

Naval fouled anchor in red on a Navy blue background: Orkney and Shetland Defences **105**

Black anchor, with a red figure 2 entwined, set on a blue circular background, with a black border: No. 2 Area S.E.A.C. (Singapore) **120**

Anchor in black, suspended by two links from the horizontal blade of a black sword, set on a red background: No. 2 District, C.M.F. **114**

Naval fouled anchor in red, with white rope set on a black background, the letters 'AA' (or 'RA') in white, set either side of the anchor: Maritime Anti-Aircraft Artillery **136**

Naval fouled anchor in yellow, set on an inverted red equilateral triangle with a narrow yellow edge on two sides, superimposed on a dark blue shield: Amphibian Support Regiment, Royal Marines **96**

ARMOUR

White knight in armour on white charger, lance at the point, set on a scarlet background: 8 Corps **28**

Knight's helmet, plumed, in white on a red square: 2nd Armoured Division **33**

Mailed fist in white on a black square: 6th Armoured Division **33**

Mailed hand and arm raised, holding aloft a sword in pale blue on a red background: 2 A.A. Corps 53

White knight in armour on a white horse on a black square: 3rd Australian Armoured Division 69

WEAPONS

ARROWS, SPEARS, etc.

Two spears in black crossed over a native carrier's head-band in black on a yellow shield: 82nd (West African) Division 92

Black arrow, representing a Naga spear, pointing upwards through a blue wavy line on a white circle with a black border: 202nd (Assam) L. of C. Area 117

White spearhead on a red diamond: 1 Corps 27

White spearhead on a red diamond, with two dark blue diagonal bands: 1 Corps Troops, R.E. 140

Gold arrow on a black square: 7th Indian Division 79

Black bow and arrow, held by a black arm and hand, set on a red square: Anti-Aircraft Command 52

White arrow, pointing upwards, on red shield with central black band: Northern Command (India) 20

Red arrow piercing the centre of a black and white target set on a black square: 6th A.A. Division 55

DAGGERS, KNIVES, Etc.

Two white daggers crossed on a red background: Waziristan District 119

Arab dagger, white curved blade, black hilt, set on a square red background: H.Q. Palestine and Transjordan 107

Arab sheathed knife in black, set on white jagged-edged background, set on dark green square: Iraq Base and L. of C. Area 113

Commando dagger in silver (white), hilt uppermost, the letters 'SS' set on either side of the hilt: No. 2 Commando 94

Crossed daggers in white, the blades forming a 'V'—and a letter 'V' superimposed on the hilts which rests on a croll bearing the word 'Force.' All set on a light green circle: 'V' Force 97

Two silver (white) Commando daggers set horizontally on a black rectangle. The hilt of each dagger in the shape of letter 'S': H.Q. Special Service Brigade 94

Dagger in yellow, held by a yellow hand and forearm, set on a red square: 19th Indian Division 81

Dagger, unsheathed, point uppermost on a black background: Commando Brigades 94

Kris, Malayan dagger, with wavy-shaped blade in yellow on a dark green background: Malaya Command 22

Kukris, a pair, crossed, in white on a dark green background: 43rd Indian Lorried Infantry Brigade 87

Panga upright, white blade and black handle, set on a red shield with a black border: 28th (East African) Brigade 92

Pangas, a pair, crossed left over right, silver (white) blades, black handles, set on a green background or on a red circle with a black border: East Africa Command 21

OTHER WEAPONS

Battleaxe, in yellow, on a black circle or square: 78th Division 48

Battleaxe in white, held aloft by an armour-clad hand and arm on a black background: 1st Australian Armoured Division 66

Battleaxe in white on a black background: 1st New Zealand Division 71

Battleaxe in yellow on a royal blue rectangle: 116th Indian Infantry Brigade 88

Bayonet, vertical, point uppermost, in yellow set on a black shield: 150th Indian Infantry Brigade 88

Lances with red and white pennants; a pair crossed below a stringed bugle horn in white on a black background: 60th Indian Infantry Brigade 87

Crossed lances in white behind a white tank set on a blue cross on a red shield: R.A.C. Training Centre, B.A.O.R. 143

Spiked mace, held aloft by a mailed fist on a red shield, divided diagonally by a yellow band: 34th Armoured Brigade 126

Seaxes, three in white, on a red shield or red square: Essex County Division 58

Two seaxes, with blue blades and yellow hilts, set on a black shield within a yellow border: 2 Corps District 103

Three seaxes in blue set on a red square: 223rd Independent Infantry Brigade 223

Sword bayonet, point uppermost, set on a rectangle divided horizontally into three bands, blue, red and blue: 33rd Guards Brigade **129**

SWORDS

Crossed Cavalry Swords and an upright pike set behind a Cromwellian helmet, all in black and white on a red background: East Central District and Central Midland District **104**

Crossed swords, hilts uppermost, in yellow on a blue cross on a red shield: H.Q. 21st Army Group **16** and H.Q. British Army of the Rhine **121**

Red sword, held aloft by a white hand and arm rising from three wavy blue lines, set on a black rectangle: 77th Division **49**

Red sword, point uppermost, blade passing through a yellow crown, set on a dark blue background: London District **99**

Rapier and cutlass in black, crossed on a yellow background: South Caribbean Area **115**

Small white sword, point uppermost, on a black shield set on a red cross on a white background: No. 21 Area M.E.F. **113**

Sword, white blade, yellow hilt, set on a blue cross on a white shield: Second Army **23**

Sword, white blade, yellow hilt, set on a red cross on a white shield: First Army **23**

Two black (Mahratta) swords, crossed above a circular black shield on a red background: 110th (Poona) Area **117**

White sword, point uppermost, red flames leaping from the blade, set on a black shield, the upper portion of which is occupied by a sky blue band and narrow bands of rainbow colours: Supreme Headquarters Allied Expeditionary Force (S.H.A.E.F.) **14**

White sword, with curled hilt, set on a red shield, a black band set across the centre bearing the Roman figures 'XIV' in white: Fourteenth Army **25**

White sword pointing upwards on white shield across which a band blue, red blue: 6th Tank Brigade **123**

White sword (tulwar), raised aloft by a white hand and arm on a black background: 20th Indian Division **81**

White sword, held aloft by a brown hand, set on a green circle: 39th Indian Division **83**

GUNS

Black cannon on a red rectangle: Lahore District **118**

Two crossed cannons in dark blue set above a dark blue cannon ball on a red square: 301st Infantry Brigade **133**

Muzzle-loading gun and a stack of cannon balls on a circle divided into red and blue: Coast Artillery Units **136**

LETTERS

'AA' in white, the letters overlapping, set on an evenly divided rectangle, top half red, lower dark blue: Anti-Aircraft and Coast Units, R.A. (C.M.F.) **136**

'AA' in white, set on either side of a red anchor with a white rope on a black square: Maritime A.A. Artillery **136**

'AF' in white on a saxe blue circle with a red border: Allied Force Headquarters **15**

'GF' in dark green in the centre of a yellow five-pointed star on a dark green circle: General Reserve Engineering Force **98**

'GO' in black on a green circle on a square black background: 8th Armoured Division **34**

'HD' conjoined in red within a red circle on a blue square: 51st (Highland) Division **45**

'JP' conjoined in blue on a red circle: 54th (East Anglian) Division **46** and 162nd Independent Infantry Brigade **131**

'NM' conjoined in black on a khaki rectangle: 148th Independent Infantry Brigade **131**

'P' in white on a black square: G.H.Q. Liaison Regiment **134**

'R' in white on a black shield: 'R' Force **97**

'RA' in white, set either side of a red anchor, with a white rope on a black square: Maritime Anti-Aircraft Artillery **137**

'T' in red: Tunnelling Companies, R.E. **139**

'TT' in red on a black square: 50th (Northumbrian) Division **44**

Three black 'V's on a red background: 15 Indian Corps **75**

'W' set on a base line in red on a khaki background: 53rd (Welsh) Division **46**

'Y' in white on a khaki square: 5th Division **37**

'Y' in white on a black circle: 5th Division **37**

'Y' on a white shield on a red circle: Yorkshire County Division **59**

GEOMETRICAL

Circle, divided in centre, top half yellow, lower half dark green: 2nd South African Division **73**

Circle in red on a black square: 5th Indian Division **78**
Red circle, one quadrant displaced, set on a white square: 4th Division **37**
Red circle on black square: 72nd Indian Infantry Brigade **87**
Black circle with red border: British Troops in Berlin **121**
White circle above a white rectangle, set on a green square: 10 Corps **29**
A quarter of a circle in red: 4th Division **37**
Diagonal bands of red (or pink) and blue forming a cross on a black square: 10th Indian Division **80**
Diamond, divided in centre, top half yellow, lower half green: 1st South African Division **73**
White Diamond: 12th Division **38**
Red diamond on a blue square: 61st Division **47**
Diamond, horizontal, in red, with a central dark blue band: First Canadian Army **60**
Diamond, horizontal, scarlet: 1 Canadian Corps **60**
Diamond, horizontal, dark blue: 2 Canadian Corps **61**
Diamond, horizontal, in black, with a central red band: 1st Canadian Armoured Brigade **63**
Diamond, horizontal, in black, with a central dark blue band: 2nd Canadian Armoured Brigade **63**
Small white equal-sided diamond superimposed on a larger red equal-sided diamond: 42nd Armoured Division **35** and 42nd (East Lancashire) Division **41** and 42nd Armoured Engineer Regiment **140**
Hexagon, with six equal segments—red, blue, French grey, green, maroon and black: Canadian Army Pacific Force **64**
Oval, scarlet: 44th (Home Counties) Division **42**
Oval, scarlet, with narrow white border: 44th (Home Counties) Division **42**
Pyramid, composed of three inner triangles, grey, salmon buff and green, within a blue border: 204th Independent Infantry Brigade **131**
Rectangle, red: 1st Canadian Division **62**
Rectangle, royal blue: 2nd Canadian Division **62**
Rectangle, French grey: 3rd Canadian Division **62**
Rectangle, dark green: 4th Canadian Armoured Division **62**
Rectangle, maroon: 5th Canadian Armoured Division **62**
Red ring on a black square: 72nd Infantry Brigade **130**
Ring in white on a black background: 29th Independent Brigade Group **128**
White ring linked with a red ring on a black background: 36th Division **40**
Red ring on a black equal-sided diamond: Central Command (India) **20**
Black square, set on the centre of a black cross on a yellow background: 18th Division **39**
Square, divided in centre, top half yellow, lower half green: 3rd South African Division **73**
Square, quartered, top quarters red and green, the lower green and red: Colombo Sub-Area **120**
Equilateral triangle in white: 1st Division **36**
Small red inverted equilateral triangle set on a black equilateral triangle: 3rd Division **36**
Triangle, equilateral, in yellow, in the centre of a larger dark green triangle: 6th South African Armoured Division **74**
Two equilateral triangles, one inverted above the other, top triangle green, lower black: 33rd Armoured Brigade **127**
Equilateral triangle, divided horizontally into three equal bands, light blue, yellow, and light blue: 66th Division **47**

STARS

Four red stars with white edges on a square black background: New Zealand Expeditionary Force **71**
Red four-pointed star on a white square: 6th Division **37** and 70th Division **48**
Royal Blue nine-pointed star on a black circle: 9th Indian Division **79**
Five white stars (conventional representation of the constellation of the Southern Cross) on a shield. Field of the shield varying in colours (eighteen different variations): Southern Command (U.K.) **18**
White five-pointed star on a rectangle, divided evenly, top half light blue/grey, lower half dark blue: Military Adviser-in-Chief, Indian State Forces **89**
Four yellow stars on a square background, evenly divided into three horizontal bands, red, black and red: Southern Army (India) **75**
Yellow five-pointed star, set on a rectangle or a shield evenly divided, top half red, lower

half dark blue: G.H.Q., India **14**
Yellow (gold) five-pointed star set on a dark blue background: Indian Units, B.C.O.F. **89**
Star, nine-pointed, in royal blue on a black circle: 9th Indian Division **79**
Star, eight-pointed, composed of eight diamonds, four red and four blue, in alternate colours: 32nd Independent Guards Brigade **129**

BUILDINGS, MONUMENTS, etc.

Castle gateway in white on a square divided evenly into red, black and red horizontal bands: North-Western Army (India) **75**
Frontier fort in white (Jamrud Fort, Khyber Pass) on a red background: Peshawar District **118**
The Great Cromlech of Stonehenge in red, set on a yellow background on a green grass base within a black and red circle: Salisbury Plain District **101**
Indian triumphal arch (the Gateway of India, Bombay) in black and white on red background: 108 (Bombay) L. of C. Area **116**
Two Greek columns in black on white square: Cyrenica District **112**
Moorish gateway with letters 'TD': Tunisia District **113**
Mosque (the Mohamed Ali Mosque in Cairo) in black on a white background: No. 17 Area, M.E.F. **112**
Martello Tower in black and white on a black diamond: 11 Corps **29**
A pyramid in red, and two palm trees in red on a white background: British Troops in Egypt **109**
Land's End lighthouse and rocky coast in black on red background with narrow black border: 12th Bn. Cornwall Home Guard **148**
Windmill in pale blue (with Dutch dyke and sea): Netherlands District **111**

TORCHES

Black torch, red flames, set on a white shield with three blue wavy lines in the lower portion: H.Q. Central Mediterranean Force **15**
Black torch, red flames held in a white hand, set on a buff or yellow background: No. 56 Area, C.M.F. **114**
Yellow torch, red flames, on a black diamond: 218th Independent Infantry Brigade **132**
Yellow torch on a blue cross set on a red shield: B.A.O.R. Training Centre **147**

KEYS

Crossed keys in white on black square: 2nd Division **36** and 5th Infantry Brigade **128**
Yellow key on a red rectangle: Gibraltar Garrison **106**
Yellow key set on a rectangle divided diagonally into red and dark blue: R.A. Units, Gibraltar **138**

CROSSES

CRUSADER'S
Blue cross on a red shield with two gold swords in saltire: H.Q. 21st Army Group and H.Q. B.A.O.R. **16**
Blue cross on a white shield with a gold sword on the vertical arms of the cross: Second Army **23**
Gold Cross on a white shield on a dark blue background: Eighth Army **24** and British Troops in Austria
Red cross on a white shield with a gold sword on the vertical arms of the cross: First Army **23**
Red cross on a small white shield against a background of a white crusader's and gold wings set on a light and dark blue rectangle. Allied Land Forces South-East Asia **15**
Red cross on a white shield: Vienna Area **121**
Red cross on a blue shield: 8th Division **38**
Blue cross on a red shield: G.H.Q. Troops, 21st Army Group **111**
Blue cross on a yellow shield: L. of C., 21st Army Group **111** and British Troops in the Low Countries **109**
MALTESE
White Maltese cross on a black band on a red shield: Malta Command **21**
White Maltese cross on a red shield: 231st Independent Infantry Brigade **132**

Dark blue Maltese cross with red edges on a black square: H.Q. R.A. Malta **138**
Maltese cross, arms divided evenly dark blue and gold, on a black square: Heavy A.A.
Brigade R.A. (Malta) **138**
Maltese cross, arms divided evenly dark blue and gold and with a narrow white border, set
on a black square: Light A.A. Brigade R.A. (Malta) **138**
ST. ANDREW'S
St. Andrew's cross in white on a light blue shield with a black border: 52nd (Lowland)
Division **45**
ST. DAVID'S
St. David's cross, with a red rose in the centre, in a red circle on a black background:
Western Command **18**
St. David's cross in yellow on a black shield: 38th (Welsh) Division **40**

HORSESHOES

Black horseshoe on a red square: 13th Division **39**
Red horseshoe on a black circle: 3rd Indian Motor Brigade **85**
Two white interlocked horseshoes on a black rectangle: H.Q. Pack Transport Group
R.A.S.C. **144**

BELLS

A pair of red bells, suspended from a red bow, set on a dark blue background: 47th
(London) Division **43**
Yellow bell on a blue shield: South Midland District **102**

CARDS

Black Ace of Spades on a green square: 25th Indian Division **82**
Black Ace of Clubs on a white square: 11th (African) Division **91**

GATES

Red three-barred gate on a black background: British Troops in Northern Ireland **105**
White three-barred gate on a light green background: Northern Ireland District **105**

MUSICAL INSTRUMENTS

Trumpet in white on a black background: 9 Corps **29**
Side drum in yellow, red bands top and base, white cords (Drake's Drum), set on a khaki
background: 45th (Wessex) Division **42**
Stringed bugle horn in white, superimposed by a crown and the figures '95' superimposed
on the cords, set on a square divided diagonally into green and black: 61st Independent
Infantry Brigade **130**

DOMINO

Dark blue and white domino on a horizontal diamond in red: 12th A.A. Division **57**

SHEARS

Pair of sheep shears in yellow on a dark green background: Durham and North Riding
County Division **58**

FEATHERS

Prince of Wales's feathers in red on a dark green circle: North Wales District **100** and
Midland West District **100**

DRAGONS

Burmese dragon (Chinthe, pagoda custodian) in yellow and white, set on a square divided
into three bands—red, yellow, red, the Roman figures 'XII' in white on the lower red
portion: 12th Army **25**
Burmese dragon in gold (yellow) on a dark blue circle: 3rd Indian Division **77**

Red (Welsh) dragon on a green background: South Wales District **100**
White dragon on black square: 4th New Zealand Armoured Brigade **71**
Wyvern (dragon) in yellow on dark blue square: 43rd (Wessex) Division **41**
Yellow (Chinese) dragon, set on a red rectangle with a central black band: H.Q. Land Forces, Hong Kong **108**

PHŒNIX

Head of a white Phœnix rising from red flames, in its beak a white torch with red flames, set on a dark blue circle with a white border: 219th Independent Infantry Brigade **132**
Head of a blue Phœnix rising from red flames, in its beak a torch, set on a white oval: British Military Headquarters in the Balkans **135**
Phœnix in blue, rising from red flames on white circle with blue border: Supreme H.Q. South-East Asia **15**
Yellow Phœnix, wings outspread, arising from red flames surmounted by a red seven-pointed corona, set on a black square: Madras District, 105 (Madras) L. of C. Area **116**

IMPS, DEVILS, etc.

Green imp, set on brown rectangle: Lincolnshire Home Guard **148**
Red devil behind a dark blue diabolo, set on a yellow circle: 16th Armoured Brigade **124**

HOME GUARD COUNTY DISTINGUISHING LETTERS

A	Anglesey	**FT**	Flintshire
AB	Aberdeenshire and Aberdeen City	**G**	City of Glasgow
ABK	Aberdeenshire (3rd Bn.)	**GLN**	Glamorganshire
(Kincardine)		**GLS**	Gloucestershire
ANG	Angus	**H**	Hampshire and Isle of Wight
ARG	Argyllshire	**HD**	Lincolnshire (Holland)
AYR	Ayrshire	**HDS**	Huntingdonshire
BDF	Bedfordshire	**HFD**	Herefordshire
BHM	Birmingham (Warwickshire)	**HTS**	Hertfordshire
BNF	Banffshire	**IOM**	Isle of Man
BR	Brecknock	**IN**	Inverness-shire and Nairnshire
BRX	Berkshire	(1st Bn.)	
BUX	Buckinghamshire	**INV**	Inverness-shire and Nairnshire
CA	Caithness	**K**	Kesteven (Lincolnshire)
CAM	Cambridgeshire	**KT**	Kent
CC	Caernarvonshire	**L**	Lindsey (Lincolnshire)
CDN	Cardiganshire	**LEI**	Leicestershire
CH	Cheshire	**LF**	Lancaster (East Lancs. 21, 22, 27,
CLN	Clackmannanshire	41, 42, 43 & 45th Bns.)	
CO	Cornwall	**LK**	Lanarkshire
COL	City of London	**LON**	County of London
COV	Coventry (Warwickshire)	**LR**	Lancashire (East Lancs. 24th Bn.)
CRM	Carmarthenshire	**M**	Merionethshire
CT	Lincoln (Lincolnshire)	**MAN**	Manchester (East Lancs. 23, 25, 26,
CUM	Cumberland	44, 45, 46, 47, 48, 49, 50, 51 & 56th Bns.)	
DBT	Dunbartonshire	**ML**	Midlothian
DDE	City of Dundee	**MON**	Monmouthshire
DEN	Denbighshire	**MRY**	Montgomeryshire
DFS	Dumfries-shire	**MX**	Middlesex
DHM	Durham	**ND**	Northumberland
DOR	Dorset	**NK**	Norfolk
DVN	Devonshire	**NN**	Northamptonshire
EHG	City of Edinburgh	**NRY**	North Riding of Yorkshire
EL	East Lancashire (28th to 32nd Bns.)	**NS**	North Staffordshire
ELY	Ely	**NTS**	Nottinghamshire
ER	East Riding of Yorkshire	**ORK**	Orkney
ESX	Essex	**OXF**	Oxfordshire
F	Fifeshire	**PEM**	Pembrokeshire
F & D	Denbighshire (7th Denflint Bn.)		

R	Ross and Cromarty
REN	Renfrewshire
R–L	Lewis
RR	Radnorshire (Radnor Rifles)
RU	Rutland
SB	Scottish Border (Roxburghshire)
SF	Sherwood Foresters (Derbyshire)
SFK	Suffolk
SHR	Shropshire
SKR	Scotland (Kirkcudbright)
SOM	Somersetshire
SS	South Staffordshire
STG	Stirlingshire
SU	Sutherlandshire
SX	Sussex
SY	Surrey
TAY	Tay (Perthshire)
TWD	Tweed (Peebles)
UTP	Upper Thames Patrol

	(12th Berkshire and 31st Middlesex)
WAR	Warwickshire
WES	Westmorland
WL	West Lancashire
WL	West Lothian
WNM	Wigtownshire (2nd Bn.)
WNR	Wigtownshire (1st Bn.)
WOR	Worcestershire
WR	West Riding, Yorkshire
Z	Zetland

HIGHER FORMATIONS

Supreme Headquarters, Allied Expeditionary Force (S.H.A.E.F.) **14**
Supreme Allied Command South-East Asia (S.A.C.S.E.A.) **15**
G.H.Q. Home Forces **14**
G.H.Q. India **14**
G.H.Q. Middle East Forces **14**
Allied Force Headquarters (A.F.H.Q.) **15**
Allied Land Forces, South-East Asia (A.L.F.S.E.A.) **15**
H.Q. Central Mediterranean Force **15**
H.Q. 11th Army Group **16**
H.Q. 15th Army Group **16**
H.Q. 21st Army Group **16**
Canadian Military Headquarters (C.M.H.Q.) **60**

HOME COMMANDS (U.K.)

Northern Command **17**
Western Command **18**
Southern Command **18**
Eastern Command **17**
South-Eastern Command **17**
Scottish Command **17**
Anti-Aircraft Command **52**

OVERSEAS COMMANDS

India Command (Supreme Headquarters, India) **20**
Eastern Command (India) **20**
Central Command (India) **20**
Northern Command (India) **20**
Ceylon Army Command **20**
Malta Command **21**
Persia and Iraq Command (P.A.I.C.) **21**
West Africa Command **21**
East Africa Command **21**
Malaya Command **22**

ARMIES

First Army **23**
Second Army **23**
Eighth Army **24**
Ninth Army **24**
Tenth Army **25**
Twelfth Army **25**
Fourteenth Army **25**
First Allied Airborne Army **26**
First Canadian Army **60**
First Australian Army **65**
Second Australian Army **65**
North-Western Army (India) **75**
Southern Army (India) **75**

CORPS

1 Corps **27**
2 Corps **27**
3 Corps **27**
4 Corps **28**
5 Corps **28**
7 Corps **28**
8 Corps (and 8 Corps District—U.K.) **28**
9 Corps (and 9 Corps District—U.K.) **29**
10 Corps **29**
11 Corps **29**
12 Corps **30**
13 Corps **30**